Long Distance Walking
IN BRITAIN

DAMIAN HALL

ROBERT HALE

First published in 2016 by Robert Hale
An imprint of The Crowood Press Ltd,
Ramsbury, Marlborough,
Wiltshire SN8 2HR

www. crowood.com
www.halebooks.com

British Library Cataloguing-in-Publication Data
A catalogue record for this book is available from the British Library.

ISBN 978 0 7198 1556 0

Dedication
For Indy and Leif.

Frontispiece: More than anything, a long distance walk is about chucking an apple and some spare socks (if you're feeling fancy) in a pack and heading outdoors for an adventure.

Typeset by Julie Laws, Stroud, Gloucestershire
Printed and bound in India by Replika Press Pvt Ltd

Contents

Acknowledgements		6
Picture Credits		7
Chapter 1	Why Go Long Distance Walking?	8
Chapter 2	Walking Form and Fitness:	
	How to Walk Naturally and Efficiently	17
Chapter 3	Long Distance Walking Equipment:	
	The Gear You Need and the Gear You Definitely Don't Need	26
Chapter 4	Picking and Planning:	
	What to Decide and Do Before Starting Out	36
Chapter 5	Life on the Trail: Tips for Staying Safe and Happy	39
Chapter 6	How to Use This Guide	48

The Top 100 Trails

England
South-West	52
South-East	64
North-West	78
North-East	111

Wales
North	119
Mid	121
South-West	122
All	124

Scotland
South	129
North	160

John O'Groats to Land's End	170
Further Information	171
Index	174

Acknowledgements

Putting this book together was a genuinely heart-warming experience that made me feel grateful and proud to be a part of the outdoor community – and indebted to a great number of fine people in it. To make this guide happen, many have gone well beyond reasonable levels of assistance in providing their time, expertise, words and photos, all without charge. I thank you one and all, and I hope you can take some satisfaction in the final product.

Those amazing people are (deep breath …): James Alsop, Sioned Bannister, Sandra Bardell, James Begg, Shane Benzie, David Binney, Emma Black, Lesley Blundell, Andrew Bowden, Debby Braund, Ian Brodie, Krysia Brodie, Mike Brockhurst, Anthony Burton, Genni Butler, Euan Calvert, David Canning, Alan Castle, Bryan Cath, Brian Cowan, Jenny Davidson, Adam Dawson, Sally Dench, Paddy Dillon, Becky Duncan, Keith Foskett, Ross Gemmell, Tristan Gooley, Tony Gowers, Sheila Gordon, Stuart Greig, Chris Grogan, Tony Grogan, Iain Harper, Leigh Hatts, John Henderson, Sophie Hewitt, Dave Higgins, Alastair Humphreys, Rick Jillings, Dennis Kelsall, Susan Kevan, Louise Kyle, Andrew Lafferty, Sian Lewis, Tim Lewis, Sarah Matthews, Dave Maclachlan, Renee McGregor, Keith McKenna, Cameron McNeish, Jacquetta Megarry, Laurence Mitchell, Mark Owen, Robert Peel, Simon Pilpel, David Pitt, Heather Pitt, David Pott, Paul Prescott, Rachele Quayle, Kev Reynolds, Carol Rowntree Jones, Ian Ritchie, Fiona Russell, Colin Saunders, Ron Scholes, Keith Sharp, Brian Smailes, Phoebe Smith, John Sparshatt, Tom Stevenson, Roland Tarr, John Tennant, Julie Thompson, George Tod, Ashleigh Tooth, Chris Townsend, Ronald Turnbull, Anne Urquhart, John Urquhart, Martin Wainwright, Julie Welch, Philip Werner, Steve Westwood, John White, Vyv Wood-Gee and David Yates.

Also, a big heartfelt thank you – you all know why – to Alexander Stilwell, Lavinia Porter, Jonathan Manning, Jenny Walters, Mario Cacciottolo, Alyssa White, Paul Simpson, Celso de Campos Jr, Elizabeth Leader, Clair Reynolds, Paul Hansford, Ryan Sengara, Tessa McLean, Vickie Bevan, Bevo, Jo, Kelvin, Barbara, Amy, Indy and Leif.

Picture Credits

All images Damian Hall, except for p63 and p64 (Tim Lewis), p66 and p67 (Sophie Hewitt/Explore Kent), p68 and p69 (Footprints of Sussex), p72 and p78 (Robert Peel), p73 and p75 (Kev Reynolds), p81, p82 and p91 (Tony Grogan), p83 (Mike Brockhurst), p84 and p85 (Brian Waters), p86 and p87 (Cheshire East Council), p88, p108 and p168 (Stuart W. Greig), p89 and p96 (David and Heather Pitt, and Colin Bywater), p90 and p91 (Frank Gordon), p93 (Kevin Tebbutt, 2020vision/Ben Hall), p94 (Diana Jarvis), p95 (Mike Williams), p103 (Tony Grogan/ Skyware Press), p103, p104, p112, p131, p132, p139, p145, p148, p150 and p165 (all Rucsacs.com), p105 and p106 (Chris Grogan), p107 (Sarah Matthews), p109 (Cannock Chase AONB Unit), p112 (North York Moors National Park Authority and Malcolm Hodgson), p115 (Ron Scholes), p119 (David Canning), p123 and p124 (PCNPA), p125 (Tom Bailey), p126 (George Tod), p127 (Tony Gowers), p130 (Susan Kevan), p130, p131, p135, p136, p137, p155, p156, p159 and p164 (Becky Duncan), p134 (James Begg), p141, p142 and p153 (Vyv Wood-Gee), p142, p143 and p163 (John Henderson), p143 and p144 (Brian Cowan), p146, p166 and p167 (Sandra Bardwell), p147 (Paul Prescott), p149 (Tom Stevenson), p151 (East Ayrshire Leisure), p157 and p158 (John and Anne Urquhart) and p161 (Iain Harper).

CHAPTER I

Why Go
Long Distance Walking?

'To tell you the truth, I'm amazed we've come this far,' he said, and I agreed. We had hiked 500 miles, a million and a quarter steps ... We had grounds to be proud. We were real hikers now. We had shit in the woods and slept with bears. We had become, we would forever be, mountain men.'

Bill Bryson, author of *A Walk in the Woods*

What's This Book All About Then?

I remember my first multi-day walk fondly. Of course, when I say fondly, I mean it makes me wince, shudder and want to bury my red face in my armpit in shame. It was all my own stupid fault.

My girlfriend and I were shopping for last-minute supplies in Launceston, Tasmania, before embarking on the 82 km/50-mile Overland Track. 'We'll need sleeping mats as well,' she said. With a macho streak I hope I haven't exhibited before or since, something made me snort, 'Pah. Sleeping mats are for girls! I don't need one.'

I did need one. I needed one for every one of the five, long, cold, uncomfortable nights of the otherwise massively enjoyable trek. 'If only I had a book,' I thought, during one of those long, dark, cold uncomfortable nights, inexplicably trying to lay the blame for my chronic folly elsewhere. A phantom wise, learned book, all about long distance walking for beginner types, that could have told me I definitely needed a sleeping mat. I think I felt a bit better once I blamed it squarely on a book. A book that didn't exist.

After the trek, I went looking for a sleeping mat, some humble pie and a book that might advise me better on long distance or multi-day walking. I have since bought a sleeping mat, several in fact, and the humble pie didn't taste that great really so I've tried not to eat it much since. But the book I never did find.

However, as I hiked all over the world – from New Zealand's Southern Alps to the Andes, and the Himalayas to the Pennines – I kept looking and, more importantly, I kept learning (a euphemism for 'making mistakes', of course; I've learnt a lot) until I realized that really, over a decade later, I knew enough now to write the book I couldn't find. So here it is. Finally.

And if it tells you nothing else useful (though hopefully it does) about long distance walking, let it be this: if you're camping or bivvying out, only a massive buffoon would do so without a sleeping mat.

Wessendon Reservoir on the Pennine Way, England's oldest National Trail.

Yes, Very Amusing, but Who Is This Book for Exactly?

Well, you, really. If you already enjoy a walk – and after all who doesn't enjoy a leisurely stroll somewhere pretty? – but have yet to try a long distance trail, or even if you have walked long distances before, this book is for you. I'm about to tell you why completing a long distance footpath is about the best thing you can ever do. Well, you know, apart from have children, travel the world and get over ten 'likes' on Facebook.

Multi-day walking is no longer a niche sport. In 2007 (the most recent figures), some 16 million people – 38 per cent of the population – used a long distance trail in Britain in some way. Hopefully this book gives you everything, including the encouragement, to help you to join all the people having a brilliant time on the country's many, excellent, long distance footpaths.

Long distance walking is called different things around the world, around this country and even throughout this book. And the words are used fairly interchangeably here. People will have their own definitions about what a long walk is – 5 miles is a legitimately lengthy stroll to my 5-year-old daughter. What this book concentrates on is multi-day walks. So that's usually trails of upwards of 20 miles, often many more. These distances aren't comfortable for most people to cover in just one day, so the route is usually covered over several days – though many people tackle long distance paths in stages; a

day here, a weekend there, maybe a week next time around. Whichever way it's done, there's a very real and specific joy, and a lasting sense of accomplishment and satisfaction to be had in completing a long distance trail. For many, it's life-changing.

Why Go for a Long Distance Walk? (It All Sounds a Bit Tiring …)

Yes, walking can be tiring sometimes, especially if hills are involved. But it never needs to be exhausting. Besides, the best things in life don't come easily and the pay-off is well worth it. And anyway, all that tiring stuff is making you incredibly healthy and fit.

Few things are more certain in this world than the simple, irrefutable fact that walking in green places is utterly brilliant. You see butterflies, rabbits and big dramatic views, feel a bit smug because it's all so ridiculously healthy, and have a pint afterwards or some chocolate during (ideally both) without feeling guilty about it.

However, if you spend a day in the great outdoors, then retreat back to 'civilization' (as places with TVs tend to get referred to) for the evening and call that job done, you're only getting a small taste of the experience. What about that starry sky, that ethereal pre-dawn light, that frolicking-fawns-at-dawn scene I paint in a few paragraphs' time (that I probably should have written about earlier for this bit to really make sense)? You want a bit of that, don't you? Think how happy a walk in the countryside normally makes you. Then imagine doing that again the next day. And the next. And the next … It's about exploration. A sense of achievement. Vital, meditative time in green places. And much more.

Nowadays long distance walking isn't nearly as tough as many people think. It certainly doesn't need to involve lugging a back-breaking pack up dales and through bogs (though I can't guarantee there won't be bogs …). If you really don't want to, you don't even need to carry a bag. Long distance walking can be easy. Almost too easy (more anon).

This book is all about the art of long distance walking – in Britain. Because Britain's a truly wonderful place to go long distance walking – people come from all over the world to walk this green and pleasant land (when I was last on the Pennine Way I met Americans, Aussies, Belgians, Swiss …). This is partly because of our combination of well-marked trails, lack of dangerous animals (though Yorkshire Dales' sheep sure can get a bit grumpy), painfully beautiful landscapes that are relatively risk free and the fact they often call into welcoming villages at day-walk intervals, meaning a tent often isn't necessary. You can get your hat blown off on the moors and mountains, but still have a glass of red by the fire at night. The best of both worlds. It's a sort of comfortable wildness. Like me, these welcome, foreign yompers know that long distance walking is a brilliant thing to do, one of life's greatest joys.

The Happiness of the Long Distance Walker (including the fawns at dawn bit, as promised …)

Imagine waking at first light to see a pink sky over dragon's-back mountains, a giant lake, motionless, like glass, reflecting back the jagged peaks, fawns frolicking unaware in the morning dew – views exclusively yours. A while later (the exact time of day has become liberatingly irrelevant to you) you brew up some tea (and tea *always* tastes fan-*ruddy*-tastic in the outdoors, regardless of how milky or stewed) to go with your chocolate porridge, sling

your pack on your back and amble merrily on your way whistling a tune without a care in the world.

Okay, some days it's more like you wake from a cold night of fitful sleep, put on wet socks, eat a stale cereal bar and sling a heavy pack on a sore back. But not usually. Not if you've done things right (and that's what this book's all about).

You'll have an adventure. You're likely see and do things you'll remember forever. You'll feel alive. You'll very likely gain a huge sense of achievement, new confidence in your self-sufficiency, self-empowerment and independence, some perspective and distance from any troubles, a new happiness, a giddy sense of freedom. And you'll feel happy. Even if it doesn't all go to plan (and it rarely does), you'll have some great stories to tell. And, to top it all, you'll come home with a more shapely backside.

Long distance walking is also cheap. It's green. It's really, really good for your body (well, apart from the blisters, but we'll talk about those later) and mind (ditto). And it directly combats many of the computer- and car-obsessed ills of contemporary life.

There are ridiculous amounts of very good reasons to go trekking. For me, perhaps above all else, is the refreshing simplicity of the days and a giddy sense of liberation. A day out walking is much simpler than most people's average day. All you're really concerned with is going from A to B and eating chocolate. So there are fewer distractions – no phone calls, emails or any texts (assuming you've turned off your smartphone, of course).

It's my own fault really, but in my average non-walking day I spend a lot of my time thinking of things I should have done (the past) and other things I need to do (the future). And not so much time thinking about what I'm doing right now. This. Here. Typing and thinking. Which is a massive shame, because at the day's end what did I remember about it? Did I really *live* it? I'm not a Buddhist, but I can see much value in the idea of living life in the now. The past has already happened and the future may never happen. Now is what's important.

Through taking in changing scenery, watching your footing on a stony path, spying a sparrow-hawk circling above, eyeing that black rain cloud with concern, checking the map to find out exactly where the bog that you've just positioned yourself up to your waist in is … all those things keep you in the present moment.

A long distance walk is almost all to your own timetable, too. Get up when you want, have breakfast when you want, walk when and where you want. Stop and stare whenever and wherever you like. Or as the brilliant Bill Bryson put it in *A Walk in the Woods*: 'Life takes on a neat simplicity, too. Time ceases to have any meaning. When it is dark, you go to bed, and when it is light again you get up, and everything in between is just in between. It's quite wonderful, really.'

That's called freedom. Freedom is perhaps the greatest thing we have. Yet a lot of the time we're trapped – tied to desks and steering wheels. I can't resist quoting W.H. Davies (1871–1940), aka Supertramp – albeit partly because he lived in Nailsworth like me – who penned the brilliantly timeless words: 'What is this life if, full of care, we have no time to stand and stare?'

I also love the sense of self-sufficiency, which goes foot in sock with the aforementioned freedom. Stick a tent and a cooker in your pack and off you go. Stop and sleep where you want. The world is your shell-based seafood delicacy. You know, like Laurie Lee, but without a violin. And that can feel giddily emancipating.

A Certified Stress-Buster

In September 2014 researchers from the University of Michigan and Edge Hill University in England evaluated 1,991 participants and found that nature walks were associated with significantly less depression and stress. Much has changed since the nineteenth century. Or has it? A novelist from that era, George Borrow, found walking was one of the few ways he could escape depression.

Go for a long walk and watch your concerns disappear, or at least see problems with real perspective and a clear, cleansed mind. I once walked England's Coast-to-Coast walk when I had some big life decisions to make, and it somehow magically sorted everything out for me.

So for me there's a deeply meditative aspect to being outdoors in nature. Do it day after day and it can become very affecting, calming, peaceful, meditative, restorative, healing and life-affirming. It's certainly changed my life for the better.

Free Your Mind (the Rest Will Follow)

My long-suffering wife often suggests I'm not your average person (I see it as a compliment – though I'm not sure she means it that way). But it's taken me about half my life to realize I'm at my very happiest when exercising in the great outdoors (before becoming a parent anyway – now I just bring the little rapscallions along, for double happy points). My mind – presumably half asleep the rest of the time – seems to come alive.

Better circulation means more energy and oxygen, which makes our brains perform better. Good ideas (well, ideas anyway) are most likely to come to me then too. Indeed, as Robert Macfarlane notes in his excellent *The Old Ways*, numerous poets, writers and philosophers have been walkers and it isn't a coincidence. 'The compact between writing and walking is almost as old as literature – a walk is only a step away from a story, and every path *tells*.'

Charles Dickens, Bruce Chatwin, Henry David Thoreau, George Orwell, C.S. Lewis (who thought talking spoiled a walk), Thomas De Quincey and many others were serious ramblers. Nineteenth-century philosopher Thoreau said, 'The moment my legs begin to move, my thoughts begin to flow.' Nineteenth-century Danish philosopher and poet Søren Kierkegaard said: 'I have walked myself into my best thoughts and I know of no thought so burdensome that one cannot walk away from it … but by sitting still, and the more one sits still, the closer one comes to feeling ill.' Though, not uncharacteristically, Friedrich Nietzsche took things a little too far when he proclaimed, 'Only those thoughts which come from walking have any value.'

Romantic poet William Wordsworth is thought to have hiked somewhere between 175,000 and 180,000 miles in his lifetime (and not always while high on opium). He was often composing verse as he went. It's said friend and fellow Romantic poet Samuel Taylor Coleridge once strode from Nether Stowey in the Quantocks to Lynton/Lynmouth and back again – some 90 miles – in just two days. He's also said to have covered the 40 miles from Stowey to Bristol in a day, to attend a meeting (we hope it was a good one). When living in Somerset in the late eighteenth century, Wordsworth and Coleridge adopted the unusual habit of night walking, which aroused suspicion that they were French spies and a government agent was sent to investigate.

This was Coleridge's most prolific period and produced the defining works of the early Romantic era. In fact we have the Romantic poets to thank for places such as the Lake District. The Romantic movement was a response to industrialization, a celebration of the precious and beautiful landscapes we have in this green and pleasant land. Wordsworth claimed the Lake District as 'a sort of national property, in which every man has a right and interest who has an eye to perceive and a heart to enjoy'. This new attitude led ultimately to the formation of the National Trust and later the Rights of Way and National Parks in England and Wales.

The Call of the Wild

'My first overnight camp was a revelation,' says revered Scottish outdoor writer and broadcaster Cameron McNeish (more from him on page 154). 'I camped high below Cairn Toul and woke to see reindeer grazing nearby. I then realised that to know a mountain fully, to really connect with the landscape, you have to sleep out on it … Multi-day walking gives me the opportunity to connect with the landscape, something I find quite difficult to do on day walks. It takes me a bit of time to feel a part of the landscape, rather than someone just passing through it.'

On a trek you'll spend most of that time in various types of what we often call nature. There's direct joy to be had in green places: in wildlife spying, rare wild-flower spotting, beguiling bird song, kookily twisted tree trunks, weird insects, beech woods ablaze in autumn, virginal blankets of frost, massive leaves, curious red berries, replenishing rain, elusive hill-tops, coy valleys, otherworldly sunsets, menacing mushrooms, mysterious standing stones, apocalyptic mud, the majestic, uncontrollable

Descending into Langdale in the Lake District – the land of Wordsworth and Wainwright.

sky above (admittedly when the sky blackens and opens up on you it's a less enjoyable experience) and much, much else besides.

Scientists talk of the 'biophilia effect' and how we as creatures subconsciously long to be in nature. We live mostly in cities, identikit suburbs, busy towns and ever-expanding villages. But that's not what our species is used to. That's not what we're comfortable doing. Humans have spent the vast majority of our existence in wild places. Sure it hasn't all been comfortable, before television, refrigerators and eyelash curlers, but I've just got this feeling that we're happier outdoors. We're animals not robots. We long for landscapes. Trees are better for us than traffic. We belong in nature. Don't believe me? Go out walking for a week and see how you feel after. A walk is a commune with nature. And we could all do with more of that in our lives. On a multi-day walk, you can simply get further away from everyday irritants – and further into nature.

An Antidote to Modern Life (Which is Rubbish)

For me and many others, distance walking is something of an antidote to the perils of modern life. We've become slaves to technology and social media, hassled by things that aren't really important, stuck in cars and offices, too far from green places and big open skies. The things that are really important are health and happiness (and loved ones, too – though you should just bring them along!). Take a day off, a weekend away, a week away, ideally more. It's amazing how deeply unimportant those things that niggled you – that email with a self-important red exclamation mark you haven't replied to, that admin you haven't done, that thing that needs fixing on the car – can seem. It opens my mind to the unnecessary over-complications of life too. All those things we think we need, but clearly don't. Especially those plastic clips for bread bags.

'The draw of being able to spend several months in the great outdoors and indeed pristine

wilderness is what lures most people to the trail,' says Keith Foskett in his account of walking North America's Pacific Crest Trail, *The Last Englishman*. 'Leave your mundane job, kiss your bills goodbye and experience life at its simplest and most uncluttered. Trail life educates you. It becomes apparent that we don't need most of our luxuries, we can live without shopping, TV becomes a distant memory and realizing how uncomplicated life can truly be is an absolute revelation.'

In *The Old Ways*, Robert Macfarlane says the idea that we may go walking to find something of a previous, less complicated, age isn't new. 'I've read them all, these old-way wanders, and often I've encountered versions of the same beguiling idea: that walking such paths might lead you – in [W.H.] Hudson's phrase – to "slip back out of this modern world".'

A real sense of achievement is possible – covering a distance you mightn't have suspected was possible all under your own steam. Accomplishing a big challenge can have positive repercussions in everyday life, not least new confidence. 'Suddenly we realise that if we can walk for a long time supporting ourselves,' says Keith Foskett, 'then all the areas of our life we once perceived as being difficult, suddenly are easy.'

Many people find long distance walking gives them a sense of journey, exploration and discovery. You'll be uncovering new places – hills and valleys, and maybe villages you've never heard of but won't want to leave.

It sounds clichéd, but there's usually an emotional journey and many of us finish a route feeling like we're different people. You'll also probably discover things about yourself – such as you don't like wet toes.

Britain *is* Great

I long took Britain for granted. I used to see it as humdrum, a crowded, post-industrial island with not much remarkable about it, other than our passion for potatoes and over-politeness. It took me several years of living abroad to realize how special

Britain is – in many ways, but especially its geography and scenic splendour. I remember coming back one summer and visiting my parents in the Cotswolds where I mostly grew up and being gobsmacked by how very, very green it all was. Bundles of the stuff – brilliant, vivid green, and so very many shades of it – tumbling down the hillsides. A few years later I returned with a huge appetite for exploring Britain's green, wild and lumpy places. Almost the first thing I did after saying hello to my mum was to go walking, from coast to coast. And it helped me fall in love with my country.

You see, Britain is a remarkable place. We haven't got deserts, volcanoes or really big mountains, but we've still got a whole lot of good stuff. The melodramatic, purple- and yellow-dotted moors of Yorkshire and Dartmoor (we have 75 per cent of the world's heather moorland), the chalky downs (with their white horses and rude giants) in the south, endless views from the Cotswold Edge, the sheer green walls of the Brecon Beacons, incredible coastal scenery, craggy Snowdonia, the remote Cambrian mountains, stone circles and hill-forts, castles and history, clandestine valleys and ancient woodlands, long whistling rivers and crashing waterfalls, the peaty Peak District (the world's second most visited National Park) and – oh my – the Lake District. Plus the tangible history of World Heritage-listed Hadrian's Wall. Then you cross the border to the north and all that looks like the black-and-white version. Up there, everything's bigger, wilder and more colourful. Proper mountains. Proper remoteness and wilderness. We're really lucky on this island.

Doug Scott, the first Briton to climb Everest, said: 'I'm always asked what my favourite mountain is and am expected to say Everest – but I always say [the Lake District's] Blencathra.' We should get out and make the most of it, get to know it. And there's no better way to do so than on your own two feet.

Luckily, Britain also has an amazing network of trails. The Long Distance Walkers Association estimates approximately 1,400 trails, with the country's path network as a whole covering some 150,000 miles.

Many of the footpaths are ancient routes, historical trails our ancestors took to travel to markets, places of work and worship, or for a bit of a biff with those pesky Vikings. Footpaths used to be our transport network and they're still cobwebbed across stout hills and wind-tickled dales, linking rustic villages and remote places of forgotten wildness.

Let's Get Physical

As well as having fantastic mental benefits, walking is ridiculously good for your health, too, and we talk about that in more detail on page 17. It's probably the most healthy activity you can possibly do in fact – it even helps combat the ageing process (it's even good for your skin). Sure, you can get fit in a gym. But given the choice of staring at MTV or being enchanted by a view of 100 miles of coastline, I know which I'd choose.

So many of us are unhealthy – mostly with problems stemming from unnatural, lazy and over-indulgent lifestyles or simply sitting down too much – and walking is the simplest, least risky way to get healthy again. Exercise also triggers endorphins. Endorphins are brilliant. They make you feel brilliant. They're addictive (in a safe way).

Long Distance Walking is Much Easier Than You Think

Completing a long distance path all in one go, being fully self-sufficient (bar the odd pub and shop visit), is doubtless the most satisfying way to go. But it doesn't suit everyone and it would be a crying shame if people weren't tasting the joy of distance walking because they were unaware of how accessible it is.

Firstly, as previously mentioned, many complete long distance trails in sections. There's no rule stating it must be done in one continuous journey. Secondly, the image of a little old man bent double under the weight of a pack twice his size, pots and pans swinging wildly, is long out of date. Trekking need no longer be a hellish, back-breaking slogathon. Equipment is so much lighter now than it was twenty, ten or even five years ago (see page 26 for more) that you can carry all you need without it being a real burden. Thirdly, on more popular trails, you don't even need to carry most of your gear. You could hike, say, the 192-mile Coast to Coast walk for two weeks, without carrying much more than a coat and a credit card. Nowadays many long distance trails are serviced by 'Sherpa services' or baggage couriers (heck, it could even be a suitcase) who'll transport your baggage (though not necessarily the emotional type) on to your next destination. As well as this door-to-door service, many will also book accommodation for you (which sometimes includes an evening meal and/or breakfast), and advise on the route and facilities, saving you a lot of admin hassle.

For some people this offers a more relaxing – physically and mentally – experience. It also means you're more likely to meet local people and contribute more fully to local economies, get a good night's sleep, a good feed and that big bubbly bath you've been fantasizing about for half the day.

Purists may bemoan the non-eco-friendly transportation of the luggage, or the fact it isn't in keeping with the original spirit of backpacking. But if it means those who otherwise might not be getting out to enjoy the great outdoors now are, then it's surely a good thing. Not everyone has a back strong enough to carry 10kg or even 5kg (although most people can manage that), for 200 miles. Of course, using these services also increases the cost and carbon output of an activity traditionally seen as a cheap and green pastime, so it is worth considering whether you can do without them.

A Little Bit of History

Almost nothing is as natural to us as walking and running. It's how we outlived the Neanderthals. They were bigger and cleverer than us, but we could cover bigger distances, so we persistence-hunted, tracked prey for hours and hours until it keeled over from exhaustion (the fact we cool down by sweating effectively was a big help too). So those types of movement are entirely natural – certainly more so than sitting hunched over a screen all day. It's what allowed us to survive as a species. Moving upright is what defines us.

Throughout history armies have marched huge distances with their packs and walking was our primary mode of transport for the vast majority of our existence. Then the wheel came along and we all got lazy.

It's safe to say that until very recently we've always walked long distances, but the modern way in which we walk as a leisure pursuit probably began towards the end of the 1800s when walking clubs started springing up. Early in the

In the dramatic West Highlands of Scotland, you can walk long distances while carrying very little.

next century, the Romantic poets, Byron, Coleridge and Wordsworth, were big walkers and Coleridge is sometimes credited with inventing the concept of hill walking – he wrote numerous paeans to the countryside.

The version of long distance walking we know today was first documented in 1935, when two American girls wrote to the *Daily Herald* newspaper asking for advice on a walking holiday in England. Was there anything here like the Appalachian Trail in the USA, they wondered? The short and shameful answer was 'No'.

Tom Stephenson – a journalist, a walker, the future secretary of the Ramblers' Association and countryside correspondent for the *Daily Herald* – recognized that the wilds of the 'lonely entrancing' Pennines were an excellent place for a long distance trail and put forward the idea in the same newspaper. 'Wanted – a long green trail' was the headline and he called for 'A Pennine Way from the Peak to the Cheviots'.

It's hard to imagine now, but many upland areas were legally out of bounds to outdoor types, despite being public land. There was already a groundswell of frustration, which had led to the seminal Mass Trespass on the Peak District's Kinder Scout in April 1932. The protest saw groups of ramblers scuffle with gamekeepers and five people jailed. A few weeks later 10,000 ramblers assembled for an access rally in the nearby Winnats Pass.

Secretly Stephenson hoped to use the Pennine Way idea as an excuse to open up the moorlands of the Peak District and South Pennines to the public. Both of Stephenson's wishes would happen, but he would have to fight for another thirty years for the Pennine Way to exist.

Britain's first National Trail finally opened on 24 April 1965, thirty-three years to the day after the legendary Kinder Mass Trespass. Stephenson finally got his bigger wish too, as in 1949 the National Parks and Access to the Countryside Act opened up England's glorious countryside for the likes of you and me to get wet and muddy in.

The Pennine Way was followed by the opening of the Cleveland Way National Trail in 1969, the Pembrokeshire Coast Path National Trail in 1970, Offa's Dyke in 1971 and the West Highland Way in 1980. England and Wales now have fifteen National Trails, and twenty-five of Scotland's twenty-six Great Trails (not including the Great Glen Canoe Trail, which is what its name suggests), are detailed in this book (from page 129).

It's worth remembering when we're blithely taking selfies along the Coast to Coast that a lot of people have worked incredibly hard, and put themselves at real risk (Benny Rothman and others were imprisoned) to help open up the hills and moors for us. And we shouldn't forget their sacrifices.

The Future

We shouldn't assume the threat to the accessibility of hills and wilder places has completely gone. Panicky governments will think up wayward excuses (or ignore problems such as climate change) and we should remain vigilant to those who might impinge on our rights to enjoy these wonderful places as they are. To that end, and to inspire others to join us, don't be shy about sharing your outdoor experiences, even if it's through social media (in fact that's perhaps the best way …). Tell people what you're doing. Put it on Twitbook and the rest. Write a blog. Heck, write a book. Try to share and inspire.

This may sound presumptuous and patronizing, but some people in this world are unhappy and getting them out in the hills might make them just a tiny bit less unhappy. Also think about joining the Long Distance Walkers Association, Ramblers, the Backpackers Club, wildlife trusts and similar organizations. They're usually dirt cheap, with great benefits. There is strength in numbers and wildlife and wild places can't speak up, so sometimes we need to speak for them.

And lastly. Please try to shop locally. Rather than stocking up in a mega-profit-making, tax-dodging supermarket before your big trip, why not try to support local businesses – cafes, shops, pubs – en route. It's just a small thing, but it will help make the world a better place. Politicking over. Promise.

CHAPTER 2

Walking Form and Fitness: How to Walk Naturally and Efficiently

'You don't stop hiking because you get old; you get old because you stop hiking. While you're moving your body the right way you're keeping it strong.'

Shane Benzie, movement specialist and technique coach

Walking is Ridiculously Good for Us

Walking is so good for you it's quite frankly ridiculous – and better for you than almost every other activity (running and cycling stress the body much more, for example, while the gallon of chlorine I consume every time I go swimming can't be healthy).

Low-intensity exercise benefits almost every part of your body, making you stronger and healthier in both body and mind (some would say soul, too). 'Regular walking has been shown to reduce the risk of chronic illnesses,' says the NHS website, 'such as heart disease, type 2 diabetes, asthma, stroke and [colon and breast] cancer.'

Walking also improves lungs, cholesterol, core strength, helps combat back problems, helps aid metabolism, blood circulation, weight loss

(a 60 kg person burns about 100 calories an hour when walking just 3 mph (4.8 kph), says the NHS), proprioception (our sense of balance and body awareness), and reduces the risk of Alzheimer's disease and having a stroke by 20–50 per cent. It also improves muscles and joints, even our skin – and our mind.

'Walking is incredibly healthy,' emphasizes Shane Benzie, who's a qualified running technique coach, movement specialist and founder of

Shane Benzie, movement specialist.

Running Reborn (runningreborn.com). He teaches a natural and more efficient technique for running and walking and is collaborating with *Born to Walk* author James Earls. Shane has trekked in the Indian, Pakistani and Nepalese Himalayas, Wales and Scotland.

'It's even good for our bones, too,' he says. 'Ten per cent of our bones are remodelled each year and if we're walking with good posture, they'll be remodelled in the correct way to support our physique better. When we're walking we tend to be in our aerobic zone, so it's also really, really good for our cardiovascular system (i.e. general fitness). It's very good for our mental state as well,' says Shane. 'We produce a lot of endorphins when we're exercising – a natural drug which makes us feel very good.'

Exercising for just twenty minutes a day three times a week has noticeable effects, said a 2006 University of Georgia study. 'Regular Exercise Plays a Consistent and Significant Role in Reducing Fatigue' found what many of us knew already, that physical activity gives us more – not less – energy and improves our mood – thanks to the happy hormones it produces. But there's more.

Naturally (pun intended), walking on hills and trails rather than on tarmac is better for you too. 'You'll be using more of your muscle groups – lateral muscles for example,' explains Shane, 'and getting more of a whole body workout. Softer terrain will be kinder for your joints, too, by as much as 30 per cent difference. The air's fresher, you're seeing great views, so it has a feel good factor.

'A multi-day walk will give you fantastic fitness and core strength. It's taking a hobby and turning it into an event, an adventure. So there's some excitement and adrenalin involved, too. It's an exciting thing to do.'

Now for the Bad News …

So that's the good news. Ready for the bad? Most of us are doing it wrong. We're walking with bad technique, or form. 'Most people walk with bad technique,' says Shane. 'That leads to the body

Bad posture and overstriding can injure your muscles when walking.

being stressed in the wrong places and, ultimately, injury.

'The most common errors are overstriding and bad posture. Lots of people overstride, especially men, when they're trying to get somewhere quickly – meaning there's too much pressure going through the heel, impacting the knee especially. Heel strikes are effectively braking and you can get stuck in a cycle of braking, pushing off, braking, pushing off. We all tend to lean back a bit even when not walking, so we tend to walk like that too. That promotes over-striding. Posture is even more important when you have a heavy pack on, meaning yet more force going through your knees.

'If we don't support ourselves properly, by aligning our skeleton,' says Shane, 'it's our muscles that are working hard to hold us up. But they should be used for propelling our body, rather than being overstressed by extra posture and weight-carrying

Good posture means walking efficiently (see the numbered points in the text).

than the ball of the foot, but you're missing out on that proprioception.

'Your head should be up, meaning you can see where you're going, but you'll be breathing more easily too. The head weighs quite a lot so we don't want it lolling around. We want it in the centre of the body, balanced by our skeleton. We also want the head to be relaxed.

'Often when we walk, especially if we're carrying a pack, we tense up – usually in the shoulders or glutes (backside). But we want to be as relaxed as possible. Everything works much better if it's relaxed.

'Let your arms swing easily – you want some natural swing, which helps your legs, via elastic recoil, meaning the other arm will swing back too – using the body's natural system of fascia tissues (think of it like a stretchy latex suit under our skin). For every movement we do, there's a counter-movement, meaning it's creating energy as we walk and making half the effort for us.

'Lots of us lean backwards, but we need a lengthened spine, a tall gait, especially when we're carrying a pack.

'A level pelvis is fundamental. It gives us structural integrity and gets our abdominal muscles engaged. If we lean back it creates an anterior tilt in our pelvis. We need a level pelvis for the abdominal muscles to work for us.

'Legs, like the shoulders, should be very relaxed and soft. The softer everything is the better it works, so we want nice and relaxed.

'We can move just as quickly and much more efficiently with a smaller stride. As you bring your back foot forward, try to bring it higher than the ankle of the other foot – this will help prevent heavy heel strikes. And a faster cadence or stride.'

work, especially if we have 10kg on our back. Overuse and misuse are what injure muscles. Bad posture usually means the quads and lower back are doing more work than they should be doing.'

How to Walk More Naturally and Efficiently: Best Posture

'The best way to walk is in the most natural and efficient way possible,' explains Shane. 'Moving with the least impact on the body means we're using less energy, stressing our body – muscles, tendons, joints – less. To walk more efficiently we use the body's natural supportive structure, the skeleton, so our posture is vital.

'Your feet have 200,000 nerve endings, all sending information back up towards your brain – that's proprioception. If you're coming down strongly on the heel not only is it much less stable

Good Posture: Warm-up

To ensure we have good posture before a walk, here's a little routine we can do:

1. Make sure your feet are facing forward, hip width apart and centred on the ground.

ABOVE: *Before you start, make sure your feet are together and facing directly forward.*

RIGHT: *To help align the skeleton, stretch your hands above your head.*

BELOW: *Also remember to level up your pelvis.*

2. Lengthen your spine by putting your arms above your head and straightening yourself out. This will allow you to walk nice and tall – you can also do this periodically as you walk along.
3. Most of us have bad posture and need to engage our core – do this by levelling your pelvis. Put the thumb of your right hand in your belly button and the back of the other hand in the small of your back and level the pelvis, by tilting it up and towards you – this engages your abdominal muscles.
4. Look down. We are looking for a straight line from ear to shoulder to hip to knee to ankle. If you can't see the knot on your shoelaces, tilt yourself from the waist slightly until you can.

Hiking Uphill

'Walking uphill is about getting up the gradient in the most efficient way – without getting into oxygen

Good posture while walking uphill is crucial to avoid injury.

Bad posture can put an unnecessary strain on your body.

debt. The one time above all we want our posture to be right is when we're coming up a hill, because our muscles are already working hard. What people tend to do is lean into the hill, even put their hands on their thighs.

'But your quads and lower back muscles are working really hard. Bending at the waist also means you lose the recoil of your fascia and, by limiting your lungs, you're probably reducing oxygen production by up to 30 per cent.

'Instead, stand tall – it feels counterintuitive, but biomechanically it's right – so the bones take the weight. You should have strength and integrity from neck to pelvis. Everything else super soft, like a rag doll. Your feet will mostly be contacting the slope with the balls. But letting your heel regularly go all the way down to touch the terrain stresses your Achilles tendon. So keep the steps small, with relaxed legs.

'And enjoy it – walking up a hill should be fun. You should have your head up, looking around. Stop and take in the view. That's what hill walking is about, not a head-down trudge. We tend to think when we're doing something tough we have to really attack it, but you should be relaxing your way up the hill.'

Hiking Downhill

'Downhill is about damage limitation. Because of gravity it's tempting to go too fast and the biggest mistake here is overstriding, which often means the heel hitting the floor with a straight leg.

'On the flat, when you put your foot down you get around five times your body weight coming back up your leg through impact. Going downhill, it's twelve times. So, on a straight leg, landing heel first, the average person could have literally a tonne of pressure going through their knee every time their foot lands.

'So bend your knees slightly. The heel will lead you, but it should be soft, rolling impact. Let the foot roll forward, rather than planting the heel into the

Bend knees slightly when walking downhill.

Avoid going downhill too fast – don't overstride.

ground. Small strides gives you more control and stability.'

Everyday Posture

'We can't just put £170 boots on and suddenly expect to walk with amazing form. Our walking form is an extension of who we are, and how we stand and sit, every day. So if we practise good posture in daily life, we'll be better walkers – and ultimately happier ones.

'You need to be thinking about your posture every day, when you're at your desk, on the phone, standing in a queue. Think about having a tall, straight spine, feet together, pointing forwards – not splayed outwards, which is a common problem – tilt your pelvis to get your abdominals engaged. When standing ensure you can see the top of your laces, head up, feel centred. Practise this and, when you go trekking, ideal posture will come more naturally.'

In a Nutshell

If all that information seems overwhelming, here's an easy way to simplify it: try to walk tall and with smaller strides.

How to Wear Your Pack

'I see lots of people wearing backpacks badly,' says Shane, 'with space between shoulder straps and shoulders, without the belt done up. That means you're stressing your body unnecessarily.

'If your backpack is getting sweaty on a hot day a lot of moisture builds up. As well as the potential for chafing and other discomforts, sweating is losing vital water. If it's comfortable, consider taking your pack off one shoulder at a time to air your back as you move. Plus it might give your shoulders a rest too.

A badly packed (see page 35 for more) – or badly worn – pack can feel twice as heavy. It should fit

POST-WALK STRETCHES

'Exercise causes muscles to compact. Make sure your body is ready for the next day, by stretching your muscles back to their previous state.'

Calves

After your walk, spend a few minutes stretching out your calves – your body will thank you tomorrow! Your calf muscles may well take a bit of a beating on the uphills, so it's good to stretch them out afterwards. Hold this position, applying pressure on the back leg and calf, for about fifteen seconds. Then switch over.

Hamstring

Feel the stretch in your front leg. Hold for fifteen seconds. You're not trying to increase flexibility necessarily, just trying to get the muscle back to its natural shape.

Quads

Grab your ankle under your backside and hold it for five seconds.

Stretch out your arms by first pointing up, then pointing out to the sides (like an airplane), then pointing down to the ground. By stretching your arms out in three directions, and holding each one for five to ten seconds, you're also stretching out your neck muscles, upper back, shoulders and arms, which can all get pretty stiff after a long day with a pack on.

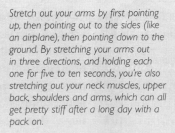

snugly around the shoulders, so there's no sideways movement. The waist belt should be done up and on your hips – people often have them too high or too low. That way it can properly take the weight of the pack, which shouldn't be on your shoulders as that will bend you forward and stress back and quads.'

Trekking Poles

Poles are really popular with walkers on the Continent – it's sometimes also called Nordic walking. They're excellent for taking impact off your legs, knees, ankles, and feet, sharing the weight around better, and for helping maintain an upright posture, especially when tired (which may help your back too). They can also be a great aid for climbing uphill, and downhill. They give your arms and upper body a workout, help you test out peat bogs and give better balance on any terrain. Nordic walking advocates also say poles enable a faster, harder pace.

The main downside of poles is that you're likely to be expending more energy – but to some that's simply burning more calories. In terms of technique, the pole needs to impact the floor before your foot or the benefit isn't being utilized.

Personally I take poles on some walks and not others, depending on the terrain. But many people find them a revelation, especially if you're rehabilitating from an injury. To find out more it might be worth looking into the Nordic walking movement.

How Fit do You Need to be for a Long Distance Walk?

There isn't a definitive answer. As you'll see from the Q&As with expert hikers in this book, many don't specifically train to get fit before a trek (though they're generally pretty active folk) and there's an argument for saying you can get fit as you go (in which case, don't plan to do big days of mileage early on, build up gradually). Of course, if you haven't done much exercise leading up to a multi-day walk, then it will be harder work – mentally and physically – and you may not enjoy it as much. Good fitness isn't a macho, muscle-pumping thing. It's being healthy. And the more hill health you have, the more you'll enjoy those fine lumpy things. You won't be too tired to appreciate an extraordinary panorama, or so fatigued you start getting topographically embarrassed. You'll simply be happier.

SIX-WEEK TRAINING PLAN – GET FIT FOR A LONG DISTANCE WALK

If you want the reassurance and motivation of a plan to follow, here's a carefully designed schedule to take walkers who might do a 4–8-mile walk once a week to being fit enough for a multi-day hike.

The best way to get strong for a long distance walk is simply by walking. Then you're using the exact same muscles and other body parts that you'll use on your walk. The key thing is to gradually increase your distance over time, ideally until you've matched the approximate distance you'll be doing on the average day on your trek. Jotting down weekly mileage can really help maintain focus and you can even start getting competitive with yourself.

Take your pack with you, because it makes a big difference. Take it empty at first, but gradually fill it.

Make your training as specific as possible, within reason. If your trek will be mountainous, sandy or marshy, try to do some training hikes in similar conditions. Different terrain tests your body in different ways and you don't want it to be a big surprise, mentally or physically.

Don't stress about doing the exercise on the exact days, missing a session, or even sticking strictly to the mileage. As long as you're building gradually and getting used to a pack, you should be fine.

Running, cycling and swimming (sometimes called cross-training) are also excellent cardiovascular workouts that will benefit your overall fitness. You may experience aching muscles and soreness at first, but that's the body adapting to the task and becoming stronger. Pain that increases, however, could be an injury. Use the Rest, Ice, Compression and Elevation (RICE) technique and if that doesn't alleviate the pain after a week or two, see a physio. And don't forget to practise a more natural and efficient walking form.

Week 1		Week 4	
Mon	Rest	Mon	Rest
Tues	Walk 2–4 miles, focusing on good form	Tues	Walk 6–10 miles on hills/mixed terrain
Wed	Rest	Wed	Rest (or cross-train)
Thurs	Walk 2–4 miles, focusing on good form	Thurs	Walk 3–4 miles
Fri	Rest	Fri	Rest
Sat	Rest (or cross-train)	Sat	Walk 12–14 miles on hills, with nearly full pack
Sun	Walk 6–8 miles on mixed terrain, with empty pack	Sun	Walk 6–8 miles with nearly full pack
Week 2		**Week 5**	
Mon	Rest	Mon	Rest
Tues	Walk 3–5 miles, focusing on good form	Tues	Walk 4–6 miles, focusing on good form
Wed	Rest	Wed	Rest
Thurs	Walk 3–5 miles on hills or mixed terrain	Thurs	Cross-train
Fri	Rest	Fri	Walk 6–8 miles on hills with full pack
Sat	Rest (or cross-train)	Sat	Rest
Sun	Walk 8–10 miles on mixed terrain, with pack with a few items in	Sun	Walk 8–10 miles with full pack
Week 3		**Week 6**	
Mon	Rest	Mon	Rest
Tues	Walk 4–6 miles on hills/mixed terrain	Tues	Walk 3–4 miles, focusing on good form
Wed	Rest	Wed	Rest
Thurs	Walk 4–6 miles, focusing on good form	Thurs	Rest (and get some extra sleep)
Fri	Rest	Fri	Rest (double-check you've got everything)
Sat	Rest (or cross-train)	Sat	Start out on your long distance walk
Sun	Walk 10–12 miles on hills, with pack with a few more items		

Long Distance Walking Equipment: The Gear You Need and The Gear You Definitely Don't Need

'There's no such thing as bad weather, only unsuitable clothing.'

Alfred Wainwright, guidebook writer

Outdoor Gear

Should you wear leather or Gore-Tex boots? And what are gaiters actually for anyway? There's lots of gear about nowadays, much of it expensive, garishly coloured, confusingly named and making outlandish claims about keeping you warm, dry and making you invisible (or similar). So getting the right equipment can be confusing.

Do your outdoor-equipment shopping with a degree of scepticism. Newest, most expensive and lightest aren't always best. 'I think most outdoor gear is over-hyped and over-expensive,' says outdoor writer and broadcaster Cameron McNeish on page 154. You certainly don't need everything that's being pushed at you. After all, grumpy guidebook guru Alfred Wainwright only ever walked in his tweed suit and leather shoes.

(Though he did seem quite miserable, so maybe that was why?)

That said, amazing advancements have been made – not least Gore-Tex and much lighter-weight staple items such as sleeping bags – over the last twenty years, which has made the distance walker's life much more enjoyable. Some bits of equipment are fantastic – especially the warmth that can be achieved with such little weight.

When you find something that really works for you, look after it (for cleaning tips, see pages 24 and 31), especially boots and waterproofs. Treat them well and they'll repay the favour. Chuck them, still dirty, in the bottom of the cupboard and they'll get their revenge on you, especially those boots and waterproofs, probably the kit you'll spend most money on.

Indeed, good outdoor kit can be expensive, so if possible look to buy things at the end of the season they're most appropriate for – tents at the end of summer, waterproofs at the end of winter/ spring – when stock will be reduced. If you suspect something is faulty, don't be afraid to return it. The industry is generally very good with returned kit and some companies will replace items that are many years old if it has performed badly. I've even returned boots that I bought in Sydney to the same company's store in Bristol.

Though there are bargains to be had online, testing, touching and trying on an item in the flesh is often crucial. Also staff in outdoor shops are usually seasoned outdoor types, so pepper them with questions. If they're using industry jargon, don't be afraid to ask what PrimaLoft or ProShell actually is and does. It's a bit sneaky, but I sometimes try on an item in a shop then buy it more cheaply online – though if we all do that all the time there won't be any shops left, so it's not particularly clever. Outdoor magazines, such as *Outdoor Fitness*, *Country Walking* and *Trail*, are useful for reviews (see page 173), especially if they're doing a group test on an item you're after.

Manufacturers were slow to acknowledge that women tend to have different body types to men, but nowadays most things, especially footwear, packs and jackets, are made in two styles, male and female.

The Essentials: What do You Really Need?

The number one error new distance walkers make is to carry too much gear, which can easily ruin your trip. It'll make you slow, tired too soon, uncomfortable, fed up and contribute towards bad posture, which may cause more problems.

We're persuaded by a consumerist society that we need so many things that it can be surprising how long we can happily go without most of them. Some backpackers take pride in how little they can get by with. But some items are essential.

Even if you've opted to use a baggage courier, you should always have a map and compass – and know how to use them. Always take a little extra food, in case you're out longer, or energy levels dive (you'll need more calories than average anyway). Liquid is crucial too, to deter dehydration (you'll likely be sweating more than normal and therefore

losing fluids). Even if the forecast is for a dry sunny day, always take one extra layer; as well as deflecting rain, a waterproof works well as a barrier against wind, but isn't usually very warm if stationary. Hilltops are windier and colder than valley bottoms, plus if you stop for a picnic lunch you can quickly get cool. Or perhaps you're out for longer than anticipated and the temperature drops (often it's wise to pack a head-torch too).

Most experienced hikers wouldn't hit the hills without some sort of first aid kit (more anon). A whistle too is essential and much as many walkers are trying to temporarily escape the bind of technology, turn your phone off and chuck it (ideally fully charged) in your pack. It could be crucial if you need to summon help (not necessarily for yourself) – or inform your B&B you're running late.

Optional but often recommended items include: an emergency shelter of some sort, a space blanket, survival bag or bothy bag. And might a hat and gloves come in (pun not intended) handy? Waterproof trousers and gaiters are two more optional items.

Then if you're going self-sufficient there is a sleeping system (as a tent/bivvy, sleeping bag and mat tend to get called nowadays) to think about and probably cooking equipment ...

Long Distance Footwear

Shoes/boots

The most important item a walker can have is his or her footwear. Make sure, above all else, your boots or shoes are comfortable. Ill-fitting footwear could ruin your trip, by helping cause blisters or other major annoyances.

Other things to look for are good grip; some level of cushioning or shock absorption is usually preferable too. The importance of ankle support is open to debate. Some people comfortably cover long distances in running- or multi-terrain shoes (i.e. trainers), or even robust sandals, as gear guru Chris Townsend often prefers, though the more weight on your back the more support you may need for your ankles.

KIT CHECKLIST

Day walker and overnight walker (essentials)

Backpack ☐
Footwear ☐
Underwear ☐
Socks ☐
Trousers/shorts ☐
Base layer top ☐
Mid-layer/shell layer (usually both) ☐
Map ☐
Compass ☐
Torch (with new batteries or spares) ☐
Whistle (many packs include these as
    standard now – but check they work) ☐
First aid (including any personal medication) ☐
Food – more than you think you need ☐
Drink ☐
Mobile phone (fully charged) ☐
Tissues ☐

Day walker and overnight walker (optional)

Waterproof trousers ☐
GPS unit ☐
Camera ☐
Gaiters ☐
Shelter (bothy bag/survival blanket/bag) ☐
Hat ☐
Gloves ☐
Spare layer(s) ☐
Sun hat ☐

Sunglasses ☐
Sunscreen ☐
Knife ☐
Trekking poles ☐
Guidebook ☐
Insect repellent (especially for Scottish midges) ☐
Water filter and/or purifying tablets ☐
Map case ☐
Binoculars ☐
Evening sandals ☐

Overnight walker (essentials)

Tent or bivvy bag ☐
Sleeping bag ☐
Sleeping mat ☐
Water container ☐

Overnight walker (optional)

Stove ☐
Fuel ☐
Pot/metal mug ☐
Spork ☐
Lighter or waterproof matches ☐
Hygiene products (toothbrush and paste,
    wet wipes/tissues, liquid soap) ☐
Reading book ☐
Pen ☐

It's definitely an item to buy from a shop – ask an assistant for advice on fitting. Anything that feels even slightly tight is too small – your feet will expand during a long walk. It's better to go boot shopping in the afternoon of a warm day, when your feet have already expanded, rather than a cold morning, when they're small. Take your favoured or thickest walking socks along and try to visit a shop with an incline board so you can test boots for downhill walking. If your foot slips forward it's not the right boot for you. If you can't find boots that fit well, look into footbeds or insoles.

Manufacturers often classify boots as one-, two-, three-, or four-season. Four is aimed more at winter and will fit crampons, so in most cases they'll be too big and cumbersome. One-season may be too lightweight for most cases, whereas two-season will give limited ankle support – not a problem if your ankles aren't used to it. Three-season will best suit most long distance walkers and is the most versatile footwear choice. Also, consider how heavy boots feel. Heavier may mean less robustness, but more spring in your stride means a faster pace. Don't ever start a long walk in new boots – you're pretty much saying 'please give me some big painful blisters'. Wear them in first.

Leather boots especially need breaking in. Leather is the traditional material for boots and

CARE FOR YOUR BOOTS ...

And your boots will care for you. Look after boots and they will last and retain waterproofness for longer. Any lingering mud will aid rot, so it needs cleaning off.

To re-waterproof, look to the manufacturer's instructions, but you'll usually use a reproofing agent such as wax or Dubbin. Similarly Gore-Tex boots will need re-proofing, usually with a spray or lotion (see the manufacturer's information for details).

It's often the last thing you want to do after a long walk, but, like the washing up, the sooner you get at cleaning your boots the easier it is. I usually sneak my boots into the shower with me when the wife's not looking. To dry them, fill them with newspaper and place them away from direct heat. By the fire, or next to a radiator or a hairdryer is bad news for leather.

it's still popular for good reason. Leather lasts and lasts if well looked after, keeps water out for a good length of time and is rugged and subtly adapts to the shape of your foot.

Gore-Tex boots in comparison will keep water out for longer, be lighter, quicker-drying and won't usually require breaking in. However, once water gets in it won't easily leave. And Gore-Tex boots aren't usually as durable or rugged, but they're perhaps the more beginner-friendly option. I have a pair of each, but still prefer trustworthy leather on most occasions.

Socks

Don't neglect socks. I like wool as it usually provides good cushioning, but more importantly stays warm when wet. Always ensure there are no seams or ridges across heels or toes – turn them inside out if need be – as this encourages blisters.

Other socks claim to ventilate well or wick away sweat, while some are even waterproof (though they need to breathe too or they'll be counterproductive). Never wear cotton socks as they retain moisture and make blisters much more likely.

A big thick pair may look uber-comfy, but in summer they'll make your feet too warm and increase the chance of blisters.

Gaiters

My wife mocks my gaiters. She says they're pointless. I love my gaiters. They're often invaluable. They're best seen as foot protection, for keeping unwanted things out of your boots – water, stones, snow, but most of all mud (and saving your legs from scratchy vegetation).

Without gaiters, water can often collect on a sock top and sneakily make its way down into your boots. Yes, like a slug. It might seem counterproductive to tuck gaiters under trousers if it's raining, but otherwise rain will likely slide down the top of them, too, rending them half-useless. Look for Gore-Tex gaiters or at least a breathable pair. I don't take them on every walk, but certainly if I know it'll be boggy.

Backpack

The three key items to spend your money on for a long distance walk are boots, a waterproof and a backpack. As with boots, an ill-fitting pack may make your trip miserable.

For a day walk (if you're using a luggage courier), a 20–30-litre-capacity pack should do for most people. Experienced, self-sufficient hikers may go as small as 35 litres, but they'll have their kit list honed to perfection. Try to aim for more like 50–70 litres

Backpacks come in various sizes. Around 25–35 litres (packs either side) are good sizes for day hikes or supported treks, whereas the 65–80-litre range is better suited for self-supported, multi-day walks.

– 75 litres and above is probably too much and there may be a temptation to fill it. You'll be carrying the weight of the pack as well as your gear, so try not to go far north of 2kg. But comfort is paramount.

You're looking for an adjustable well-padded harness, a strong, comfy hip belt and an overall feeling of comfort and stability. The hip belt should sit well on the hips – helping balance the load equally between hips and shoulders. Try it on in the shop and ask for it to be filled with items – you'll gain little from trying it on empty. Try on several, even if the first one feels good. Some have adjustable back harnesses so play around with them.

Also look for compression straps (to make the bag compact when not full), a fortified bottom (as it'll often be plonked on rocks and wet grass), a slim profile (i.e. no large side pockets), so you're not bashing into things/people, and a reasonable level of water resistance. But most of all, as with your boots, it's about comfort. For how to wear a pack, see page 22.

Layers

A 'layering system' is a buzz-phrase at the moment and all it means is wearing two to four layers on your torso, instead of perhaps one or two big, thick, heavy ones. They usually comprise a base layer, mid-layer (perhaps two in winter; often none in summer) and an outer shell (a waterproof). Layers can be taken off or added as the day progresses.

But layering isn't the only way. Companies such as Buffalo Systems and *Páramo* produce innovative products that negate both the layering philosophy and the obsession with waterproof fabrics. The former is based on observations of how the Inuit dress (using animal hides), the latter how animal fur naturally deters rain. Neither are strictly waterproof in the conventional sense, but both pledge to keep you warm in the wet.

Cotton is the devil (no, really) and should be avoided at all costs, especially for any layers touching skin. It absorbs and retains sweat, makes you cold and encourages chafing and blisters in the bathing suit area and feet respectively.

If you're starting an outdoor wardrobe from scratch, some of the items below aren't essential. A non-cotton T-shirt, a wool jumper and/or a track-suit top are all half-decent options.

Base layers

A base layer is meant to keep you insulated, and, when you warm up, not let you get too warm (because that creates moisture, which makes you cold again) by ventilating and wicking away sweat. To wick well, a base layer should fit well. Collar zips are a good way to regulate temperature, too. Polypropylene and polyester are popular materials as they dry quickly (though can get pongy). Merino wool is warmer and a great autumn or winter option. Wool doesn't wick as well and instead absorbs moisture, but stays warm when wet. I tend to wear a synthetic, quick-dry top in summer and perhaps merino in winter. Similarly with underwear, avoid cotton. I like SmartWool products, but there are other thermal options.

Mid-layers

A good mid-layer will be warm, but allow moisture from the base layer to escape easily, and yet retain much of its insulating properties even when damp.

Waterproof jackets, such as these from Berghaus, come in all sorts of levels of protection, from those designed for winter mountaineering (left) to extremely lightweight items best suited to runners (right).

The most popular mid-layers are fleece, down, synthetic (like down but man-made) and softshell.

Down jackets are wondrous things, so light and warm (the best warmth per gram ratio). But they're more expensive and traditionally don't retain warmth when wet and that could get you in trouble if your waterproof misbehaves (and no waterproof keeps rain out indefinitely). Berghaus and others are bringing out clever down materials that still work well when wet, but generally speaking synthetic (such as PrimaLoft, ThermoBall, Thermolite, Polartec …) will work much better when wet. Down is also often too warm for walking and better kept in your pack for lunch on a windy plateau edge. Insulation jackets are lighter than fleeces but heavier than down and they work when wet, so perhaps present the best of all worlds.

There are a wide range of thicknesses and warmth levels for fleeces – from 'micro' fleece tops that weigh just over 200g, through to large jackets close to 1kg. Fleeces generally have good wind resistance as well as warmth, but tend to be heavier than other options, and are certainly heavy when wet. Both down and synthetic insulation layers are noticeably warmer, but I always feel a good fleece offers psychological comfort – you think you're warm.

Gilets and vests – be they fleece, down or synthetic – can be excellent as they allow armpits to breathe while warming your core – but again they need to fit snugly to work. There's nothing wrong with a woollen jumper really (just ensure it's not combined with evil cotton, hiss). They provide great warmth that will still work if wet, but they can be heavy – heavier still when wet – and slow to dry.

Softshell – What is It Anyway?

One disadvantage to a layering system is that if you're getting too warm and it's raining, it's the middle layer that needs to come off. Taking off that outer layer means losing warmth and/or getting a bit wet. The softshell (as opposed to an outer, 'hard' shell – i.e. a waterproof) helps combat this. It's like a tracksuit with a sci-fi makeover really. Softshells usually have more warmth than a waterproof and some weather resistance (i.e. wind and rain), but aren't fully waterproof. So they'll keep the elements off for a while. Some waterproofs will get you a bit too warm if worn all day, so a softshell is a good alternative as they're more breathable. They're not essential kit, but I love them.

Outer Shell/Waterproof

An outer shell or waterproof will probably be one of your biggest investments. It should keep the elements – rain, wind or snow – off but also allow excess warmth to escape – so you can breathe, through 'membranes'. But the jacket that's 100 per cent waterproof and 100 per cent breathable hasn't been invented yet, so there will be a marginal compromise in one direction.

As well as Gore-Tex, eVent and NeoShell technologies are breathable and waterproof and most jackets, whether made by Berghaus, Rab, North Face or whoever, use these materials – and will have a label clearly saying so.

RE-WATERPROOFING

Few things look as miserable as the walker with the waterproof that has just been found out to no longer perform the task that gives it its name. Like with boots, jackets need care and re-waterproofing to retain effectiveness over time (as do other waterproof items such as gaiters and packs).

Based more on suspicion than science, I wait as long as possible to wash a new jacket, as it may never seem quite as effective afterwards. Most jackets have a Durable Water Repellency (DWR) coating, which gradually wears off and needs replacing. Carefully follow both the manufacturer's and reproofing agent's (Nikwax and Granger are the two most popular makes) instructions. These usually include washing a jacket at 30°C, on its own, and without fabric conditioners.

To test whether your waterproof still does what its name suggests, run it under a tap and the water should 'bead' on the material. If it doesn't, it needs re-proofing. Breathability too dwindles with a build-up of dirt (visible and otherwise).

Like fleeces and most upper body items, there's a range of thicknesses, from ultra-lightweight 'packaway' jackets that weigh just over 100g (designed more for occasional summer showers), to monstrously heavy-armoured items designed for Himalayan winters.

Check the jacket is tape-seamed. Some extra tape along the seams – areas especially vulnerable to water – goes a long way to keeping you dry. Also look for a good hood, ideally with strengthened peak/visor for adjustability (usually pull cords), and so it stays off the face. Flaps over the zips also help protect a vulnerable area. I like big pockets, but think about whether they'll be accessible with your backpack belt done up?

Look for cuffs that do up tightly to keep rain out. And make sure it's long enough in the arms – fully stretch your arms out with gloves tucked into cuffs to see if a gap appears. You want room underneath for two to three layers, but not much more as it'll mean wind can sneak up there. With the zips, see if it's easy to operate with gloves on – some aren't. In a downpour, I also like to be able to hide my chin away from the elements. I'm a bit of a coward like that.

Jackets' waterproof ratings are surprisingly badly (perhaps intentionally?) signposted and you may have to ask about them. Waterproofs all go through a Hydrostatic Head test to meet the British Standard. Test scores range from 0 to 1,500 mm ('water resistant' and appropriate for 'dry conditions or very light rain') all the way to 10,000–20,000 mm (branded 'highly waterproof' and suitable for 'heavy rain'). In between, a rating of 1,500–5,000 mm is seen as suitable for 'light to average rain'. So for my jackets I usually want at least 5,000–10,000 mm, which earns the label 'very waterproof' and is suitable for 'moderate to heavy rain'.

A Moisture Vapour Transfer Rate (MVTR) tells us how breathable a product is. The results are normally stated as grams per square metre per day. The larger the number, the greater the performance. For more active use (stout hill walking rather than field or woodland bimbles), where you're likely to sweat, look for features such as underarm zips and big pockets, both can be undone to increase ventilation.

Waterproofs and many softshells also have a layer of Durable Water Repellancy (DWR), which wears off gradually and needs to be replaced by re-waterproofing.

Leg Cover

Most of the year I wear shorts for walking. They're breathable, less restrictive, there's little material to dry after a shower (wet trousers are 'orrid!) and I rarely feel the cold in my legs. That way I don't usually need to bring waterproof trousers either (though I've regretted that at times). However, outside of warmer months, once stopped, you can quickly feel the wind. There's also the threat of brambles and ticks.

If going for full-length trousers, ensure they're light, perhaps stretchy and definitely quick-drying. Jeans are a very bad idea. Like cotton, they absorb and retain water, drying very slowly, growing heavy and encouraging chafing, plus they're inflexible. Along with cotton, they're the worst things you can wear if there's a hint of moisture about.

I've always considered waterproof trousers a luxury – but less so if you're looking at more than an hour of driving rain. Nowadays they can weigh less than 100g and are often just as breathable as jackets, made with Gore-Tex and suchlike.

Don't underestimate the brilliance of the buff (bottom), a super-versatile bit of kit that can be a scarf, a hat or used for wiping your snotty nose or tearful eyes.

Accessorizing

It's often colder up on the hills and you'll be out in the evenings and early mornings, so contemplate whether gloves and a hat are needed. Again wool and fleece are good options, while companies such as SealSkinz make waterproof products. Buffs, too, are brilliant. I hardly go anywhere without one. These could, unkindly, be mistaken for a metal music fan's bandana, but they're so much more than that. This magically versatile addition can be a headband, light hat, ear warmer, scarf that won't blow away and hankie or cloth for miscellaneous purposes – and there are always miscellaneous purposes.

Head-torches mean hands are free, and I prefer ones with standard AA or AAA batteries as it's easier to get hold of more batteries en route. I usually take a tiny back-up light too.

Tents

Companies who make kit with mountain-marathon runners in mind, such as Vaude, Terra Nova, Nemo, Big Agnes, Mountain Hardwear (ultra-lightoutdoorgear.co.uk is a good starting point for lightweight kit) and others are often the best places to start. One-man tents weigh as little as 552g nowadays, and two-man tents less than 1kg. But be aware there will be some comfort sacrifices, and these super-lightweight tents cost more. A three-season tent will suffice for most scenarios.

Sleeping Bag

Traditionally a sleeping bag would rival your tent as potentially your heaviest and most expensive item. But bags are as light as 300g now (though they're not super warm at that weight – but you can get a lot of warmth, especially in a down bag, for well under 1kg) and as with most things, there's a ridiculous amount of choice.

Your biggest decision will be whether to go with down (natural fibre, more warmth per gram, packs up smaller, but doesn't work well when wet, costs more and difficult to clean), or synthetic (heavier for the warmth, but works much better if wet). Personally I just love the feeling of being snug as a bug in a down sleeping bag and I'm happy to put effort (well, an extra dry bag anyway) into keeping it dry.

Sleeping bags have a rating system based on one to four seasons, which is pretty self-explanatory. They also have a Comfort rating, which again should be easy to guess at, and an Extreme rating (slightly alarmingly, it's based on the lowest temperature in which a woman can survive).

For summer camping in the south, a one-season sleeping bag may well suffice in Britain, but it's a pretty limited option. For spring and autumn in higher places you'll need at least a three-season-rated bag; for winter, it can get cold enough to warrant an 'Extreme' rating (–10°C), so consider adding a liner to make a bag up to 5°C warmer (e.g. silk is warmer but more expensive than polyester, polycotton, cotton, fleece, and others).

Sleeping Mat

As I learned the hard way (see page 8), you won't get much sleep without a mat – it's as much about insulation from the cold ground as it is about comfort. However, after a long day's stroll you'll probably be fairly tired, and will sleep in conditions you probably wouldn't normally manage. Old-school foam mats are cheaper, often lighter and more durable, but less comfy and more bulky than inflatable mats. I usually go for a three-quarter length inflatable mat to save weight. My feet don't need padding (I chuck a spare layer down for insulation from the cold). Around 200–400g is a good weight for a comfortable, inflatable (sometimes called self-inflating, though you'll still need to puff your cheeks) sleeping mat.

Food

Cans of baked beans may be what cowboys seemingly ate around the campfire but I wouldn't recommend it for a backpacker. They're heavy and there are much cleverer options nowadays, especially dehydrated food, which is very light and available in most outdoor shops. All you do is add water (sometimes it doesn't even need to be heated, though that invariably tastes better) and you can have a chilli con carne or spag bol. Desserts are usually to die for and breakfast options abound too.

Breakfast is perhaps the hardest meal from home to replicate in the wilds, with neither toast nor cereal being practical (powdered milk is best for teas and coffees). For me it's often dried noodles and a flapjack or banana (if I've been able to pick one up en route). Don't carry much more food than necessary, but you should always have a little bit extra in case of unforeseen circumstances. For more on good walker nutrition, see page 40.

As with all outdoor clobber, cooking kit is getting lighter and lighter, with titanium (which the two pots here are made from) being especially light.

Cooking

There are plenty of well-priced high-quality pocket rocket-style stoves around, which are small, lightweight (the Alpkit Kraku stove is just 45g, without gas) and take mere minutes to get your brew on. There are various types of fuel, but I stick to gas as although it's not as quick as others, it's more readily available on or near long distance trails. For lightness, buy titanium for your pot or mug and spork. I tend to add a brew kit – tea bags/coffee/hot chocolate (small amounts in plastic bags) and dried milk (fresh milk is impractical) to keep morale up.

For a water container some prefer bottles, as they're easier to top up from streams. While hydration bladders encourage you to drink more regularly, the user is oblivious to how much water is left and they're a faff to refill.

First Aid and Safety

First aid kits in shops are usually bulky and include many things you're unlikely to use. This probably isn't a view endorsed by St John Ambulance, but I only take painkillers/anti-inflammatories, plasters (primarily with blisters in mind) and possibly some antiseptic cream (the Ramblers website also considers bandages, sterile dressings and disposable gloves to be essential). And I've regretted not having

Vaseline, too, for weather-battered lips and chafes in unmentionable places. If I need a large bandage I'll use some clothing. Minimum safety equipment should be phone, survival blanket or bag (if you're not carrying a bivvy), whistle and torch.

Hygiene

There are some obvious differences with standard holiday packing. For example, there's no way I'd carry a week's worth of spare clothes on a week-long trek. I'd take just one spare set and even then probably only clothes that will be directly against skin – a dry set (and a warm layer) for sleeping and evening wear. If there's no one around but sheep, who cares if you're a bit pongy?

Materials such as merino wool often have no whiff even after several days' usage. Modern outdoor fabrics dry quickly and the best way to dry out wet kit is by wearing it. There might be a chance to give it a rinse in a stream at some point (though I did once meet a chap who always scheduled in a wash day at a laundrette into his walks). A small bottle of liquid soap, too, can be an asset.

If you want to be more considerate of fellow hikers or don't want to be refused entry to pubs en route and there are no enticing mountain streams for a wash, wet wipes are a good way to freshen up

Dry bags, such as these from Exped, can be very useful for obvious reasons. Brightly coloured ones are less likely to be left behind after a picnic.

– but again, not a full packet; they're as heavy as a brick. I always take two or three spare plastic bags, for rubbish and wet kit.

How to Pack Your Pack

Pack packing is a compromise of practicality balanced against weight. The heavier but hopefully softer items should be against your back and ideally about halfway up it. This helps good posture (too much weight at the bottom will encourage a forward lean) and balance (a top heavy pack may swing about and make you unstable).

The idea is to create a centre of gravity close to your back, neither too high nor too low. Your tent, sleeping bag, food, mat and stove are usually the heaviest items. Though the sleeping bag always seems to end up at the bottom of my pack, partly because it's the last thing you need when you set up camp, you don't want to have to spread everything out on wet grass to get your tent out. So that's where practicality comes in. Be careful about tent poles running against your back though. Stuff any spare clothes around the central bulk, trying to have equal weight at either side so it doesn't subtly unbalance you.

Practicality comes into play again when considering which items you may want to access – snacks, water, a warm/waterproof layer, navigation aids, etc. – without tipping the entire contents of your pack out into a bog.

Despite manufacturers' claims, hardly any packs are reliably waterproof and you really don't want a wet sleeping bag (especially if it's down), so it's best to either have your kit in extra dry bags inside your pack, or a cover over your pack (the former is preferred as it won't blow away). A third and better option is one big dry bag inside your pack, which has the risk of rain getting in if you're fumbling about looking for something, but makes packing easier (individual dry bags will trap air) and simpler.

See the Light

The lighter your pack weight, the happier you'll probably be (as long as you haven't forgotten to put the tent in). I read a magazine feature recommending taking a polystyrene cup and cutting the handle off your toothbrush, which is taking things to a new level of gram-geekery. But one common mantra is that each item should have two uses. Will rolled up clothes suffice as a pillow? Can a fleece double as a towel? Will a titanium mug double as a pot? If you have a penknife, do you need a cutlery knife? Every gram counts. Could items such as toothpaste and sunscreen be decanted into something smaller? With food, is there excess packaging that could be binned?

Luxuries

Many experienced hikers allow themselves one luxury item, a pillow perhaps (shame!) or a Kindle. I always like to take a good book and a pen to make notes in it, though think *The Diving Bell and the Butterfly* rather than *War and Peace*).

A backpacking mantra is 'nothing new on the day' – the day being the first of your long distance walk. Make sure you've tried out everything beforehand, ideally in similar conditions. You don't want to find your new socks cause you ferocious blisters when you're miles from anywhere.

CHAPTER 4

Picking and Planning: What to Decide and Do Before Starting Out

'Nothing is more damaging to the adventurous spirit within a man than a secure future. The very basic core of a man's living spirit is his passion for adventure. The joy of life comes from our encounters with new experiences, and hence there is no greater joy than to have an endlessly changing horizon, for each day to have a new and different sun.'

Christopher McCandless, aka Alexander Supertramp, *Into the Wild*

Some Motivation

'Don't keep thinking about doing a hike,' says *The Last Englishman* author Keith Foskett, 'because you'll never do it. Set a date, even if it's two years distant. The hardest part of any thru-hike is not actually doing it, but having the guts to make the definite decision to go and do it in the first place.'

But Which Trail?

Try to pinpoint what it is you want from the experience. Is it a taste of wilderness you're after? (think Scotland). Do you like the idea of a trail with lots of history (Hadrian's Wall, The Ridgeway, Offa's Dyke Path)? Do you want to stay near home (there are long distance trails in and near London; the Thames Path; the London Loop and the Capital Ring)? Do you want to get away from all the bothersome people (the Pennine Way, northern Scotland, the Cambrian mountains in central Wales)? Or prefer the idea of chancing into a few friendly faces (Coast to Coast has never been more popular, thanks to Julia Bradbury's TV series)? Do you want big hills and big views (all the aforementioned paths, but plenty of others too), or something a bit flatter and not too exposed to the elements (look at trails in the south)? Do you particularly like railways (Settle to Carlisle), rivers, canals or the coast (in each case, there are plenty to pick from)? Is there a part of the country that's always sounded like worth a visit – the Yorkshire Dales or Peak District? Is wildlife part of the appeal (think coastal walks, such as the South West Coast Path, Norfolk, or the Scottish islands)? Flowers (try the Cotswold or Pennine Way)? Or is your motivation primarily for a fitness challenge (any of them, just shift your backside)?

To avoid becoming one of those unfortunate anecdotes National Park or Mountain Rescue staff will exchange at the pub, it's advisable not to make something as long and challenging as say Coast to Coast or Cape Wrath your first multi-day walk. Start with something smaller – even a weekend trip – on the same trail. You'll see if you enjoy it if nothing else. It'll be great for fitness and testing out kit, too.

National Trails and Great Trails

If you want a path that will be well signposted, well maintained and not too remote, consider a National Trail, the Champions League of British trekking. There are fifteen National Trails in England and Wales, and twenty-six Great Trails (well twenty-five really – one's a canoe route) in Scotland. They're government-backed, so they're clearly marked on the ground and on maps, and usually planned out so there's a village or accommodation option at approximate day-walk intervals.

Each National or Great Trail showcases a different part of the country, a different type of terrain, with a unique character. The downside is they'll be busier, especially during summer – but you may find that comforting. Most distance walkers start out on the National Trails, often working their way through them over a period of years.

National Trails also have individual trail officers and excellent websites which make planning your trip easier, and several guidebooks to choose from. But there are hundreds of trails that don't have National Trail status that shouldn't be ignored.

When to Walk?

The attractions of summer walking are obvious, but it's the busiest time, especially during school holidays (mid-July to end of August), so booking ahead – even weeks ahead – for accommodation is wise.

Spring can mean colourful splashes of flowers and playful bleats of lambs; it's less predictable weather, but magical if the planets align for you. But again, be aware of Easter holidays and extra demand for services around then.

In Britain there is no reason why you cannot do a long distance trail at any time of year, provided you are properly prepared.

Autumn can be beguiling, perhaps the best time of the lot, with the special colours of trees. I love a late-August stroll in heather, which turns to a sea of vivid purple on the North York Moors and Exmoor.

Winter is underrated (except perhaps in Scotland, where the nights become very long). There's less daylight of course and it'll probably be cooler, but you'll probably have most of the trail to yourself and the pleasure of being the first to place footprints in fresh, crisp frost or snow. However, some accommodation providers and even transport in remoter places (crucial ferries on the South West Coast Path for example) may not be running, so it will involve some research. Also, remoter and higher trails, such as in Scotland, may get more severe weather and aren't for the inexperienced.

Pillow Talk

How you're going to sleep – carry a shelter or stay in accommodation en route – will be perhaps your biggest decision. For me, half the joy of long distance walking is in being self-sufficient. It's just you and your pack against the world, you're an independent soul, a freelancer, an adventurer, a renegade cast adrift by society … (okay, perhaps I'm fantasizing now). The extra weight of tent, sleeping bag and mat mean your shoulders mightn't vote for this option, but your wallet will. Plus hiking with a tent or bivvy makes you much more flexible. If you've booked accommodation you're committed to a certain distance every day. The availability of campsites varies though, so research the trail before setting off.

The Backpackers Club lists campsites in remoter areas on its useful Long Distance Footpath Site and Pitch Directory. The LDWA website is excellent for searching for accommodation options, too – and everything else for that matter.

Wild Camping

The ultimate option for the purist is wild camping, which simply means camping out, but not at designated campsites (though nothing's stopping you switching between the two). Wild camping can be exhilarating and liberating. It's cheap, more peaceful, adventurous and closer to nature. It's controversial though. In England and Wales wild camping is officially only allowed with the permission of the landowner, otherwise you're technically trespassing. But that often isn't practical (where is the landowner? Should you knock on doors after 9 p.m.?).

There's a tradition of backpackers arriving in the evening and breaking camp early, and wild camping is largely tolerated on the basis that it's for one night only and no sign of your stay is left. That includes rubbish and fires – which are bad for local ecosystems, leave an eyesore and you don't want a wildfire on your conscience. And always avoid polluting water. If you need to, ahem, lighten the load, do so 30 m away from water, 50 m from paths and not anywhere that might be used for shelter such as a sheepfold or cave.

Wild camping also offers little to local economies. But the Ramblers Association openly support it, you're invited to wild camp in wonderful Dartmoor National Park and anywhere in Scotland (away from dwellings and roads), so it's hardly a criminal activity. Wild camping tends to make for a more solitary experience of a trail, for better or worse.

Bunk to Basics

If you'd rather not turn feral, you'll find a variety of accommodation options, including some surprisingly plush ones. Youth hostels cost from around £15 for a dorm bed, and often offer good-value evening meals and cooked breakfasts, plus the chance to compare blisters with other walkers. But be wary of group bookings of hostels (where they book it all) during holiday periods and some weekends. Bunk houses and camping barns are usually just a wooden barn with a sleeping platform and toilet facilities (you'll need a sleeping bag and mat), from around £6, though they're fairly rare. There are even rarer opportunities to sleep in bothies/refuge huts, which are much more prolific in Scotland. They're free, but basic. B&Bs, guesthouses, hotels and pubs offering accommodation (all around £25–£60) feature in most villages and towns and using local accommodation means you're helping local economies too.

National Trails' official websites are usually the best starting points for accommodation listings, and transport, and other trails have good websites, often run by enthusiasts. But new places spring up (and down) all the time, so have a search about too. Local tourist information centres can be helpful as well.

Solo or Team?

'Walking alone, you see a lot of wildlife and scenery,' says Jacquetta Megarry on page 133. 'There's nothing to disturb your tranquillity nor to interrupt your train of thought.' She also applauds wilderness hiking conservationist John Muir's quote: 'Only by going alone in silence, without baggage, can one truly get to the heart of the wilderness.'

I too prefer to go solo, then I'm free to make all the decisions, rather than debating and compromising on every little one. However, a walking holiday with a friend is one of life's great joys (especially if they do all the map-reading). I usually feel a tiny bit sad when I'm seeing something amazing and there's no one to directly share it with. In a nutshell: it's a win either way.

CHAPTER 5

Life on the Trail: Tips for Staying Safe and Happy

'What is this life if, full of care, we have no time to stand and stare?'

William Henry Davies, *poet and walker*

Topographical Embarrassment: 'Er … Where am I?'

Unless with someone more experienced, you shouldn't start out into the UK hills without navigation skills. But even the experienced can get a little, *um*, topographically embarrassed occasionally. Most of the time that just adds some time and distance to your day's walk. But being unsure of your location, somewhere remote, in hostile weather, can have consequences. So for your own safety – and potentially anyone you might be walking with – it's vital that you know how to use a map and compass before you set out on a long distance walk. Getting lost isn't itself dangerous, but as part of a chain of events it can lead to a bad situation.

I'm perhaps not the best person to give advice on navigation (my wife thinks I get lost on purpose, and she's probably right). But three things I've learned through my countless errors are:

1. Check a little ahead on your map or route description in your guidebook to see what the next junction or significant landmark is, so you're expecting it. You should always know approximately where you are on the map.

2. When the penny drops and you realize you're temporarily topographically perplexed, the simplest solution is usually to retrace your steps. This will often lead you back to the trail, rather than carrying on regardless. Which, I know from bitter experience, usually gets you more lost.

3. If you're trying to work out where you are from the map, look to the landscape around you first – are there any high points, edges of woods, walls, telegraph pylons, lakes, rivers, buildings, roads or steep gradients? – and try to apply that to the map, rather than the other way around. Looking at the map first and trying to fit it to the ground often means you force it to fit what you want to see, when it doesn't really.

If you're intimidated by the idea of navigation, pick up a book or do a course, spend time in the hills with someone who can teach you, formally or informally, even check out instructional videos on YouTube. As a minimum you should know how to read a grid reference, and make and march on a bearing. It's not as complicated as it may seem and can be great fun to learn.

Natural Navigation

If you enjoy navigation and reading the landscape, have a think about learning some natural navigation. Some of it's really clever, real-life Crocodile Dundee stuff, while some of it is common sense. I was very lucky to be sent by *Country Walking* magazine to meet adventurer and *Natural Navigator* author Tristan Gooley (for more details, see page 120) and do a story on him and his outdoor skills. It was revelatory.

He taught me how to find north from looking at a tree – most trees bend towards the sunnier south – and even from puddles on a track (he chuckled indulgently when I called him 'the Puddle Whisperer'). More than that though, he taught me to really think about the landscape: what made it, what's under it, what does it tell us? The natural world – and even urban areas (moss tends to grow on north-facing places, where it's damper; most satellite dishes point south–south-east) – hasn't looked the same to me since. There's excellent information on his website (naturalnavigator.com), including about his courses, too, and in several more of his must-read books.

Food and Drink: Why Eating and Drinking the Right Things – and in the Right Amounts – Will Make Your Hike Safer and More Enjoyable

As former Pennine Way trail officer Steve Westwood confesses on page 101, he had no knowledge of suitable hill food when he set off to walk the National Trail as a 16-year-old. 'I recorded what I ate in my guidebook,' he says. 'Malham – two litres of cola and seven packets of cheese and onion crisps!'

Of course, that's not the type of food armies – or indeed healthy distance walkers – march on. 'One of the common mistakes long distance walkers make is underestimating how much energy or fluid loss there will be,' says Renee McGregor (eatwellfeelfab.co.uk), a registered dietitian and sports nutritionist with numerous years' experience working with a range of athletes, from elite to recreational level, and herself a keen ultra runner and hiker. Her excellent book *Training Food* makes the science of sports nutrition practical and accessible.

'Some may think that walking isn't going to be as energy demanding as running or cycling the same distance,' she says, 'but that's not the case. The length of time on feet means your body's energy demand will be just as high.'

Energy dependence

If you're exercising in the outdoors all day you'll need more fuel (calories) to produce more energy. Add to that the extra energy you need to carry a pack, the possibility of some stiff hills, a cold wind perhaps ... you'll need a lot more calories.

Fuelling properly begins with the right breakfast. 'A good breakfast made up of slow release carbohydrate and protein is essential for sustained energy,' says Renee. 'A wholegrain bagel with two poached or boiled eggs, or porridge made with milk, topped with a banana and nut butter are all great options.'

Carbs are most people's main energy source and that's what our muscles prefer to use for fuel. Carbs are sugary foodstuffs (including fruit, which has lots of natural sugar), starches (bread, rice, potatoes, pasta) and fibres (plant-based foods). Some carbs are better fuel sources than others: sugar is good for a quick pick-me-up, but soon leads to another crash as you burn through it quickly. The NHS website says, 'Sugar steals your stamina' (meaning added sugar, rather than naturally occurring sugars in fruit and similar). Slow-burning starches (potatoes, bread, cereals and pasta) give a more sustained energy release. Fruit is often watery so helps with hydration too.

The trick when out in the hills is to eat and drink little and often. Renee says the best energy snacks for hikers are: 'trail mix, flapjacks, salted peanuts, peanut butter sachets or sandwiches, dried fruit, malt loaf or fruit loaf, chocolate-covered Brazil nuts and filled bagels.'

But don't rely wholly on carbs. 'Adding snacks that are high in fat and protein will help to sustain energy levels and slow down the release of energy from the carbohydrate stores. Nuts, seeds and nut butter are all ideal, making trail mix a great choice.'

Running low on energy doesn't mean you'll suddenly keel over and fall asleep in the middle of the trail. However, if it's raining, windy or cold and perhaps you're a little bit topographically embarrassed, lacking energy at a key moment can lead to bad decision-making. If you're keeping energy levels topped up, you're going to have a more enjoyable experience overall and make better decisions.

'Top up with snacks and fluid on a regular basis,' says Renee. 'Exact requirements will be dependent on age, gender and size of the individual, but working on a principle of needing around 30g of carbohydrate an hour is a good place to start. That's equivalent to a large banana, or three dates, a slice of bread with peanut butter, one and a half slices of malt loaf, a small square of flapjack or 500 ml of energy drink.'

Snacks you really enjoy can be great for morale, after a shower or long, stiff climb, especially.

Fluid arrangement

'It's really important to keep on top of hydration, too, especially on hot days,' says Renee. 'Dehydration will not only hinder performance by enhancing fatigue and encouraging cramps, but will also affect concentration and the ability to make decisions. Water or squash are ideal hill drinks. If it's particularly warm, you will probably be losing more water through sweat. But also iodine, sodium, potassium and calcium, so add some electrolyte tablets to your water to help replace what's been lost. In warm conditions aim for 200–250 ml of water every twenty minutes. In less warm conditions you will need 100–150 ml.'

Though there's an argument for isotonic drinks being helpful in replacing sodium (salt) and glucose (a rapidly digested carbohydrate), sugary fizzy drinks aren't clever. Metabolizing all the sugar uses up water that should be used for hydration and can potentially imbalance the body's sugar and insulin (leading to mood swings). A bubble-filled tummy can also mask real thirst.

Paradoxically and a little confusingly there's real danger in drinking too much water. It can eventually cause your brain to swell, stopping it regulating vital functions such as breathing, and causing death through water intoxication. In the 1990s several news-making deaths of young people who'd taken ecstasy were because the drug made them thirsty and they drank too much.

A good way to see if you're hydrated is when you pee … if it's yellow, you're dehydrated to a degree; if your self-made water is transparent, you're hydrated. If you're going to the toilet more than twice an hour you may be over-hydrating. The best way to think of it is to drink when you're thirsty – but don't force yourself to.

Recovery food

'With back-to-back days of walking, the key for keeping on top of fatigue is combining good fuel options during the day, but also really thinking about recovery nutrition' says Renee. 'A long day of walking will mean depleted glycogen stores and ideally these need to be replaced in preparation for the next day. Protein – meat, fish, eggs, dairy – helps muscles that will have been damaged during a day's exertion repair and recover.'

Wild camping nutrition

But what about wild campers who mightn't be sitting in a pub or restaurant each night? 'You want to maximize on nutrient-dense foods to ensure you can replenish appropriately. Rehydrated food is good, as it's light and easy to prepare. Whether you go for state-of-the-art specialist meals or cobble together something yourself is up to you.

'Simple options include mixing together dried soup packets (which adds vital salt) with either noodles or couscous,' says Renee. 'The only drawback of this tactic is that it can be low in essential protein required for good recovery. One way to get over this is to include a milk-based pudding such as custard, fortified with skimmed milk powder, followed by a hot chocolate also fortified with skimmed milk powder. Just 20g (or 4tsp) of skimmed milk powder will give you an additional 10g of protein. For a recovery meal, most people will need 20–25g of protein dependent on weight. For campers, preparing a breakfast based on oats, skimmed milk powder, nuts and dried fruit, which

you can just add boiling water to, will be a great start to the morning.'

Weight loss

Some may see walking as a good way to lose unwelcome weight and they're right to do so. 'Walking is a great form of exercise to aid weight loss,' says Renee, 'as it's carried out at an intensity where you can tap into your fat stores. Trying to keep carbohydrates to a minimum but filling up on high fat or protein choices will ensure fat stores are utilized for energy.

'If weight loss is not a target, be sensible about your choices. Aim to fill up on protein and vegetables. For breakfast, instead of a fry-up, opt for wholegrain toast with poached eggs, grilled tomatoes and mushrooms for a nutrient-packed start to the day.'

Wild camping is one of life's most underrated joys.

What about pub grub?

What if you're in the pub at the day's end, treating yourself to an ale but not wanting to write off all the good you've just done to your body? 'There is no problem in having a celebratory meal or pint. However it's important to remember that alcohol slows down the absorption of nutrients needed for recovery. I would suggest trying to take on a small amount of recovery food on completing your day's walk, having a shower and then having a pint.'

Staying Safe: the Weather, Hypothermia and Other Hazards

'But what happens if you twist your ankle?' asked my friend. 'You'd be stuffed.' We were discussing our weekend plans over a drink on a Friday night after work. I was off on a two-day coastal hike in Royal National Park just south of Sydney and my friend, a non-walker, thought the idea was reckless verging on lunacy. Okay, it was Australia, where everything seems to be against you – the hot hot heat of the sun, a scarcity of water, all those animals with big sharp teeth. But to me his attitude was really ironic.

Here we were in a busy city centre, drinking alcohol, while all around us did the same, releasing the frustrations of a working week. Outside the bar, on two sides, were roads teaming with fast traffic. There were real hazards all around us in a hectic urban environment – Friday night is a pretty busy time at A&E. The next morning I felt far safer on my own, away from alcohol-fuelled crowds and speeding vehicles.

Hiking is incredibly safe and healthy – and it makes you safer (because you pick up more skills and confidence) and healthier. But like almost anything, in the great outdoors there is a chance not everything will go entirely to plan, especially when the great British weather is involved. But that's part of the appeal. It's a real place, not a video game or smartphone app, outside of our control and all the better for it. But it's important to know which things are more likely to go wrong and what to do if they do.

Tell someone

Anyone who's read *Between a Rock and a Hard Place* or seen the film version *127 Hours*, will know the importance of letting someone know where you're going. Aron Ralston, despite being an experienced hiker, went exploring in Utah's canyons without telling anyone his plans. He got his arm stuck under a boulder – really, *really* stuck. And he remained there for five days, until, out of desperation, he cut off his own forearm to free himself. If anyone had known where he was he would probably still have two hands.

Bear in mind though you may be relying on an SMS message or phone call to notify someone you've made it to Dufton and there may be no signal. You don't want to trigger a big search operation needlessly. My message is usually something like, 'I'm walking the XX Way, starting from XX on XX and it should take me about XX days. So if you haven't heard from me by [twenty-four hours after my latest expected finish date], please contact the police/Mountain Rescue.' I'll also try to get in touch with that person a couple of times en route, just to let them know all's well. If any accommodation or transport is booked, I pass on those details too.

Admittedly this may seem like overkill for something like the Cotswold Way where you're never far from a road or village – there's little that can go wrong for you. But get into good habits and when you're attempting something far more remote such as Cape Wrath you'll be safer.

The weather

Us Brits are obsessed with the weather, but for good reason. We live on an island so the skies change quickly and not always predictably. Get a daily weather forecast if you can. It's worth knowing if rain or strong winds are forecast for a certain time of day. Would you consider setting out earlier or later to dodge the worst of it? Do you need to take extra layers, or waterproof trousers? Are you in for a cold night? The weather plays a massive part in the enjoyment of your trip so be aware of it. Just remember that if you're going up into the hills or mountains, the forecast for the little village down in the valley may be very different, so try to get a hill forecast.

Lightning

They're rare, but a direct lightning strike can cause a fatality. A partial lightning strike, often using rock as a conduit, can also cause long-term health problems. Storms are often indicated by dramatic towering clouds. A good way to determine how close a storm is is to count slowly between cracks of thunder and flashes of lightning. Six seconds is equivalent to about a mile and a half (2 km). Then repeat the procedure several times to work out whether it's getting nearer or further away.

Lightning likes summits and other protrusions, as they're easier to reach. So when a storm is detected it's best to calmly but swiftly move away from the highest ground – you also don't want to be the highest thing around on, say, a plateau. Then sit on your pack or a sleeping mat and keep your hands off the floor, until the threat passes.

River crossings

With river crossings, if a safe jump isn't certain it can be better to get wet feet than to slip on a rock on landing and make the situation worse. If wading though, the place where the river is narrowest is often less safe, as the current is usually stronger and the water deeper. Loosen your pack so if you do stumble you can cast it off quickly and it won't drag you underwater. Facing upstream makes you more stable. Again trekking poles or a stick can be a great aid. If the river is intimidating you, consider whether crossing it here is really necessary. There may be a bridge or access to an easier crossing further along.

Drinking water

Is water in streams and rivers safe to drink? Might be. Might not. I tend to add water-purifying tablets. Nowadays they work fast and have little taste, but mean you definitely won't have a week-long puking bug. Contaminated water is commonly caused by animal carcases, but also droppings. Never drink from still water sources. Running water is much more likely to be safe, and the higher up it is the less things may have contaminated it – and the faster it runs, the safer it's believed to be. Boiling water is another way to make it safe.

Magic mushrooms

When it comes to foraging, unless you know your *Agaricus macrosporus* from your Slippery Jack, don't eat wild mushrooms. Some of them are so toxic that they will ensure they are the last things you will ever eat.

Carbon monoxide poisoning

I used to cook with my gas stove in the tent without realizing how dangerous it is. But backpackers die from carbon monoxide poisoning, often in their sleep. Poisoning occurs when gas or similar fuel fails to fully combust due to a lack of oxygen in the surroundings. So always cook outside your tent. If it's a monsoon outside, okay, bring it into the porch, with great care, but make sure there's as much ventilation as possible – and leave the tent open for a time after cooking. Carbon monoxide is undetectable by smell or taste. Symptoms to look out for include dizziness, headaches, nausea and drowsiness.

Blister-busting

Probably the most common ailment of the long distance walker is the cursed blister. 'Blisters are caused by heat, moisture or friction,' says movement specialist Shane Benzie. 'Firstly, think, are your socks and footwear appropriate to the conditions?' Wearing super-thick socks in mid-summer, no matter how comfy they are initially, is likely to cause overheating and sweat. Look for socks that ventilate and wick. Some boots (Gore-Tex) are more breathable than others too.

'The best way to combat moisture build-up is to air your feet regularly,' says Shane. 'Whenever I sit down, to stop for lunch or admire a view, I take my shoes and socks off. That way, the heat goes, the moisture evaporates and you can get rid of any stones or mud too. In one move you eradicate

Looking down towards the Edale Valley from the Pennine Way National Trail in the Peak District.

the three evils of blister creation. As long as your walking partner doesn't mind, of course.

'Alternatively, take them off the moment you stop at the end of the day. Many people might stay in the same socks to cook, eat and even sleep. Getting those feet aired is massively important, especially if you're walking for several days. And if you feel a hot spot on your foot, deal with it. That usually means a sturdy plaster over it, or tape, to reduce the friction.'

If you realize too late and a blister has sprung up, official advice is not to pop it as it can lead to infection. But lots of people take a sterilized (with a lighter flame) needle to it, let the fluid out, and then apply a firm plaster over the top or apply a sterilized plaster.

If you struggle with blisters, experiment with different types of boots and (more economically) socks, but there are also pre-emptive measures, such as Vaseline, (the excellent) Camphor Spray or talcum powder on feet, or if you know from experience exactly where hot spots are likely, pre-tape your feet.

Hardened feet are less susceptible to blisters and regular walking hardens feet. At risk of sounding like an oppressively interfering parent, trim your toenails. People lose toenails because the foot is banging into the end of the boot. So clip them a few days ahead of the walk. Beware – you can cut them too short, and if mud gets into your boots and into your toenails infection can occur.

Chafing and sprains

Like blisters, the best way to discover if you're susceptible to chafing in certain places or from certain garments is to wear the equipment you're likely to take on your long distance walk on training walks. Nevertheless, I've become accustomed to carrying a little tub of Vaseline close to hand to deal with irritant areas. And it can happen in the most unexpected places. Yes, those sorts of places. Try to ensure nothing you wear or carry rubs against your body. Again, cotton is more likely to lead to chafing because it retains sweat and water next to the skin. On a long walk a minor rubbing can become a big unforgettable sore.

For a sprained or twisted ankle, remember the RICE principle:

Rest
Ice
Compression
Elevation

Rest your ankle and, to reduce any swelling, add ice (if you don't have any to hand, drip some cold water over it). Then wrap your ankle firmly (though not tightly) in a bandage and raise your ankle so that it is just above the height of your heart. Don't be a hero: take painkillers if you have to.

Hazardous animals

Cows

I used to think people who got frightened of the big bovines were proper scaredy cats. Turns out they were right. For whatever reason (possibly new species have been introduced after the Foot and Mouth epidemic), increasingly walkers are attacked and even killed by cows. So approach them with great care. Sometimes trekking poles can lend a bit of confidence to the situation.

Most attacks occur when there are calves present and it seems to be protective behaviour by parents. The presence of dogs can also make cows nervous. The British Mountaineering Council advise that: 'If you find yourself in a field of suddenly wary cattle, move away as carefully and quietly as possible, and

if you feel threatened let go of your dog's lead and let it run free rather than try to protect it and endanger yourself. The dog will outrun the cows and it will also outrun you.

'Those without canine companions should follow similar advice: move away calmly, do not panic and make no sudden noises. Chances are the cows will leave you alone once they establish you pose no threat. If you walk through a field of cows and there happen to be calves, think twice; if you can, go another way and avoid crossing fields.' Bulls are best approached – or rather, not – as you would cows. Try to be alert but not alarmed.

Ticks

Ticks are right little blighters. These tiny bloodsucking arachnids can be found in areas of dense vegetation, such as long grass or bracken. They seek to attach themselves to you and feed on your blood like tiny, mostly harmless vampires. Ticks are known to carry diseases however, the most serious of which is Lyme Disease, which you don't want to get.

For areas of dense vegetation, you'll be more tick-proof in a long-sleeved shirt with cuffs fastened and trousers tucked into socks. Think about wearing shoes or boots rather than open sandals, and perhaps use insect repellent.

If you find a tick (ugh!), remove it quickly – preferably with a tick removal tool. You can use tweezers, but at the risk of squashing the tick and releasing fluids into your skin. Another tried-and-tested method of removal is to loop a thread of cotton around the tick's mouthparts, then pull steadily upwards. If part of the tick breaks off or you think any part of it may be left in your skin, consult a doctor as soon as you can. If possible, take the tick with you so it can be sent for analysis.

Other irritating insects

Insect repellents containing DEET are good for discouraging most types of biting insect, including mosquitoes, midges and gnats, and are a good idea if you're walking in areas where midges are likely, such as Scotland in summer. Midges tend to dislike lightly coloured clothes. And midge repellent.

Horsefly bites often result in a painful itchy welt. They cut the skin, rather than piercing like a mosquito. So clean the bite while it heals to prevent infection.

If you are stung by a bee the stinger may remain in your skin. The safest way to remove it is by scraping something hard, like a credit card, over the skin. Do not attempt to pinch it out as this can squeeze more venom into your skin.

Snakes

Britain's only venomous snake, the adder, can be a variety of colours but is best identifiable via a black zig-zag pattern on its back. While adder bites should not cause too much damage to a healthy walker, they are painful and require medical attention regardless. The venom may have more impact on a child or dog.

Bites are more common in summer when reptiles emerge to enjoy the sun, but because of their camouflage can easily be trodden on by accident. Most of the time they're shy creatures, but don't try to touch them. No one has died from an adder bite in Britain for over twenty years. With proper treatment, the worst effects are nausea and drowsiness, followed by (sometimes severe) swelling and bruising.

Hypothermia

Because Britain's high and wild places are often wet and windy, cold exhaustion and hypothermia are real possibilities. Hypothermia is genuinely dangerous and can lead to the worst outcome. Things can spiral quickly if fatigue also comes into play. It sounds obvious, but especially in wet, cold or windy conditions, it's key to stay warm. Staying dry helps a lot, eating regularly is also key. Getting damp from sweat can lead to problems if you stop for a while.

If the early signs of hypothermia are spotted, take on more food and drink (ideally sweet), add warm layers and remove wet or damp ones. Moving generates warmth and you should be moving down off the hills. But if that's not possible, see if the person can be further sheltered, using a bivvy, bothy or survival blanket. Then summon help (see opposite).

Signs of mild hypothermia include (among others): shivering, cold, pale skin, blue lips and pale, white hands and feet, and lethargy.

Signs of moderate hypothermia include (among others): violent shivering, slurred words and lack of co-ordination, confusion, difficulty with tasks, personality change and odd behaviour.

Signs of severe hypothermia include (among others): cessation of shivering, cold, pale skin, blue lips, unconsciousness, unresponsiveness, rigid muscles, possible absence of signs of life (breathing, pulse).

Summoning help – call 112

If your phone shows no signal and 999 does not work, dial 112 and it will hunt for an alternative network. A 112 call is prioritized over other calls, even when your phone says 'busy network'. If you're having to use someone else's phone and don't know the pin number to use it, again dialling 112 overrides that function. Phones with no credit can also still make 112 calls. Some phones will even allow a 112 call without a SIM card.

Wait for a full minute for a call to connect. Then if it hasn't got through, turn 180 degrees and try again. If it's windy, turn your back on the elements to talk to an operator. If you've pre-registered your mobile phone with the emergency services (which you should: to do so, just text 'register' to 112 to receive an automated reply; read it and follow instructions to text back with 'yes') a text to 112 may still get through. State who you are, where you are, what the incident is and how many people are hurt. Then wait for three minutes for a text back.

If phones aren't working at all, the emergency signal is six blasts on the whistle or six flashes with the torch. Another way to signal is with a mirror or reflective object, again, six flashes, pause, then six more. Lighting a fire can be an option – and a triangle of three fires will be understood by a helicopter as a distress signal. If you have a bright jacket or sleeping bag or pack, that might be worth waving. Another international signal is waving with two arms.

CHAPTER 6

How to Use This Guide

'I only went out for a walk and finally concluded to stay out till sundown, for going out, I found, was really going in.'

John Muir, *American author, conservationist and long-distance walker*

This isn't a definitive list of the country's top 100 trails. How could it be – has anyone walked all 100 to be an authority on them? And what makes one trail supposedly superior to another is subjective. But included are those that seem to be the most highly rated ones. And that definitely means the fifteen National Trails (plus Coast to Coast and the new, very exciting, Wales Coast Path) in England and Wales, and Scotland's twenty-six Great Trails. After that there are some obvious classics to include. And almost any trail that has a guidebook made the list, because it's assumed an author and publisher both think the trail popular enough to merit one. There are plenty of beginner-friendly paths here and I've gone for a good geographical spread, too. It was tough sticking to 100 though. So just because a footpath isn't on the list, it certainly doesn't mean it's not worthwhile. We're spoilt for choice in Britain.

If this book has given you the walking bug and you want a truly comprehensive list (and plenty of helpful information for each walk), go to the Long Distance Walkers Association's excellent website (ldwa.org.uk) or pick up their *The UK Trailwalkers Handbook*. Ldwa.org.uk should be your next port of call anyway. It's a brilliant resource for long distance walks.

Baggage Couriers

Many of these trails have baggage courier services, ranging from larger companies covering the whole country (such as Contours Walking Holidays, contours.co.uk), to smaller local, one-man-and-his-van operators. We haven't listed them here because things change and information like this can quickly become out of date. But a quick internet search for the name of a long distance path and 'baggage' or 'luggage' and 'courier' or 'service', or even 'sherpa service', will usually get you the information you want. The more popular the route (National Trails especially), the greater the chance the path is serviced this way.

Trail Experts

What makes this directory different to any other is that an expert with first-hand information provides each entry. We can all use the internet to find dry stats and figures, but I really wanted people who'd actually walked each trail to share their views, their passion, their wisdom and tips.

Usually the trail expert is a guidebook author. If they weren't able to help or there wasn't a printed guide for the route, the expert either works for the local council in the relevant department (often looking after the trail is their job), runs an online guide, belongs to the society for the path, or is a member of Ramblers or the Long Distance Walkers Association and has walked it. Occasionally we've been lucky enough to get a contribution by the person who devised the route.

Waymarking, Maps and Guidebooks

Most long distance trails are also clearly marked on maps. Occasionally they're not though, for various reasons – which to some will seem fun, to others less so – but we've let you know in each case.

Relevant maps have been suggested and they're usually Ordnance Survey. OS maps come in two scales: 1:25,000 (Explorer) and less detailed 1:50,000 (Landranger). But for most long distance walks you'd need a big bundle of them – nine for the Pennine Way for example, which is expensive and heavy. Alternatively, Harvey Maps provide excellent maps for many long distance trails on

waterproof paper, at a scale of 1:40,000. For the Pennine Way you'd need just three from Harvey, and only two from a third option, Footprint Maps. Footprint's offerings aren't as detailed, in fact they're quite rudimentary, but for that reason they appear clearer to the eye. Some are waterproof and their scales vary from 1:40,000 to 1:50,000. Rather than a coding system like OS, both Harvey Maps and Footprint Maps name their maps after specific trails: Pennine Way South, Pennine Way Central and Pennine Way North, for example, for that National Trail.

Guidebooks always have some sort of mapping in them too, along with detailed route descriptions (plus information on history, flora and fauna, and where the best pubs are), and in my experience that can be enough. A guidebook may cost you £13. Four OS maps would be well over £30, and heavier. Guidebook maps can vary from full-page OS mapping to hand-drawn efforts. Guidebooks can be a major asset. But then I would say that because I'm a guidebook author.

Occasionally a trail is waymarked on the ground but isn't (yet, in most cases) detailed on OS or other maps. In these and similar cases we've still listed the maps needed to navigate the area.

The North York Moors on the Coast to Coast walk in late summer, when the heather turns purple. DAMIAN HALL

The Top 100 Trails

KEY

GT = Great Trail
NT = National Trail

South-West England (15)

Bournemouth Coast Path
Clarendon Way
Coleridge Way
Cotswold Way (NT)
Great Stones Way
Heart of England Way
Icknield Way Path
Mid Wilts Way
Monarch's Way
Ridgeway (NT)
Somerset Coast Path
Shakespeare's Way
South West Coast Path (NT)
Wessex Ridgeway
White Horse Trail

South-East England (15)

Capital Ring
Chiltern Way
Downs Link
Greensand Way
London Loop
New Lipchis Way
North Downs Way (NT)
Pedlars Way and Norfolk Coastal Path (NT)
Saxon Shore Way
Sandlings Walk
South Downs Way (NT)
Suffolk Coast Path
Thames Path (NT)
Vanguard Way
Wealdway

North-West England (23)

Coast to Coast
Cumbria Way
Cumbria Coastal Way
Dales High Way
Dales Way
Dales Celebration Way
Derwent Valley Heritage Way
Gritstone Trail
Herriot Way
Howgills and Limestone Trail
Lady Anne's Way
Limestone Way
National Forest Way
Pennine Bridleway (NT)
Pennine Journey

Pennine Way (NT)
Raad Ny Foillan (Isle of Man Coastal Footpath)
Ribble Way
Settle to Carlisle Way
Six Peaks Trail
Staffordshire Way
Tributaries Walk
Two Saints Way

North-East England (7)
Cleveland Way (NT)
Hadrian's Wall (NT)
Ravenber Way
Six Dales Trail
St Oswald's Way
Viking Way
Yorkshire Wolds Way (NT)

North Wales (1)
Isle of Anglesey Coast Path

Mid Wales (2)
Glyndŵr's Way (NT)
Wye Valley Walk

South-West Wales (1)
Pembrokeshire Coast Path (NT)

All Wales (3)
Cambrian Way
Offa's Dyke Path (NT)
Wales Coast Path

Southern Scotland (23)
Annandale Way (GT)
Arran Coastal Way

Ayrshire Coastal Path (GT)
Berwickshire Coastal Path (GT)
Borders Abbeys Way (GT)
Centenary Way
Clyde Walkway (GT)
Cowal Way
Cross Borders Drove Road (GT)
Fife Coastal Path (GT)
Forth and Clyde Canal and Union Canal Paths (GT)
John Muir Way (GT)
Kintyre Way (GT)
Mary Queen of Scots Way
Mull of Galloway Trail (GT)
Rob Roy Way (GT)
River Ayr Way (GT)
Romans and Reivers Route (GT)
St Cuthbert's Way (GT)
Scottish National Trail
Southern Upland Way (GT)
Three Lochs Way (GT)
West Highland Way (GT)
West Island Way (GT)

Northern Scotland (9)
Cape Wrath Trail
Cateran Trail (GT)
Dava Way (GT)
Great Glen Way (GT)
Formartine and Buchan Way (GT)
Moray Coast Trail (GT)
Skye Trail
Speyside Way (GT)

Other (1)
John O' Groats to Land's End

England

South-West England

Bournemouth Coast Path

Leigh Hatts, author of *Exploring the Bournemouth Coast Path*
Swanage to Lymington: 37 miles/59 km
Difficulty rating: 1
Average days to complete: 4
Waymarking? Yes (although under various names – E9, Bournemouth Coast Path, Christchurch Coastal Path – the route passes through several local authority areas)
Maps: OL 15, 22
Baggage courier? No
For more details: bournemouthcoastpath.org.uk
Describe the trail
A route linking the Dorset Coast Path to the Solent Way by way of a spectacular bay at Bournemouth. A mainly cliff-top walk featuring high chalk cliffs, sandy chines, salt marshes and natural harbour entrances. The entire route can be in view on a clear day.
Highlights
Old Harry Rocks, Poole Harbour's chain ferry and Hengistbury Head.
Lowlights
The brief road walk past very expensive gated houses at Sandbanks.
Why do you love it?
The views, which have been likened to the Bay of Naples and admired by Benjamin Disraeli, Henry James and many others.
History/background
Check out Churchill's wartime lookout at Studland and Highcliffe Castle, where the last German Kaiser stayed shortly before World War I.
How challenging?
One steep path ascent and two cliff staircases. Signage varies in design due to county and borough boundaries.
Accommodation and transport
Plenty of B&Bs and budget hotels. Camping is difficult. All sections can be easy day-walks.
Best day-walk: Bournemouth Pier to Boscombe Pier. It's short but this gives an overview and there is the opportunity to be tempted further east.

Clarendon Way

Andrew Bowden, ramblingman.org.uk
Salisbury to Winchester: 26 miles/42 km
Difficulty rating: 1
Average days to complete: 2
Waymarking? Yes
Maps: OS Explorer 130, 131, 132
Baggage courier? No
For more details: ramblingman.org.uk
Describe the trail
A walk between two cathedrals. Forming part of the (modern) Pilgrim's Way, it's an easy and pleasant walk across the south of England. Much of it runs over downland, with a close similarity to the South Downs Way which connects with the Clarendon Way.
Highlights
Two stunning cathedrals to admire at each end.
Lowlights
The arrival into Winchester requires a fair amount of time wandering around suburban streets.
Why do you love it?
Pleasant, easy-going walking through quiet villages. Looks especially nice in the autumn and spring.
History/background
Part of the (modern) Pilgrim's Way, which, when connected with the St Swithun's Way and North Downs Way, allows the modern pilgrim to get all the way to Canterbury.
How challenging?
The walking is simple and easy-going, with few climbs. There are no long days, and few hills. However, waymarking is often not brilliant and using a map is highly recommended.
Accommodation and transport
There's plenty of good accommodation, and there are regular bus services along the trail. Train services run from each end. Using bus services, the trail could be split into two day hikes.
Best day-walk: Salisbury to Kings Somborne – quiet villages, pleasant pubs and good views.

Coleridge Way

Bryan Cath, coleridgeway.co.uk

Nether Stowey to Lynmouth: 51 miles/82 km

Difficulty rating: 3–4

Average days to complete: 6–7

Waymarking? Yes

Maps: OS/OL 9, 140

Baggage courier? Yes

For more details: coleridgeway.co.uk

Describe the trail

Follow in the footsteps of the Romantic poet, Samuel Taylor Coleridge, from where he lived to cross the Quantock Hills, the Brendon Hills and Exmoor. From open moorland to deep wooded valleys with rushing streams, to wide panoramas and coastal vistas. It passes through AONBs and a National Park.

Highlights

Coleridge Cottage (NT) at Nether Stowey; Moorland Hall and the stained-glass window celebrating the poetry of Samuel Taylor Coleridge in the village hall at Wheddon Cross; Coleridge Garden, Porlock; Oare church (the setting of R.D. Blackmore's romantic novel *Lorna Doone*); Lynton and Lynmouth (pretty, unspoilt villages on the coast); and Lynton and Lynmouth Cliff Railway, a water-powered funicular railway.

Lowlights

It is often thought of as harder than expected because of the height lost and gained (9,450 ft/2,879 m).

Why do you love it?

The beautiful scenery along its whole length. It passes through unspoilt villages with B&Bs who welcome walkers. It is perfect for the long distance walker or as a first attempt at a long distance walk taken at an easier pace.

History/background

There's lots of history found on this walk: Coleridge Cottage, The West Somerset Mineral Railway, Oare church, Watersmeet House and the Lynton and Lynmouth Cliff Railway are just some.

How challenging?

More challenging than one thinks, as the terrain is quite hilly. It's well waymarked, with a quill to mark the route. There are downloadable route directions on the website.

Accommodation and transport

It breaks easily into sections, using villages for B&Bs. Public transport is the main problem – getting back from either end to your start point is not really possible. If you came to the walk by public transport, then you can get a bus from Taunton to Nether Stowey and you can get a bus from Lynmouth to Barnstaple Station.

Best day-walk

Difficult to pick. But if forced, the start from Lynmouth to Oare church passes through some glorious scenery (but there's no way of getting back without a lift).

Cotswold Way (NT)

Anthony Burton, author of *Cotswold Way* and National Trail Video Guides (tvwalks.com)

Chipping Camden to Bath: 102 miles/164 km

Difficulty rating: 3

Average days to complete: 7

Waymarking? Yes

Maps: OS (1:50,000) 150, 151, 162, 163, 172; Harvey Maps

Baggage courier? Yes

For more details: nationaltrail.co.uk/cotswold

Describe the trail

A delightful rural route that follows the edge of the Cotswold escarpment – some of the finest scenery in the Cotswolds. There are a few sections that go through small towns and villages, but these are also very attractive. As much of the walk is on the edge of the escarpment, there are many splendid viewpoints.

Highlights

One of the great appeals of the route is the contrast between, for example, the wide-open spaces of Cleeve Common and the beech woods between Birdlip and Painswick.

Lowlights

There are very few lowlights – honestly. Right at the end there's quite a long walk through the outskirts of Bath – but it is Bath!

Coaley Peak, on the Cotswold Way, bequeaths classic Cotswold views looking south towards Dursley.
DAMIAN HALL

Why do you love it?

It's a personal favourite – but I do live practically on the Way! I love it for its wonderful scenery and the fact that it really doesn't ever have a dull section.

History/background

There is some excellent archaeology along the way, notably the Neolithic tomb at Belas Knap and several spectacular Iron Age forts.

How challenging?

There are some quite steep climbs, but always on good footpaths. The going underfoot is generally good, but in wet weather some descents can be a bit tricky. Transport isn't brilliant, but most places have some public transport. It's advisable to arrange accommodation in advance as it's quite sparse at some points – though I've walked the whole route twice myself and never had a problem. There are no actual campsites.

Accommodation and transport

Although accommodation is quite sparse it's generally very good, and there are usually choices between country pubs and B&Bs happy to cater for walkers. It would be extremely difficult to do the walk in day trips using public transport. But both ends have decent transport.

Best day-walk

Leckhampton to Painswick provides some of the best of Cotswold scenery: terrific views from the escarpment, followed by woodland, with a hill-fort along the way and ending at a typical Cotswold village.

Climbing up from the Stroud Valley on Selsley Common, with Laurie Lee's Slad Valley in the distance.

Great Stones Way

Ian Ritchie, greatstonesway.org.uk

Barbury Castle (near Swindon) to Old Sarum (near Salisbury), via Avebury and Stonehenge: 36.5 miles/58.5 km

Difficulty rating: 2

Average days to complete: 3

Waymarking? Partial

Maps: OS Explorer 157, 130

Baggage courier? No

For more details: Steve Davison's *The Great Stones Way* (Cicerone, 2014) is highly recommended

Describe the trail

The Great Stones Way links the two great stone circles of Avebury and Stonehenge. It crosses the green rolling Wiltshire Downs and passes through quiet villages in the Vale of Pewsey. It climbs onto Salisbury Plain with its wide-ranging views before, in Avon Valley, it meanders through picture-perfect villages with old churches and cosy pubs. It finishes at the ancient site of Old Sarum. All along the trail are ancient hill-forts and burial mounds and you really feel you are walking through history.

Highlights

The varied scenery and the sense of history.

The Great Stones Way. DAMIAN HALL

Lowlights

There aren't many, but perhaps the least interesting stretch is on the minor road from Woodborough to Wilsford – but it's only 3 km long.

Why do you love it?

It has a wonderful mixture of scenery, from the rugged landscape of Salisbury Plain to the sylvan delights of the Avon Valley.

History/background

The Great Stones Way is all about history – or rather pre-history. By comparison, Hadrian's Wall

The Great Stones Way visits World Heritage-listed Avebury, the largest stone circle in Europe. DAMIAN HALL

is a modern upstart. It takes in the greatest concentration of ancient sites on any walking trail in the UK.

How challenging?

This is not a difficult walk and it would be ideal for someone new to long distance trails. It is not yet well waymarked, but with reasonable map-reading skills and Davison's *The Great Stones Way*, it is an easy route to follow.

Accommodation and transport

Accommodation along the route is plentiful – visit greatstonesway.org.uk. Public transport on the northern half of the route is not good, but there's a good service along the Avon Valley. The trail can be broken up into easy day walks and there are a number of attractive circular walks.

Best day-walk

Overton Hill to Honeystreet. From ancient Sanctuary, a steady climb from the village of East Kennett gives views back to Avebury and Silbury Hill. After crossing the ancient Wansdyke there's a steep climb to the top of Walkers Hill. The views from here are stunning. As you drop down you look over the Vale of Pewsey and see Salisbury Plain looming in the distance. The villages of Alton Priors and Alton Barnes have fascinating old churches. Then there's the Kennet and Avon canal and the Barge Inn at Honeystreet, the centre of the world of crop circles!

Heart of England Way

Dave Higgins, walks secretary, Heart of England Way Association

Milford Common to Bourton-on-the-Water: 102 miles/164 km

Difficulty rating: 1–2

Average days to complete: 5–7

Waymarking? Yes

Maps: OS Explorer 244, 232, 220, 221, 205, OL45

Baggage courier? Yes

For more details: heartofenglandway.org and *The Heart of England Way* by Stephen Cross

Describe the trail

A journey through largely unspoilt English countryside. Starting on Cannock Chase (AONB), then visiting Lichfield with its magnificent cathedral, crossing the edge of the Trent Valley and continuing through the Tame Valley. On past the eastern rim of the saucer-shaped plateau that is Birmingham, descending through undulating countryside to cross the Avon Valley and the edge of the Vale of Evesham before entering the Cotswold Hills (AONB) and its honey-coloured stone villages and towns. The Heart of England Way offers a chance to enjoy countryside often bypassed or sped through by motorists, to show off some of the area's rich variety of terrain, towns and villages.

Highlights

Cannock Chase/Castle Ring, Lichfield Cathedral, Kingsbury Water Park, Baddesley Clinton, Henley-in-Arden, Alcester and Ragley Hall, Bidford on Avon, Chipping Campden, Blockley and Bourton-on-the-Water.

Lowlights

One section in Staffs (Drayton Lane near Drayton Bassett) is forced to use a busy road, due to continuing disputes over a short section of footpath designated 'private land'. Parts of the route are under threat from the HS2 high-speed rail line.

Why do you love it?

Walking variety on my doorstep.

History/background

There are several places of historical interest en route, including Castle Ring, the Katyn Memorial and Litchfield Cathedral. *The Heart of England Way* by Stephen Cross gives plenty of this type of information, always interesting and relevant to the section of walk it appears alongside.

How challenging?

It's definitely beginner-friendly. There are sections that can be a little long, but it really depends on the accommodation/transport choices made by the walker. There is ascent and descent but nothing too severe. The guidebook contains detailed maps and walk instructions; any updates to the route are listed on the website.

Accommodation and transport

B&Bs are available throughout the walk, so there's no need to camp. The guidebook has been written so that the walk can be appreciated in its 102-mile linear format, but is also incorporated into thirty-two circular walks (a total of 225 miles). The website contains pub and accommodation listings and the guidebook has transport information.

Best day-walk

Any of the Cotswolds sections, Henley-in-Arden to Alcester and Cannock Chase.

Icknield Way Path

Lesley Blundell, secretary, Icknield Way Association

Ivinghoe Beacon to Knettishall Heath: 110 miles/177 km

Difficulty rating: 2

Average days to complete: 8–10

Waymarking? Yes

Maps: There is sometimes confusion between the prehistoric route (sometimes marked on OS maps in Gothic lettering) and the modern walkers' route (in places marked in sans serif Roman lettering). OS Explorer 181, 193, 194, 209, 210 and 229 cover almost all the route

Baggage courier? No

For more details: IcknieldWayPath.co.uk, IcknieldWayTrail.org.uk; *The Icknield Way Path: a Walkers' Guide*, authored and published by the Icknield Way Association.

Describe the trail

It runs through six counties, over delightfully varied countryside including the Chiltern Hills and Breckland, through charming villages and along beautiful green lanes. The Icknield Way can claim to be the oldest road in Britain, consisting of pre-historic pathways ancient when the Romans came. It's dotted with archaeological remains and passes near or through a number of historic small towns and villages.

Highlights

The stretches of the route running from Whipsnade Tree Cathedral along the crest of Dunstable Downs to Five Knolls then on to Maiden Bower. The length of the route from Galley Hill, Streatley, across the top of Deacon Hill, Pegsdon and along Wood Green Lane down into Pirton village.

Lowlights

The stretch through Letchworth Garden City and Baldock is a pavement slog, at times through some unlovely areas and so rather boring.

Why do you love it?

Its history and archaeology together with the beauty of the chalk hills.

History/background

The Icknield Way Path can claim to be the oldest road in Britain.

How challenging?

The Icknield Way Path is clearly waymarked and beginner-friendly, with no really steep ascents or descents. Some parts may be muddy and slippery in really wet weather. The Path can be walked in a series of individual days or weekends, or as an eight- to ten-day continuous long distance walk. The Guide divides it into eight day-walks of between 10 and 18 miles, but it can easily be divided into shorter lengths.

Accommodation and transport

Much of the route is quite close to the railway although bus services to many of the rural communities along the route are sparse. The Icknield Way Association's *Walkers' Guide* and their website list contact details for bus operators and county travel information services.

Best day-walk

Streatley to Ickleford – 10 miles incorporating two of the highest hills on the route, wonderful views, two national nature reserves, prehistoric burial mounds, green lanes and a village with a twelfth-century motte-and-bailey castle, and two great pubs.

Mid Wilts Way

James Alsop, author of *Mid Wilts Way*

Ham to Mere: 68 miles/109 km

Difficulty rating: 3

Average days to complete: 4

Waymarking? Yes

Maps: OS Landranger 174, 173, 184, 183

Baggage courier? Yes

For more details: VisitWiltshire.com

Describe the trail

An east to south-west trail that seeks out the very best of Wiltshire's downland, giving a lowland walk a distinctly upland flavour at times. The Ham Hill Downs, the Pewsey Downs, Roundway Down, the Westbury Downs, Cley Hill, the Deverills and finally the Mere Downs all feature to make this an exceptional walk. Long-range views and lofty vistas make for glorious moments and memories.

Highlights

The downland delights, especially Ham Hill at the start (massive views into Berkshire), the Pewsey Downs (unrivalled in the county and beyond for downland character and long-range views), Cley Hill, the Deverills and the Mere Downs. But also some of the villages, perhaps especially Steeple Ashton.

Lowlights

The long canal stretch between Devizes and Seend Head Mill (SHM), somewhat tedious stretches between SHM and Bratton, and Cley Hill and Horningsham with some road and lane walking, but these are partially alleviated by the villages passed through.

Why do you love it?

The downland delights and the logical direction and progression of the route.

History/background

Exciting co-operation between landowners, Wiltshire Council's ROW team and an enthusiastic volunteer (yours truly) made the route possible. Its ongoing viability is largely down to the diligence of a few keen enthusiasts, especially Tim Lewis.

How challenging?

There are a few exciting ascents onto the downland but otherwise it's straightforward. Some of the low-lying route-finding can be a little challenging, but otherwise the route is exceptionally well waymarked.

Accommodation and transport

Both are somewhat limited, but there's still accommodation available in Wootton Rivers (the Royal Oak – can be a bit pricey for the average walker), Oare (the White Horse pub), Devizes, Steeple Ashton, Upton Scudamore, Horningsham and Mere.

Best day-walk

Wootton Rivers to Roundway Down, for the reasons described above.

Monarch's Way

John Tennant (@monarchsway), Monarch's Way Association (monarchsway.50megs.com)

Powick Bridge to Shoreham: 630 miles/1,014 km
Difficulty rating: 2–3
Average days to complete: 66
Is it waymarked? Yes
Maps: OS Explorer (1:25,000) OL45; 116; 117; 119; 120; 121; 122; 129; 130; 131; 132; 141; 142; 143; 155; 167; 168; 204; 205; 218; 219; 220; 221; 242
Baggage courier? No
For more details: see the official Monarch's Way website at monarchsway.50megs.com or guidebooks (page 171)

Describe the trail

This long distance walk closely follows the route of the escape of Charles II after the Battle of Worcester in 1651 and visits many historic sites. It also passes through two World Heritage Sites, one National Park and six Areas of Outstanding Natural Beauty, plus some of the finest scenery in western and southern England.

Highlights

The trail has so many highlights it's difficult to mention just one. However, the sections through the Cotswolds and along the South Downs are very impressive.

Lowlights

It goes through parts of the industrial West Midlands. However, that is part of what makes it so interesting – it passes through so many different types of landscape and scenery. Parts of the route are through areas where there are no shops within easy reach and so planning is very important.

Why do you love it?

Unlike many other trails, this one commemorates a significant historical event, where a future King of England escaped Oliver Cromwell with a huge bounty for that time (£1,000) on his head. Several times during his escape he had the most amazing good luck, which enabled him to make his escape to France.

History/background

The Monarch's Way Association believes that the period of the English Civil Wars is, at least constitutionally, one of the most important periods of British history. Also, nothing enhances a good walk more than a good theme – and the Monarch's Way enjoys both of these ingredients.

How challenging?

It covers a huge distance and so walking it on consecutive days is a big commitment. However, most people walk it on days out or do a few sections together at the same time. Parts along the south coast between Charmouth and Bridport are very hilly, however most of the route is not like that.

Like most UK walks progress is much easier during the late spring through to early autumn when the paths are drier. The route is fully waymarked and work continues to make improvements wherever they would benefit walkers. It is sensible to have 1:25,000 maps of the route and Trevor Antill's well-written guidebooks are also very useful.

The trail website contains details of any changes to or problems along the route, such as fallen trees etc. A few of the sections are long at 17 miles, however the usual length is around 8–10 miles.

Accommodation and transport

The Association has an up-to-date accommodation listing available free, by email. The walk could easily be done in sections and this is the way it is usually completed. Public transport is good in parts of the route, i.e. along the Fosse Way (Cotswolds) and also in parts of the West Midlands. However, some areas will require good planning or an overnight stay in accommodation.

Best day-walk

I've chosen three:

1. **Section 13**, Bentley Hall (the site of) to Halesowen Abbey (16 miles), is unusual as it passes for 1.75 miles through the Netherton Tunnel, which is the highlight of this section. The tunnel is unlit and has percolating water.

2. **Section 41**, Charmouth to Bridport (10 miles), is different again as it passes along the Dorset Coastal Path. The route passes over Golden Cap, at 618 ft/188 m the highest sea cliff on the south coast, with magnificent views.

3. **Sections 21 to 24**, Chipping Camden to

Cirencester (46 miles), go through the Cotswolds and would make an ideal 3- to 5-day walk. The route passes though Chipping Camden, Moreton-in-Marsh, Stow-on-the-Wold, Northleach, Chedworth (Roman Villa) and Cirencester.

Ridgeway (NT)

Anthony Burton, author of *The Ridgeway* and National Trail Video Guides (tvwalks.com)

Overton Hill to Ivinghoe Beacon: 87 miles/140 km

Difficulty rating: 2

Average days to complete: 7

Waymarking? Yes

Maps: OS (1:50,000) 165, 173, 174, 175; Harvey Maps

Baggage courier? Yes

For more details: nationaltrail.co.uk/ridgeway

Describe the trail

It follows an ancient track mainly at the top of chalk downland. This is mostly a high-level walk, but dips down to important crossing places. It's rich in prehistoric sites, particularly in the more western section.

Highlights

Not quite on the route, but anyone who hasn't already been there should certainly take a small diversion to Avebury – the world's largest henge monument. At the eastern end, there are sections of rich woodland – and you can virtually guarantee seeing red kites over the Chilterns.

Lowlights

A few sections are still byways, used by four-wheel-drive vehicles, and bridleways tend to be popular with motorbike riders as well as horses. This can lead to difficult ground especially in wet weather. Chalk paths can also be quite gooey in the wet.

Why do you love it?

I love the open downland sections, where you get immense views and the delightful, shapely scoops of the valleys.

History/background

As this follows an ancient route there are many prehistoric sites, including Iron Age forts, round barrows and Neolithic tombs – and the famous White Horse at Uffington.

How challenging?

In general the going is really quite easy. This is very open countryside for most of the way though, so if you do get bad weather it really hits you. Because it stays with the high ground, stopping places actually on the path are few and far between. Unless you want to go down the hill to find lunch and then stomp back up again it's as well to carry your own food.

Accommodation and transport

Accommodation on the whole is not difficult to find – though you may have to walk off the route at the end of the day in many places. Public transport is on the whole poor – it's very difficult to break it down into day trips without your own transport.

Best day-walk

The section from Liddington Castle that passes over the top of the Uffington White Horse and enjoys some of the best views of the whole walk. You could end either at the road down to Kingston Lisle or Sparsholt Firs.

Somerset Coast Path

Damian Hall, author of *Somerset Coast Path*
Bristol to Lynton/Lynmouth: 121 miles/195 km
Difficulty rating: 2

Average days to complete: 7–8
Waymarking? Half is waymarked as West Somerset Coast Path; the other half is unmarked.
Maps: Will be part of the fully waymarked England Coast Path by 2020. The guidebook has full OS mapping (or OS 154, 153, 140, OL9)
Baggage courier? No
For more details: nationaltrail.co.uk/England-coast-path

Describe the trail

Linking Bristol to the South West Coast Path: cliffs, birds, beaches and glorious Exmoor. The Somerset coast is a place of beauty, drama, history, charm, quirks and surprises. Until the England Coast Path is fully implemented this isn't an official trail as such, but it makes complete sense already. The dashing Mendips, the bulbous Quantocks, the glorious, kaleidoscopic moors of Exmoor, the unfairly ignored Brendon Hills, nature reserves and Sites of Special Scientific and Geological Interest, and the Somerset Levels – the largest low-lying wetlands in Britain.

Highlights

Exmoor, undoubtedly, and the section from Minehead along the South West Coast Path. But the segment following the River Avon and its abundant history out of Bristol is surprisingly enjoyable. There's drama and a sense of wildness in the big sand dunes on the way to forgotten-about

As well as big views down the coast, the Somerset coast offers beaches full of fossils. DAMIAN HALL

THE 100 TOP TRAILS

Burnham-on-Sea. The tiny, tumbleweed village of Steart feels like the end of the world, and from here it's the best bit of coast yet. Then the coast rises and falls like a rollercoaster, with sweeping views and beaches full of fossils and swirling, unearthly rock formations. Magnificent Exmoor is a fitting climax, the land of ponies and red deer, pink heather and luminous gorse.

Lowlights

Bleeping (in both senses of the word) Weston-super-Mare gets in the way a bit, as does Hinkley Point nuclear power station. The River Parrett has to be followed a long way inland to a bridge (at Bridgwater no less), then back out again. And due to not totally compliant landowners, some sections aren't strictly on the coast – at the time of writing. But that will change soon.

Why do you love it?

That sense of getting away from it all (even in some of the pleasingly old-fashioned seaside resorts) in a reasonably busy part of the world. And some deliciously quiet beautiful places.

History/background

The area has a strong connection to the Romantic poets. Eighteenth-century wordsmiths Samuel Taylor Coleridge and William Wordsworth wrote 1798's *Lyrical Ballads*, the defining early text of the Romantic movement, while Coleridge lived in Nether Stowey and Wordsworth in Alfoxton, about a mile from the Somerset coast. The men would meet for walks almost daily and their long, sometimes opium-enhanced, strolls were a deeply creative time for them both.

How challenging?

Not very. The only challenging element is the distance really. It's mostly flat walking all the way to Hinkley Point, then you do start using your calves and quads.

Accommodation and transport

Bristol is very well served of course. A few places don't have many accommodation options, especially between Bridgwater and Minehead, so book well ahead there. Likewise, there's limited public transport for that stretch. Otherwise, most of it could be done as day walks.

Best day-walk

Anywhere between Kilve Beach and Lynton/Lynmouth, where it's full of atmospheric woodlands, classic cliff views, moody moorlands, ponies and fossils.

Shakespeare's Way

Jenny Davidson, shakespearesway.org

Shakespeare's Birthplace at Stratford-upon-Avon to the Globe Theatre, London: 146 miles/235 km

Difficulty rating: 2

Average days to complete: 10

Waymarking? Yes

Maps: OS Explorer 205, OL45, 191, 180, 170, 171, 172, 173

Baggage courier? Yes

For more details: shakespearesway.org, *Shakespeare's Way* by Peter Titchmarsh

Describe the trail

A journey of imagination! Imagine walking in the footsteps of the Bard himself. Follow the route that Shakespeare may have taken when travelling between Stratford-upon-Avon and the Globe Theatre, London.

Highlights

Red kites flying over the Chiltern Hills.

Lowlights

The hustle and bustle of London after the peace and quiet of the countryside.

Why do you love it?

It's an opportunity to see the countryside as Shakespeare may have seen it.

History/background

On the evidence available, it appears Shakespeare first journeyed to London sometime between 1585 and 1588. He probably went on foot, stopping at Oxford. After that, he would have headed towards High Wycombe, a route now occupied by the M40 corridor – we have chosen a more tranquil option.

How challenging?

A good long distance path for a beginner. There are plenty of villages/towns en route so no feeling of real isolation if that is a concern. There is waymarking where permitted. There's some reasonable ascent over the Chilterns.

Accommodation and transport

It's easily completed in sections. B&Bs are plentiful, campsites are a little more sparse. Access to public transport is good.

Best day-walk

Between Stratford-upon-Avon and Oxford – Cotswold stone villages, Rollright Stones and Blenheim Palace.

South West Coast Path (NT)

Roland Tarr (rolandtarr.com), author of *South West Coast Path: Minehead to Padstow* and *South West Coast Path: Exmouth to Poole*

Minehead to Poole: 630 miles/1,014 km

Difficulty rating: 4

Average days to complete: 40

Waymarking? Yes

Maps: Harvey Maps

Baggage courier? Yes

For more details: *South West Coast Path: Padstow to Falmouth* and *South West Coast Path: Falmouth to Exmouth*

Describe the trail

It's 1,000 km of one of the most beautiful coasts in the world and includes a UNESCO World Heritage Site, with varied, dramatic and unique cliff scenery

and geology, magnificent beaches, and a good bus service for walkers.

Highlights

Exmoor, the Cornish coast, Start Point, the 'Isles' of Portland and Purbeck, the secret Lulworth Army Ranges, Lulworth Cove to Kimmeridge Bay. Massive cliffs and secret coves.

Lowlights

Some ghastly-looking caravan sites. The Lyme Regis to Charmouth section, where for the last twenty years golfers have succeeded in excluding coastal path walkers from enjoying the superb cliff-top views afforded there.

Why do you love it?

Secret coves; different scenery every day; some great pubs; some of the best long distance views anywhere.

History/background

Iron Age hill-forts; distinctive Stone and Bronze Age remains; fishing villages; and quaint Victorian seaside resorts.

How challenging?

The terrain rises from sea level to 500 ft/150 m several times most days. Competent map-reading skills will be useful. A few sections can get overgrown in summer and slippery in winter – good boots and/or sticks are handy. You will be fit after finishing it, even if you weren't before!

Accommodation and transport

Public transport along all of the South West Coast Path is well above average for England. It could be completed without a tent/bivvy bag or can easily be done in sections/day walks. I advise planning on 12 miles a day (on normal terrain I reckon on 20 miles), so don't just rely on the chapter lengths as day sections.

Best day-walk

Minehead or Porlock to Lynton. A complete round walk of Portland's cliffs. Tintagel to Port Isaac.

The South West Coast Path offers rugged, lumpy scenery, coves and curves, and more ascent than three climbs of Mt Everest..
DAMIAN HALL

Wessex Ridgeway

Anthony Burton, author of *The Wessex Ridgeway*

Marlborough to Lyme Regis: 127 miles/204 km

Difficulty rating: 3

Average days to complete: 10

Waymarking? Yes

Maps: OS (1:50,000) 173, 183, 184, 193, 194, 195

Baggage courier? Yes

For more details: dorsetaonb.org.uk, northwessexdowns.org.uk

Describe the trail

A continuation of the Ridgeway National Trail south to the coast. This is very much an up-and-down route – up over the downland and dropping again to valleys. It starts by going over Marlborough Downs to Avebury, then up again over the hills to Devizes and the Avon Valley. Much of the walk is very open and offers some spectacular views.

Highlights

It has many notable archaeological sites, including Avebury, but also some hugely imposing hill-forts, especially Hambledon hill-fort. Lyme Regis makes a splendid ending to a good walk.

Lowlights

On Salisbury Plain your route is limited to a rather dull straight line path along the firing range perimeter fence.

Why do you love it?

This very undulating country of Wiltshire and Dorset offers great variety; the countryside is very open; and you never get the large numbers of people you find in more popular areas.

History/background

Apart from the archaeology, you also get to walk along the restored Kennet and Avon Canal for a while.

How challenging?

There are a number of quite steep climbs and much of the upland is very open with no shelter – wet days can be pretty demanding.

Accommodation and transport

Accommodation on the whole is not difficult to find – transport to either end is reasonably good.

Best day-walk

I'd suggest Marlborough to Devizes, but you could have a great day just walking from Marlborough to Avebury and spending part of the day exploring the local sites – not just the henge, but also Silbury Hill and West Kennet Long Barrow.

White Horse Trail

Tim Lewis, area footpath secretary, Wiltshire Ramblers

Circular walk (Wiltshire): 95.5 miles/154 km (with alternatives and add-ons)

Difficulty rating: 2

Average days to complete: 8–9

Waymarking? Yes

Maps: OS Explorer 157, 156, 130, 143, Landranger 173, 184

Baggage courier? Yes

For more details: visitwiltshire.co.uk

Describe the trail

Not only does this take in all of Wiltshire's White Horses, but it also includes the best walking in north Wiltshire, namely the Pewsey Vale. It takes you to the area's best-known archaeological sites, being the Avebury stones, Windmill Hill, Silbury Hill and West Kennet Long Barrow.

Highlights

Walking through and above the Pewsey Vale, being the sections from Marlborough to Redhorn Hill, and

At Westbury you can view one of Wiltshire's finest white horses, originally cut in the late 1600s, probably to commemorate the supposed Battle of Ethandun. TIM LEWIS

The Kennet and Avon Canal on the White Horse Trail includes the unusual sight of 16 locks at Caen Hill. TIM LEWIS

from the Devizes White Horse to the Alton Barnes White Horse. The section along the Wansdyke also boasts panoramic views to north and south, and the views from the Westbury White Horse are also spectacular.

Lowlights

Walking along the edge of Salisbury Plain, which is tedious with (often) no views; this is the section from Charlton (before Redhorn Hill) to Westbury.

Why do you love it?

Its sheer diversity: lowland, soaring heights with great views, the Kennet and Avon Canal, the Marlborough Downs, countryside mixed with small towns and villages, with very little of the route being on roads.

History/background

The trail was a Millennium project of Wiltshire Ramblers. The oldest Wiltshire White Horse is the Westbury one, which dates from 1778, closely followed by the Cherhill figure which was cut in 1780

under the direction of a Dr Alsop, who shouted directions over a megaphone from the main road! The Marlborough white horse was designed in 1804 by a Marlborough schoolboy, and the Alton Barnes one was cut in 1812.

How challenging?

Moderately. It can be done in easy sections of no more than 14 miles. It includes several moderate to steep climbs, but much of it is flat. The terrain is mostly very easy going, except where vegetation growth may have got out of hand. The waymarking has been recently revised over the whole length of the trail.

Accommodation and transport

Much of the trail can be accessed by public transport (buses mainly, but Westbury and Pewsey have railway stations), however some of it is inaccessible by public transport (except for taxis), e.g. Knap Hill car park, Redhorn Hill, Hackpen Hill. There are several B&Bs and hotels on or near the route.

Best day-walk

From the Alton Barnes White Horse to Cherhill via Avebury, for the maximum variety of all the trail as a whole has to offer.

South-East England

Capital Ring

Colin Saunders, author of *The Capital Ring*
Woolwich to Woolwich: 78 miles/125 km
Difficulty rating: 2
Average days to complete: 8–10
Waymarking? Yes
Maps: OS maps are included in *The Capital Ring* by Colin Saunders
Baggage courier? No
For more details: walklondon.org.uk

Describe the trail

Transport for London's strategic inner circular walk. It seeks out a hidden corridor of green space around Inner London, taking in the capital's parks, woodlands, towpaths, riverbanks and historic cemeteries.

Highlights

The stretches through Wimbledon Common and Richmond Park and beside the Thames.

Lowlights

There's a lot of walking on hard surfaces and much of it goes through relatively dull residential areas, though even they are not without interest.

Why do you love it?

It demonstrates that there's some excellent walking in London.

History/background

The route passes many places of historical and cultural interest, such as the Thames Barrier, Charlton House, Wimbledon Windmill, London's old docks, the Woolwich Foot Tunnel, and the sites of Woolwich Dockyard and Richmond Palace.

How challenging?

The walking is mostly easy, though there are some steep but relatively short ascents. Some stretches can be muddy in wet weather. Signposting is mostly excellent.

Accommodation and transport

The walk can easily be completed in day trips, either from home or by staying at a central London hotel. Public transport is excellent and the walk can be broken into suitable distances as required.

Best day-walk

Wimbledon Park Station to Richmond Station.

Chiltern Way

John White, Chiltern Society
Circular walk: 134 miles/215 km
Difficulty rating: 2
Average days to complete: 8–10
Waymarking? Yes
Maps: OS 171, 172, 181, 182, 192, 193
Baggage courier? No
For more details: chilternsociety.org.uk

Describe the trail

A circular route taking in the best of the Chilterns. The trail covers a wide range of terrain, including chalk downland, beech forests and open agricultural land. The route passes hill-forts and other ancient settlements and uses some of the oldest paths in Britain. Couple this beautiful landscape and fascinating history with the many delightful villages and quintessentially English pubs en route, and you've all the ingredients for a classic long distance trail.

Highlights

The continuously changing scenery, the higher ground where views open up and the wonderful villages.

Lowlights

A few sections are relatively flat and uninteresting.

Why do you love it?

The combination of chalk downland and delightful forests.

History/background

There's lots of history – Iron Age hill-forts, ancient tracks and much more modern history.

How challenging?

Navigation is easy. Some sections have surprisingly hilly bits, and in wet conditions the chalk hillsides can get very slippery.

Accommodation and transport

Lots of accommodation options and generally decent public transport.

Best day-walk

Nettlebed to Skirmett or Stokenchurch to Pishill.

Downs Link

Andrew Bowden, ramblingman.org.uk
St Martha's Hill (near Chilworth) to Shoreham-by-Sea: 37 miles/60 km
Difficulty rating: 1
Average days to complete: 3
Waymarking? Yes
Maps: OS Landranger 186, 187, 198; OS Explorer 122, 134, 145
Baggage courier? No
For more details: ramblingman.org.uk

Describe the trail

Mostly running along the trackbeds of former railway lines, the Downs Link connects the North Downs Way with the South Downs Way, before finishing up at the seaside. The trail goes through old stations, and there's various railway memorabilia and other rail-themed paraphernalia along the way.

Highlights

Fine views of the magnificent South Downs at the southern end of the trail. At the former West Grinstead Station, there's also an old semaphore signal, which walkers can set.

Lowlights

Walking is often in a straight line. Especially in the northern half, trees block out the views. As the path goes over embankments and in cuttings, you sometimes get a bit divorced from your surroundings, meaning you can walk through villages without really realizing they are there. People who aren't railway buffs may be a little less keen on it.

Why do you love it?

I love walking up to West Grinstead Station and finding an old railway coach sat on some rails.

History/background

There are the two former railway lines, and the route starts at an isolated church with no road access.

How challenging?

Downs Link is an easy walk, along good tracks. There are few climbs and it's very well waymarked.

Accommodation and transport

It passes through many villages with accommodation. Train stations can be found near each end (Chilworth and Shoreham-by-Sea) and at the midpoint at Christ's Hospital. There are regular bus services along the trail, and it could be walked in day hikes.

Best day-walk

Henfield to Shoreham-by-Sea is a fantastic walk, with fine views of the South Downs, riverside walking and a magnificent arrival into Shoreham-by-Sea.

Greensand Way

Sophie Hewitt, Environment, Planning & Enforcement, Kent County Council
Haslemere to Hamstreet: 108 miles/174 km
Difficulty rating: 3
Average days to complete: 2–4
Waymarking? Yes
Maps: OS Explorer 146, 147, 148, 136, 137, 125
Baggage courier? Yes
For more details: kent.gov.uk/explorekent; surreycc.gov.uk

Describe the trail

The route showcases local areas of natural beauty – the Surrey Hills and the Kent Downs – as well as many Sites of Special Scientific Interest. It passes a

A statue of Sir Winston Churchill can be seen on the Greensand Way, in Westerham, where the prime minister lived for many years.
SOPHIE HEWITT/EXPLORE KENT

number of magnificent houses, gardens and parks. The trail continues through ancient and semi-mature woodland with bluebell walks in spring, cool shade in the summer and vibrant displays of colour come autumn.

Highlights

Chartwell house, bought by Sir Winston Churchill in 1922. Stubbs Wood, home for many rare animals and plants. Hampstead Lock, the deepest lock along the Medway navigation.

Lowlights

Walkers may find it difficult to get back to their original destination without the use of public transport.

Why do you love it?

Abundant wildlife and beautiful gardens, ancient architecture and history of the local villages, this trail has a little something for everyone.

History/background

The soil of the Greensand Way has long been ideal for agriculture. For many centuries, sheep rearing provided a staple industry. Cloth-making and manufacturing glass also relied on the natural resources of the area, before the arrival of mining and water-powered mills, which provided the locals with paper, iron and brass.

How challenging?

Allow yourself extra time to enjoy the sites and marvellous locations that create the Greensand Way

The Greensand Way offers some lovely scenery and inviting benches to sit and enjoy it. SOPHIE HEWITT/EXPLORE KENT

trail. It's advised to complete the walk in smaller sections if you aren't a regular walker.

Accommodation and transport

There are many places to rest along the way. There are many local public houses and convenient hotels en route, and plenty of camping and caravan sites. There are bus and train routes along the way too.

Best day-walk

Each section of the trail provides a different historic and wildlife experience.

London Loop

Colin Saunders, co-author of *The London Loop*

Erith to Purfleet: 150 miles/240 km

Difficulty rating: 2

Average days to complete: 15

Waymarking? Yes

Maps: included in *The London Loop*

Baggage courier? No

For more details: walklondon.org.uk

Describe the trail

The London Loop tracks a green corridor closely following the Greater London boundary, among green and often secret countryside that can make you forget you are close to suburban sprawl.

Highlights

Foots Cray Meadows, High Elms Country Park, Bushy Park, Hounslow Heath, the Colne Valley, Trent Country Park, Enfield Chase, Epping Forest, Hainault Forest, Havering Country Park, Thames Chase, Hornchurch Country Park, the RSPB's Rainham Marshes Reserve.

Lowlights

It's sometimes necessary to walk through relatively boring residential areas.

Why do you love it?

It shows there's some excellent walking on the outskirts of Greater London.

History/background

Places of historical and cultural interest include the site of Nonsuch Palace, Kingston-upon-Thames, Grimsdyke House, Bentley Priory and Forth Hall.

How challenging?

Mostly easy walking, though there are some steep but relatively short ascents. Much of the route is on rough paths in open countryside, which can be muddy in wet weather. The signposting is mostly excellent but there are some short gaps.

Accommodation and transport

The walk can easily be completed in day trips either from home or by staying at a central London hotel. Public transport is excellent and the walk can be broken into suitable distances as required.

Best day-walk

The string of commons on the southern outskirts from West Wickham to Farthing Downs.

New Lipchis Way

Keith McKenna and Sally Dench, footprintsofsussex.co.uk

Liphook to East Head: 39 miles/62 km

Difficulty rating: 2

Average days to complete the trail: 3

Waymarking? Yes

Maps: OS Explorer 133, 120

Baggage courier? Yes (info@footprintsofsussex.co.uk)

For more details: newlipchisway.co.uk

Describe the trail

It explores West Sussex from head to toe in all its natural beauty. The trail is aligned north–south and, thereby, crosses all the main geologies of West Sussex. It begins on the greensand ridges and follows Wealden river valleys before crossing the high chalk downland and dropping to the coastal plain. It offers a great variety of scenery, flora and fauna.

Highlights

There are great views from the high points of Older Hill and the Trundle and a really peaceful stretch along the banks of the River Rother. Finishing on the sand dunes at East Head is great fun.

Lowlights

The route into Chichester city is a long flat cycle way following an old railway line and can get a little tedious.

Why do you love it?

It's three completely different days of walking.

History/background

The trail was originally a pilgrimage route from Liphook to Chichester Cathedral; we re-routed it a bit and extended it down to the coast.

How challenging?

There are just two quite moderate climbs and one short, very steep section. Otherwise, it has good paths, and is waymarked along its entire length and clearly shown on the OS maps.

Accommodation and transport

It breaks neatly into three good days' walking with plentiful accommodation in Midhurst and Chichester. Between Liphook and Midhurst there is no public transport. South of Midhurst public bus transport is good.

The New Lipchis Way enjoys some lovely bespoke waymarking.
FOOTPRINTS OF SUSSEX

The church in the village of Iping offers a diversion along the New Lipchis Way. FOOTPRINTS OF SUSSEX

The River Rother on the New Lipchis Way. FOOTPRINTS OF SUSSEX

The postcard-perfect Chichester Harbour, on the New Lipchis Way. FOOTPRINTS OF SUSSEX

Best day-walk

The three days are all so very different and clearly described in the trail guide. Depends what mood you're in!

North Downs Way (NT)

Colin Saunders (colinsaunders.org.uk), author of *North Downs Way*

Farnham to Dover: 153 miles/246 km

Difficulty rating: 3

Average days to complete: 8–10

Waymarking? Yes

Maps: OS Explorer 137, 138, 145, 146, 147, 148, 149, 163; Harvey Maps

Baggage courier? Yes

For more details: nationaltrail.co.uk/north-downs-way

Describe the trail

The North Downs Way follows the chalk ridge across south-east England. It's a magnificently varied, and surprisingly tranquil, journey: through beech and oak woodland, across springy downland, rising to sweeping vistas from many viewpoints, and following much of the Pilgrim's Way to the ancient city of Canterbury.

Highlights

St Martha's Hill, Box Hill, River Medway, Kit's Coty House, Thurnham Castle, Wye Crown, Devil's Kneading Trough, Postling Downs, Battle of Britain Memorial, Shakespeare Cliff, Bigbury Fort, Canterbury Cathedral, Dover Castle.

Lowlights

Motorways and busy roads in several places.

Why do you love it?

The chalky landscape, the variety, the sense of history and the big views.

History/background

Much of the route follows the Pilgrim's Way, an ancient track between Winchester and Canterbury.

How challenging?

Although much of the route is on level ground, there are several very steep ascents or descents. The

Views from Older Hill on the New Lipchis Way. FOOTPRINTS OF SUSSEX

stretch between Folkestone and Dover is exposed in some places.

Accommodation and transport

Public transport is excellent and there are good facilities for accommodation and refreshments along the entire length.

Best day-walk

Etchinghill to Dover for spectacular coastal scenery. Near Guildford to Newlands Corner for lovely downland scenery. Boughton Lees to Chilham for a lovely woodland walk and first distant view of Canterbury Cathedral.

Peddars Way and Norfolk Coast Path (NT)

Phoebe Smith (Phoebe–Smith.com, @Phoebe RSmith), author of *The Peddars Way and Norfolk Coast Path*, and *Extreme Sleeps: Adventures of a Wild Camper*

Knettishall Heath to Cromer: 96 miles/155 km (if you cut out the dog-leg to and from Hunstanton!)

Difficulty rating: 2

Average days to complete: 7–8 days (you can do it faster but this way you really enjoy it)

Waymarking? Yes

Maps: OS Explorer 229, 236, 250, 251, 252

Baggage courier? Yes

For more details: nationaltrail.co.uk/PeddarsWay

Describe the trail

Big skies, wild marshland, dramatic cliff-tops and sandy beaches. It's the shortest National Trail in the UK so a perfect first long distance path. And it's flat. But don't be fooled. What it lacks in height it makes up for in ever-changing landscapes and fascinating history – from the Bronze Age to the Iceni and Boudicca's uprising against the Romans, World War II and beyond. It also offers a mix of country and coast, ancient and modern and the ease of splitting it into easy-to-manage sections.

Highlights

There are just so many but, for history, the castle and priory at Castle Acre. For views, the striped cliffs in Hunstanton followed by the seemingly endless dunes at Holkham. For great local food Stiffkey and Cley. For the sense of achievement, Cromer. And if you can do it in winter and you get snow, the memory will stay with you forever …

Lowlights

I'd say the first few kilometres on the second day from Little Cressingham and again the start of the walk from Castle Acre to about Harpley Dams on day three. It's mainly on minor roads, and the cars do go fast! All is forgiven though once you reach the priory at Castle Acre and start to spy the marl pits and ancient tumuli en route to Sedgeford.

Why do you love it?

I'm a mountain girl really, so the fact that a trail could hold my attention for a week with so much to offer at low contour lines really impressed. Plus I do passionately love the sea, so the idea of building up a thirst for it on the Peddars Way section before it's spectacularly revealed on the Norfolk coast takes some beating. I enjoy a walk where I can work hard for a big payoff and the coast certainly delivers.

History/background

So much! Definitely worth reading up on the Iceni and their fight against the Romans – this was their land and the Peddars Way traces old roads used by them way before the Romans landed. Seahenge in Holme-next-the-Sea dates back to 2,050BC. Not to mention the archaeological finds that date human habitation in the area to 700,000BC. I could go on – there's just so much here …

How challenging?

It's probably one of the easiest of the National Trails as the length is short, the coastal section has a regular bus service that provides easy escape routes and there's little ascent. Parts of it can be boggy of course. In winter wrap up very warm as those easterly winds can be unforgiving.

Accommodation and transport

The Peddars Way section is much harder to split – it is possible but timings make it hard. There are also fewer accommodation choices. Doing it in one though is certainly easy enough using public transport and staying in B&Bs in summer – though do book in advance as space is limited. The coast is a whole different ball game. A great Coasthopper bus network and rail links both ends makes it a dream.

TALKING WALKING – PHOEBE SMITH

A travel editor, writer and author, Phoebe's love of dramatic landscapes and wild places takes her on adventures all around the world – from wild camping on the Scottish islands, to watching the Northern Lights from a heated wigwam above the Arctic Circle. Formerly features editor at *Trail*, she is editor of *Wanderlust* and author of several books including *Extreme Sleeps: Adventures of a Wild Camper* and the *Peddars Way and Norfolk Coast Path* (Cicerone). Follow her adventures on Twitter @PhoebeRSmith.

Did you make any rookie errors on your first multi-day walk?

Loads! Forgetting suncream, gas for my camping stove, taking too much kit – you name it, I did it. But making errors is what it's all about when you start – it's how you learn and actually, continuing even though things go wrong makes you realize just what you're capable of.

What effect did your first multi-day walk have on you?

It boosted my confidence tremendously and made me realize that I could cope with just about anything. It also gave me space to think, to reconnect with myself and the wonderful country I call home. Do it once and you get addicted; seriously it's hard for me now not to do multi-days. I like to create my own, normally based around wild camping. I do research into places and find secret spots I want to get to and explore, then grab an OS map and start planning. Official trails are fantastic, but don't forget the joy of doing a bespoke one that no one else knows about.

What is it about long distance walks that appeals to you?

I like everything about it – from preparing and packing to being on the trail and the satisfaction you get from finishing your planned route. Most of all I like the feeling

Phoebe Smith.

I get when walking, with everything I need on my back, knowing I am totally self-sufficient.

What luxury item do you take on a trek, if any?

Inflatable pillow. Always have, always will. If you have a great night's sleep you can deal with anything in the morning.

There's also a whole host of options for where you make your bed – from high-end hotels to camping.

Best day-walk

Tricky, but I'd say the section from Hunstanton to Burnham Deepdale. You get a mix of classic British seaside, then the wilds of Gore Point, the birds at Broad Water, a short section of inland that gives you a flavour of the Peddars Way part and then an end at a lovely village with the best campsite and a lovely cafe next door.

Saxon Shore Way

Robert Peel, area secretary, Kent Ramblers
Gravesend to Hastings: 153 miles/246 km
Difficulty rating: 2
Average days to complete: 11

Waymarking? Yes

Maps: OS Explorer 163, 149, 150, 138, 125, 124

Baggage courier? No

For more details: kentramblers.org.uk

Describe the trail

It follows the coastline of Kent as it was in late Roman times. The route offers great diversity of scenery, from the wide expanses of marshland of the Thames and Medway estuaries to the majestic White Cliffs of Dover. Spectacular panoramic views follow the route along the escarpment of the old sea cliffs from Folkestone to Rye and from the sandstone cliffs of the High Weald at Hastings.

Highlights

The White Cliffs from Deal to Folkestone.

Lowlights

None really. Some of the walk is very flat and across marshes but these areas are wild, remote and full of wildlife.

Why do you love it?

The variety.

History/background

The historian is treated to the 'Saxon Shore' forts built by the Romans at Reculver, Richborough, Dover and Lympne, to the landing place of St Augustine and of Caesar and to defences of more modern times against Napoleon and Hitler.

How challenging?

There are some reasonable climbs over the White Cliffs but most of the route is very flat. Much of it is quite remote and so most appropriate for reasonably confident walkers.

Accommodation and transport

Not much of either in the northern section except at towns such as Faversham. Plenty of both at and south of Sandwich.

Best day-walk

Over the White Cliffs from Folkestone to Dover (you can get the train back).

Sandlings Walk

Laurence Mitchell (laurencemitchell.com; eastofelveden.wordpress.com), author of *Suffolk Coast and Heaths Walks: Three Long Distance Walks in the AONB*

Ipswich to Southwold: 59 miles/94.5 km

Difficulty rating: 1–2

Average days to complete: 5

Waymarking? Yes

Maps: OS Landranger 169, 156; OS Explorer 197, 212, 231

Baggage courier? Yes

For more details: suffolkcoastandheaths.org

Describe the trail

A meandering inland trail through the Suffolk coastal hinterland. It takes in a variety of landscapes – riverbanks, extensive forest, farmland and Sandlings Heath. The route also passes through the attractive and historical coastal towns of Southwold and Woodbridge.

The 163-mile Saxon Shore Way follows the coastline of Kent as it was in Roman times. ROBERT PEEL

Highlights

The stage through Rendlesham Forest between Sutton Common and Butley. Also the stage between Thorpeness and Dunwich Heath that follows the coastal path. The last stage between Dunwich and Southwold via Dunwich Forest and Walberswick Common is especially attractive.

Lowlights

It might be frustrating for some walkers to be so close to the sea yet rarely within sight of it.

Why do you love it?

A wide variety of landscapes – heath, forest, coast and farmland – with some unique wildlife. Several interesting and charming places to stay and eat along the way at Woodbridge, Snape and Southwold.

History/background

There are the UFO legends of Rendlesham Forest and the vanished medieval port of Dunwich, now lost to coastal erosion.

How challenging?

Easy throughout and beginner-friendly. Navigation is mostly straightforward. Easy walking mostly on dry heath or along forest trails.

Accommodation and transport

There are good accommodation options at Ipswich, Woodbridge and Southwold, and other possibilities in between. Public transport is limited at some of the interim points along the route but it is mostly quite reasonable.

Best day-walk

The section between Southwold and Dunwich via Walberswick Common.

South Downs Way (NT)

Kev Reynolds (kevreynolds.co.uk), author of *The South Downs Way*

Eastbourne to Winchester: 100 miles/160 km
Difficulty rating: 2–3
Average days to complete: 8–10
Waymarking? Yes
Maps: OS Landranger 199, 198, 197, 185; Harvey Maps
Baggage courier? Yes
For more details: nationaltrail.co.uk/south-downs-way, visitsouthdowns.com

Describe the trail

A scenic walk through history. Striking through Britain's newest National Park, the trail passes countless historic sites dating back to Neolithic times, while giving far-reaching views over the Weald and, at its eastern end, fabulous coastal scenery.

Highlights

The helter-skelter coastal section across Beachy Head and the Seven Sisters.

Lowlights

Chalk trails can be very sticky after prolonged rain, and some short sections turn to quagmires where mountain bikes have cut deep ruts.

The dramatic cliffs of Beachy Head at the eastern end of the South Downs Way (SDW). KEV REYNOLDS

TALKING WALKING – KEITH FOSKETT (AKA FOZZIE)

Keith is a long distance hiker, writer and blogger. His lightweight approach has resulted in three thru-hikes of El Camino de Santiago, the Pacific Crest and Appalachian Trails. He has written two books: *The Journey in Between* is an account of his first walk on El Camino de Santiago and *The Last Englishman* follows his adventures on the Pacific Crest. His website is keithfoskett.com.

Keith 'Fozzie' Foskett.

What do you remember about your first multi-day walk?

It was the 100-mile South Downs Way when I was sixteen with my best mate, Andrew. On reaching halfway, we congratulated ourselves and camped on top of Kithurst Hill near Storrington. I woke a few hours later to lightning cracks and pounding rain. Andrew had wrapped himself halfway up one tent pole, like a frightened bear cub. At first light, we dejectedly packed up and plodded back to civilization. I remember thinking hiking was a pursuit I didn't want further involvement in.

What effect did your first long walk have on you?

The walk opened my eyes. The outdoors made me relax, gifted me time to think in depth about whatever topic took my fancy and provided an escape from the normal routine of life. It was a whole different world, at a more sedate pace and where my worries faded into insignificance. I get exactly the same feeling when I walk now. It gives me the opportunity to look back on the life I lead and observe where I go wrong, how I can improve, and make plans for my future.

Do you do any fitness preparation beforehand?

I train for hikes because I've suffered from the effects of not training. A couple of months before I'll try and do a 5-mile route every day carrying a pack full of water to simulate the weight. At the weekends I'll try and put in a 15–20-miler. I will also do a little yoga which works wonders for flexibility and to prevent injury. I've suffered from blisters, so toughening up my feet (by training on tarmac) helps a lot.

What advice do you have for fellow long distance walkers?

Never give in to the temptation of giving up, because two days after getting back home you'll wish you hadn't. The achievement of a thru-hike is carried over to everyday life. Suddenly we realize that if we can walk for six months supporting ourselves, then all the areas of our life we once perceived as being difficult, become easy (or, at the very least, easier than before). Spending an extended period in the outdoors is not about giving up a few months of your life, it's about having a few months to really *live*.

Why do you love it?

Expansive views, big skies, chalkland flora and the song of skylarks, which creates a perpetual soundtrack to the walk. Heaven!

History/background

The SDW passes the vast Iron Age hill-fort of Cissbury Ring, crosses a Roman road with sections still intact, and ends in Winchester, the old Saxon capital of England, with its impressive cathedral.

How challenging?

The perfect beginner's long distance path – waymarking is exemplary, there are no stiles to cross (bridle gates only), although there are some steep ascents and descents. The longest sections are only 12 miles/19 km and the trails are mostly in good condition.

Accommodation and transport

Accommodation is plentiful (mostly B&Bs and youth hostels), but can be at a premium in the

One of many thatched houses in Amberley close to the SDW.
KEV REYNOLDS

summer months. There are few campsites and wild camping is forbidden, so backpacking is not worth considering. The SDW could be achieved in a series of day walks using public transport.

Best day-walk

Without question, start at Eastbourne and follow the SDW across Beachy Head and the Seven Sisters to either Exceat (bus back to Eastbourne) or Alfriston (overnight accommodation). To enjoy a second best, return to Eastbourne from Alfriston by the inland bridleway option via Jevington.

Suffolk Coast Path

Laurence Mitchell (laurencemitchell.com, eastofelveden.wordpress.com), author of *Suffolk Coast and Heaths Walks: Three Long-Distance Walks in the AONB*

Lowestoft to Landguard Fort: 55–60 miles/89–97 km
Difficulty rating: 1–2
Average days to complete: 4–5
Waymarking? Yes
Maps: OS Explorer OL40, 231, 212, 197

The Fulking Escarpment and its view over the Weald near Devil's Dyke on the SDW. KEV REYNOLDS

THE 100 TOP TRAILS

Baggage courier? No

For more details: suffolkcoastandheaths.org

Describe the trail

The walk takes in coastal Suffolk at its finest – a unique blend of shingle beaches, salt marshes, reedbeds, river estuaries and heath. Along the way it also passes through attractive seaside towns and villages like Southwold, Walberswick, Dunwich and Aldeburgh, all of which were once important fishing ports.

Highlights

The marshes and heathland south of Dunwich close to RSPB Minsmere; the 'Sailor's Walk' section along the Alde estuary between Aldeburgh and Snape; the deserted shingle beaches south of Shingle Street on the way to Bawdsey Quay.

Lowlights

Some of the shingle beach walking can be a bit of a slog. The section south of Lowestoft, the first you will walk if doing the walk north to south, is probably the dullest part of the trail.

Why do you love it?

Big skies; the sea within sight most of the way; excellent wildlife, especially wading birds and shingle flora. Pleasant old-fashioned resorts like Southwold and Aldeburgh that have good places to eat and drink. Plenty of characterful pubs en route serving good food and Adnams beer.

History/background

Dunwich, now reduced to just a tiny village by coastal erosion, was once an important medieval port and one of the largest towns in East Anglia.

How challenging?

Beginner-friendly, with plenty of places to stop. It can be hard work walking in shingle but there are usually inland alternatives. It's a little boggy after heavy rain. The last sections are quite long and cannot easily be shortened because they require the use of a river ferry. The landscape is flat, no ascents or descents whatsoever. Signposting is mostly good and easy to follow.

Accommodation and transport

There are some good options for accommodation in the towns, although there can be fierce competition for B&Bs in high summer. No need for a tent. It is easily done in day sections. Public transport is reasonable in the northern section but very limited in the southern section, which needs careful planning.

Best day-walk

The section between Dunwich and Thorpeness has a bit of everything the Suffolk coast has to offer – woodland, heath, bird-rich reedbeds and marshes and plenty of coastal shingle.

Thames Path (NT)

Leigh Hatts, author of *The Thames Path: London to the Source*

London to Kemble: 180 miles/289 km

Difficulty rating: 2

Average days to complete: 16

Waymarking? Yes

Maps: OS Explorer 159, 161, 162, 168, 169, 170, 171, 172, 173, 180; Harvey Maps

Baggage courier? Yes

For more details: thamespath.org.uk

Describe the trail

Along the River Thames from London to the source in Gloucestershire. Most of the trail is on a rural towpath switching banks and leading directly into the centre of country towns and villages.

Highlights

England's wonders and main heritage sites including the Thames Barrier, Greenwich, the Tower of London, St Paul's Cathedral, the Houses of Parliament, Kew Gardens, Syon House, Runnymede with its Magna Carta memorial, Windsor and Oxford.

Lowlights

The good transport links disappear after Oxford.

Why do you love it?

Not only do the seasons change the feel of the walk but so does the flow of the water upstream and the tides downstream.

History/background

In addition to the great heritage sites there are unique churches such as Iffley where the doorway decoration is only found elsewhere in Santiago de Compostela. Also there is every kind of crossing from the late nineteenth-century Tower Bridge to Newbridge where the 'new' bridge dates from 1250.

How challenging?

The remote stretches come at the end so you start with the backup of cafes and handy transport. There is only one hill. Good National Trail signage.

Accommodation and transport

There is no need for a tent, although campsites exist. In addition to B&Bs there are budget hotels in many towns. Most sections can be treated as day walks. Public transport is poor after Oxford but the source is very near Kemble Station, which has fast trains back to London.

Best day-walk

For urban walking Greenwich to Westminster. For countryside Marlow to Henley-on-Thames where you cross the water on the way.

Vanguard Way

Colin Saunders, author of *The Vanguard Way Companion*

Croydon to Newhaven: 66 miles/107 km

Difficulty rating: 3

Average days to complete: 5–6

Waymarking? Yes

Maps: See vanguardway.org.uk

Baggage courier? No

For more details: vanguardway.org.uk

Describe the trail

A quirky but fascinating route from London to the Sussex coast. It follows footpaths and bridleways through some of the best countryside in southern England. It mostly avoids built-up areas – the only ones between Croydon and Newhaven are Forest Row and Seaford.

Highlights

The trail crosses the North Downs, the Weald, the Ashdown Forest and the South Downs National Park, finishing with some of the finest views in England, of the Cuckmere Meanders, the Seven Sisters and Seaford Head.

Lowlights

Very few! There are some short stretches along country lanes that can be busy at times, and in wet weather some of the paths can get muddy.

Why do you love it?

It shows that one of the best trails in England can be

created by a small rambling club (Vanguards).

History/background

The trail passes places of historical and cultural interest such as Coombe village, Farleigh Church, Titsey Place, Haxted Mill, Starborough Castle, Dry Hill Camp, Winnie the Pooh country, Tickerage Mill, Alfriston village and Tide Mills historic village.

How challenging?

Mostly easy walking on footpaths and bridleways, but they can be rough and muddy in wet weather. There are many stiles and several steep ascents and descents. Signposting is good and mostly complete.

Accommodation and transport

Accommodation is reasonably plentiful, and public transport is good in most places. *The Vanguard Way Companion* provides full details of public transport, accommodation and refreshment opportunities.

Best day-walk

The best part is from Berwick Station to Seaford, but the Ashdown Forest section from Forest Row to Poundgate is also an excellent walk.

Wealdway

Robert Peel, area secretary, Kent Ramblers

Eastbourne to Gravesend: 82 miles/131.2 km

Difficulty rating: 3

Average days to complete: 6

Waymarking? Yes

Maps: OS Explorer 163, 148, 136, 147, 135, 123

Baggage courier? No

For more details: kentramblers.org.uk/kentwalks/wealdway

Describe the trail

It crosses the South Downs, the High Weald, Ashdown Forest and the North Downs. This is quintessentially English countryside with rolling downs, archetypal village greens on which cricket has been played for centuries, deep wooded valleys and traditional pubs. History abounds with numerous furnace and hammer ponds reminding us of the iron industry of the Tudors and Stuarts and many fine old houses. Despite its proximity to many towns and with London not far away, much of the route has a surprisingly remote feel to it.

The atmospheric Avery's Wood, on the Wealdway. ROBERT PEEL

Highlights

The middle section of the route between Uckfield and Tonbridge is exceptionally fine, crossing the superb landscapes of the High Weald.

Lowlights

The most northerly section through Gravesend lacks the rural tranquillity of much of the rest of the trail; many people walk from north to south to get this bit over with.

Why do you love it?

The combination of the delightful scenery and the feeling of remoteness. You can walk all day without meeting another human being.

History/background

Created by Sussex and Kent Ramblers in partnership with East Sussex and Kent County Councils.

How challenging?

This is not demanding terrain although there are plenty of ups and downs. An ideal choice for someone's first long distance trail.

Accommodation and transport

There is plenty of accommodation within easy reach of the route. The walk could easily be done in sections and public transport is for the most part adequate. It could also be done as a series of circular walks although the total miles walked would then be much more than the length of the walk itself.

Best day-walk

Withyham to Bidborough.

North-West England

Coast to Coast

Martin Wainwright (martinsmoths.blogspot.com), author of *The Coast to Coast Walk*

St Bees to Robin Hood's Bay: 192 miles/307 km

Difficulty rating: 5

Average days to complete: 14

Waymarking? Partial

Maps: Harvey Maps or Footprint Maps

Baggage courier? Yes

For more details: wainwright.org.uk

Describe the trail

Very long, very varied, very beautiful. It is purposeful, crossing from sea to sea and traversing two outstanding National Parks, but also takes in many gentle spots, interesting villages and the small but lovely town of Richmond (roughly halfway). It is the most varied long distance walk in the UK. Walkers are strongly encouraged to follow the advice of its pioneer, Alfred Wainwright, not to treat it as a tramline but to scan the maps for possible alternative sections, which abound. There is a campaign to fix and waymark the path, which would lose it this distinction. It's also very good to do in small chunks if the full Monty is too much.

Highlights

The crossings of the Lakes and North York Moors are unbeatable, but anyone familiar with those National Parks will also enjoy the novelty and difference of the limestone stretch between the M6 and Kirkby Stephen and the fascinating navigation across the farmland of the Vale of Mowbray in North Yorkshire.

Lowlights

It's very long and if you get consistent bad weather, it really isn't any fun and I would abandon ship and start again if your plans allow. The Pennine crossing is a boggy trudge even in perfect weather. The run-in to Robin Hood's Bay is a bit disappointing except for the very last bit. There can be rather a lot of walkers – another reason for finding your own alternative sections en route.

Why do you love it?

It is a wonderful way to see, enjoy and understand

the north of England at the pace which human beings were originally designed to take.

History/background

The creation of the journey by Alfred Wainwright is interesting, as is his description of it as 'feminine' compared to the 'masculine' Pennine Way. His qualification of that division broadly suggested that the Coast to Coast is beautiful, subtle and reveals its qualities gradually, as opposed to the in-your-face ruggedness of the Pennine Way.

How challenging?

If you're not in a hurry and enjoy navigating, it is manageable by any reasonably active person. There are a lot of ups and downs and you should be prepared for mist on high ground and know how to navigate in it. Quite a lot of the route can be boggy (yet another reason for seeking out little bypasses and alternative ways). The logistics of timing and accommodation are important and can be quite complicated. I would very much recommend doing some of the day-sections in advance to get the hang of things.

Accommodation and transport

Public transport is poor throughout and a disadvantage of the walk is that neither end is easily accessible – St Bees has an invaluable train station but the little town's quite a way from most walker's homes. Accommodation en route is adequate in the amount available but early booking is definitely recommended in summer. Tough sorts could do it with a bivvy bag and smelly clothes but most walkers have a support party at some stage to cart extra stuff or bring new clothes etc.

Best day-walk

Patterdale to Shap.

Cumbria Way

Anthony Burton, author of *The Cumbria Way* and National Trail Video Guides (tvwalks.com)
Ulverston to Carlisle: 70 miles/112 km

The Coast to Coast plunges you in at the steep end, with the Lake District fells coming near the beginning of the trail. DAMIAN HALL

The section above Patterdale is one of the highlights of the trail. DAMIAN HALL

Climbing towards Rampsgill Head, the Coast to Coast's highest point. DAMIAN HALL

Difficulty rating: 3
Average days to complete: 6
Waymarking? Yes
Maps: 1:50,000 85, 90, 96; Harvey Maps; Footprint Maps
Baggage courier? Yes
For more details: ramblingman.org.uk

Describe the trail

A walk from one side of the Lake District to the other. It begins with a quite gentle walk to Coniston, then follows the lake shore before heading north to Langdale. It then goes over the end of the valley to reach Derwent Water and Keswick. There are then two alternative routes – round or over Caldbeck Fells, ending with a final section up the river to Carlisle.

Highlights

This depends on your taste: for some it's the pleasant walk beside the two lakes; for others – me for one – it's the more rugged country at the head of the Langdale Valley.

Lowlights

It is a bit of a dull trudge for the last few miles into Carlisle – though the walk stops before the centre.

Why do you love it?

The Lake District boasts the most dramatic mountain scenery in England and this walk introduces you to some of the best of it.

History/background

It's worth looking out for the splendid steam passenger launch *Gondola*.

How challenging?

Parts of the walk are quite demanding, especially the tough climb out of Langdale via Stake Pass.

Accommodation and transport

Transport is reasonably good – no difficulty getting to either end and some bus services along the way. Accommodation generally isn't a problem.

Best day-walk

Coniston to the Old Dungeon Ghyll in Langdale. It includes lovely, lonely Blea Tarn, has a variety of scenery and ends at some of my favourite pubs!

Cumbria Coastal Way

Ian and Krysia Brodie, authors of *The Cumbria Coastal Way*

Silverdale to Gretna: 182 miles/298 km
Difficulty rating: 1.5
Average days to complete: 12–15
Waymarking? Partly (from Whitehaven to Allonby is now marked as the English Coastal Path)
Maps: All but the latest editions of OS 1:25,000 maps have the route marked: OS (1:25000) OL6, OL7, 303, 314, 315; OS (1:50000) 85, 89, 96, 97
Baggage courier? No
For more details: ldwa.org.uk

Describe the trail

A coast rich in wildlife and heritage where the pearls are linked by the Cumbria Coastal Way. Never rising above 100 m, this is a real exploration of the coast, linking its often rare natural history with its ancient and industrial heritage, as well as its literature, and providing some fantastic views to the Lake District, the Isle of Man and Scotland. The spread of fantastic estuaries and the superb evening sunsets make this a unique experience.

Highlights

The estuaries of Morecambe Bay, the Duddon and the Solway coupled with the delights of St Bees Head.

Lowlights

Until the England Coast Path (ECP) comes along there are a few sections on roads and some may find the fascinating post-industrial towns of Barrow, Whitehaven and Workington not to their liking.

Why do you love it?

The proximity of the sea, its unusual wildlife and friendly local people.

History/background

The whole coast is rich in historical sites and relics of industrial innovation.

How challenging?

Very little ascent or descent, with great support by public transport (for most of the route you link with railway stations). With the development of the ECP the poorer sections are being eliminated making the route readily accessible and easy to follow. Besides the committed long distance walker, the route offers opportunities for the less-experienced and the more senior walkers.

Accommodation and transport

It's often done in day sections, but there are some friendly B&Bs along the way. There's little opportunity for wild camping.

Best day-walk

Depends on the season and weather. We often revisit various sections at different times of the year.

Dales High Way

Chris Grogan, co-author of *A Dales High Way Companion* and *A Dales High Way: Route Guide*

Saltaire to Appleby-in-Westmorland: 90 miles/145 km

Difficulty rating: 3.5

Average days to complete: 7

Waymarking? Yes

Maps: OS OL2, OL19, Explorer 27 and Explorer 288 online. In print OL2, with rest to follow as they are reprinted

Baggage courier? Yes

For more details: daleshighway.org.uk

Describe the trail

An exhilarating 90 miles across glorious high country. This is a challenging route that covers some of the most beautiful scenery of the Yorkshire Dales and Eden Valley. It's a trail of great variety, starting in the World Heritage village of Saltaire and finishing in the traditional market town of Appleby-in-Westmorland. In between it encompasses open moorland and the dramatic limestone scars, craggy slopes, velvety folds, pretty banks and lush farmland of the Eden Valley. It takes the walker from the familiar beauty of Malhamdale and the Yorkshire Three Peaks to the less well-known delights of the Howgill Fells and Great Asby Scar. It also visits some of the most charming villages and market towns in the western Dales.

Highlights

The traverse of the Howgill Fells, the climb over Ingleborough from Crummackdale, the limestone scars of Malhamdale and Ribblesdale and the return journey on the Settle–Carlisle railway line.

Lowlights

In wet weather the muddy fields around Addingham and along Hoff Beck and the boggy descent from Flasby Fell are all a slog. The route is exposed in places and the guidebook gives alternatives in case sections are daunting in bad weather.

Why do you love it?

The variety. Every day brings a different landscape and a new high point. And I love the return journey from Appleby on the Settle–Carlisle railway line, travelling in a few hours through the landscape you've just walked.

History/background

The walk has a rich history, geology and culture,

Above Daentdale on the Dales High Way. TONY GROGAN

the best of all possibly being the Settle–Carlisle railway line.

How challenging?

It's a challenging route, not for beginners. There's 2 miles/4.6 km of ascent and it's exposed in places. Navigation is straightforward, the guidebook includes 1:25,000 maps and the route is waymarked enough to reassure, although not enough to navigate from. The route follows ancient trade routes, green lanes and packhorse trails where possible and the walking in the limestone areas is delightful. There are some wet areas on the moors and along the riverbanks.

Accommodation and transport

Accommodation is very good. The route climbs to the fell-tops but returns to villages and market towns at night. Chapel-le-Dale is the only squeeze point and should be booked first. The Dales High Way website links to accommodation providers. Much of Dales High Way can be walked in days using the Settle–Carlisle railway line and local buses, although the Sedbergh to Appleby section needs an overnight stay. It can be completed without a tent/bivvy bag.

Best day-walk

The Howgill Fells in clear weather are a joy and on the 6-mile ridge walk from the summit of the Calf to Bowderdale you are likely to share them only with the Fell ponies that roam these hills. The climb from the isolation of Crummackdale to the summit of Ingleborough is spectacular and a chance to conquer one of the Yorkshire Three Peaks. The walk beneath the limestone scars of Attermire and Warrendale Knotts between Malham and Settle is delightful.

Dales Way

Anthony Burton, author of *The Dales Way* and National Trail Video Guides (tvwalks.com)
Ilkley to Bowness-on-Windermere: 80 miles/128 km
Difficulty rating: 3
Average days to complete: 6
Waymarking? Yes
Maps: OS (1:50,000) 97, 98, 104; Harvey Maps
Baggage courier? Yes
For more details: dalesway.org
Describe the trail
A walk that takes you from Wharfedale to Dentdale and on to the edge of the Lake District. The walk starts among the gritstone crags of Ilkley Moor, continues up the valley of the Wharfe to the upper reaches of limestone, then crosses the Pennines to drop down into beautiful Dentdale, ending up on the shore of Lake Windermere.

Highlights

The walk is at its best on the higher levels, especially on the limestone pavements above Grassington and on the crossing over the hills and down to Dent, the latter one of the most attractive villages along the way.

Lowlights

There are none.

Why do you love it?

I'm prejudiced – I'm a Yorkshireman and started my walking in these dales. But I'd say the greatest appeal is the contrast between following the River Wharfe in different moods and being high in the surrounding hills. Do remember to wear a hat for Ilkley Moor. As the song says, 'Go without and you'll catch your death of cold.' (See the Yorkshire National Anthem for details.)

History/background

There is one historic beauty spot, Bolton Abbey. But there are also extensive remains of the old lead mining industry around Grassington.

How challenging?

There is nothing unduly challenging beyond what you would expect on a long distance walk.

Accommodation and transport

Transport is reasonably good – no difficulty getting to either end, and some bus services along the way. Accommodation generally isn't a problem.

Best day-walk

I'd choose Grassington to Hubberholme, for its contrasts of high-level and riverside walking and some of the best scenery along the way.

Dales Celebration Way

Mike Brockhurst, aka the Walking Englishman, walkingenglishman.com

A circular walk around the Yorkshire Dales, beginning and ending in Skipton: 130 miles/209 km

Difficulty rating: 4

Average days to complete: 8

Waymarking? No

Maps: OS Explorer OL2, OL30

Baggage courier? No

For more details: walkingenglishman.com/dalescelebrationway.htm

Describe the trail

A circular long-distance walk visiting many outstanding places in the Yorkshire Dales National Park. This unique footpath is my tribute to this fantastic National Park. At approximately 130 miles long (depending on the various alternatives) it's designed to conveniently fit into a one-week holiday window, especially suitable to starting and finishing on a Saturday or Sunday.

Highlights

The route visits as many of the National Park's attractions as possible. Most of the major hills are scaled, including the Three Peaks, and many dales are visited including Airedale, Wharfedale, Dentdale, Swaledale and Wensleydale. Major natural features such as Gordale Scar, Malham Cove, Sulber Nick, Gaping Gill and Aysgarth Falls are all on the route as are historic monuments like Skipton Castle and Castle Bolton. All the walking days are designed to end in some of the Dales' most interesting towns or villages, including Settle, Ingleton, Dent, Hawes, Reeth and Kettlewell. This gives the walker plenty of choices on type of accommodation and what to eat.

Lowlights

There are no bad stages of the walk, as all are designed with visits to enjoyable sights in mind.

Why do you love it?

This trail is a tribute to the diversity of the Yorkshire Dales National Park. Do not just think limestone, but gritstone, too. Think of ancient, medieval and

The limestone amphitheatre of Malham Cove, on the Dales Celebration Way. MIKE BROCKHURST

more contemporary sites including old lead mining areas and buildings of the Industrial Revolution. And think of the unique character of the Yorkshire people. This is a walk that welcomes the user to the Yorkshire community.

History/background

Mary, Queen of Scots, was imprisoned at Bolton Castle, and Skipton Castle, famous for Civil War mischief.

How challenging?

Fairly. Some days are long with a fair bit of climbing and descending. Despite not being waymarked, the route is on good paths and generally easy to follow.

Accommodation and transport

Accommodation is very good. The walk stages are designed in such a way that each one ends in a popular town or village. This was the intention at conception so that the local economy benefitted from the walk.

Best day-walk

They are all exceptional. But in terms of popularity, Malham Cove on day one (clockwise) and Aysgarth Falls on day six (clockwise) are the biggest for footfall.

Derwent Valley Heritage Way

Rick Jillings, assistant area manager, Derbyshire County Council Countryside Service
Heatherdene to Derwentmouth: 55 miles/88 km
Difficulty rating: 2
Average days to complete: 4

Waymarking? Yes
Maps: OS Explorer 1, 24, 259, 260
Baggage courier? Yes
For more details: nationalheritagecorridor.org.uk

Describe the trail

Follow the journey of the River Derwent through Derbyshire's beautiful countryside and discover fascinating heritage, magnificent scenery and wildlife.

Highlights

The beauty and variety of Derbyshire's countryside, the dramatic gritstone edges, the grandeur of the Chatsworth Estate, the heritage of the Derwent Valley Mills, the water voles along Cromford Canal, the Derwent Riverside path through Derby, and the heritage of Shardlow and its waterways.

Lowlights

Some people may be put off by the thought of walking through the centre of a major city – but don't be. The beautiful Darley Abbey, Darley Park, cathedral quarter and Silk Mill offer a dramatic route along the riverbank. Before long you'll be near Elvaston castle and the beautiful flood plains near Ambaston and Shardlow.

Why do you love it?

The beauty and variety of the natural countryside and early industrial landscapes.

History/background

The River Derwent and tributaries were the source of power for the Industrial Revolution. The route

Chatsworth House, on the Derwent Valley Heritage Way.
BRIAN WATERS

The Wharf at Cromford, Derwent Valley Heritage Way.
BRIAN WATERS

travels through the Chatsworth Estate and the Derwent Valley Mills World Heritage Site.

How challenging?

The walk is on well-used footpaths, often following the river, but with the option of climbing up to get the superb vantage point of High Tor at Matlock Bath and climbing above the town of Belper. With it being in the valley some paths will be muddy after rain.

Accommodation and transport

There are plenty of B&Bs and guesthouses along the route. Public transport links are good. There are excellent transport links once in the valley from Matlock to Derby and Derby to Shardlow.

Best day-walk

Don't miss out – it's all great. Heatherdene to Baslow has the beauty of the rugged peakland gritstone edges. But do continue on to discover the wonders of the Industrial Revolution in the Derwent Valley Mills World Heritage Site and the wildlife of Cromford Canal.

Gritstone Trail

Genni Butler, Discover Cheshire (discovercheshire.co.uk)

Disley to Kidsgrove: 35 miles/56 km
Difficulty rating: 3
Average days to complete: 3
Waymarking? Yes
Maps: OS Explorer 1, 24, 258, 268; Landranger 109, 118

Tranquil view near Calver, Derwent Valley Heritage Way.
BRIAN WATERS

Belper North Mill and weir, Derwent Valley Heritage Way.
BRIAN WATERS

Baggage courier? Yes

For more details: discovercheshire.co.uk

Describe the trail

The trail goes along the ridges and valleys of Cheshire's Peak District. Stride out along the Gritstone Trail and sample some of the finest walking in Cheshire. You'll visit a relatively quiet side of the Peak District, with stunning views from the gritstone ridge of hills abutting the Cheshire Plain. On a clear day you'll get views across to the Welsh Hills and the cathedrals of Liverpool.

Highlights

There's a real variety of landmarks and features along the route, coupled with the stunning views into the Peak District and across the Cheshire Plain.

Lowlights

If you get good weather, then there's nothing not to like on the Gritstone Trail. Even when you think you're warming down along the canal towpath into Kidsgrove, there's still Harecastle Tunnel and a canal aqueduct over another canal to keep your interest.

Why do you love it?

You can often see your progress along the trail by looking back at landmarks and ridges that you've already walked by.

History/background

You'll pass through the National Trust's Lyme Park, Bollington's White Nancy, Tegg's Nose and Mow Cop mining history, features of the canal network and a disused railway.

How challenging?

The Gritstone Trail is a route that follows the relatively exposed western edge of the Peak District. It is a relatively challenging route including some steep but short ascents and descents along with rewarding ridge walks. The Trail is well waymarked.

Accommodation and transport

Public transport is available to Disley in the north and Kidsgrove in the south, with the trail starting and finishing at the respective railway stations. However, although the trail is normally divided into three days, accommodation along the route is limited. So transport to and from the route stages should be arranged in advance, and is sometimes offered by local accommodation options.

Best day-walk

The stretch from the village of Disley south via the National Trust's Lyme Park, up to the landmark of White Nancy at Bollington, and finishing at Tegg's Nose Country Park near Macclesfield. This day offers a variety of historic landmarks and scenery, with views across the Cheshire Plain.

Herriot Way

Stuart W. Greig (herriotway.com; lonewalker.net; @LoneWalkerUK), author of *Walking the Herriot Way*

A circular walk starting in Aysgarth, Yorkshire Dales: 52 miles/84 km

Difficulty rating: 2

Average days to complete: 4

Ruins amidst the heather on the Gritstone Trail. CHESHIRE EAST COUNCIL

Waymarking? No

Maps: OS Explorer OL30

Baggage courier? Yes

For more details: *Walking the Herriot Way* by Stuart W. Greig, herriotway.com

Describe the trail

A wonderful introduction to the diverse scenery of the Yorkshire Dales. Along its 52-mile (84 km) length you visit beautiful valleys (dales), high, open fells and rolling, heather-clad moorland. You cross one of the highest points in Yorkshire, visit historic monuments and pass the crumbling remains of the lead mining industry high on the hills.

Highlights

There is something to delight all walkers. If you love walking beside rivers there is the wonderful section beside the River Ure in Wensleydale. If high remote hills are your idea of heaven then the ascent of Great Shunner Fell will be your highlight. Lovers of grouse-filled, heather moorland will revel in the crossing of Melbecks and Harkerside Moors.

Lowlights

The barren wasteland above Gunnerside, created by the lead mining industry of the nineteenth century is not to everyone's taste. Likened to a moonscape, it will be a long time before Mother Nature reclaims it.

Why do you love it?

The diversity of the scenery encountered along the relatively short Herriot Way are what sets it apart from the other long walks in the UK. The feeling of remoteness while still being within easy reach of civilization every day and the mix of easy strolling through the dales and the strenuous ascent of Great Shunner Fell make it a perfect candidate for your first long distance walk.

History/background

The walk is named after James Herriot, the fictional name given to the real-life veterinary surgeon who lived and worked in the Dales for many years. James Herriot was really Alf Wight and parts of this walk are first described in his book *James Herriot's Yorkshire*, a coffee-table book with stunning photographs by Derry Brabbs.

Sheep searching for their breakfast in the snow, Gritstone Trail.
CHESHIRE EAST COUNCIL

Walkers will visit a diverse array of remains from the lead mining industry that was prevalent through this area of the Dales for many years. Subtle information boards provide an insight into how hundreds of miners lived and worked in this desolate environment, changing and shaping it forever.

How challenging?

The Herriot Way is the perfect walk for a first-time long distance walker, or for an experienced walker looking for a leg-stretcher. The 52 miles are broken into four approximately equal 13-mile days, each one ending in villages with plentiful local amenities. The good mix of strenuous sections and easy walking through lowlands, beside the wide River Ure, make for an interesting walk, giving you a taste of the different kinds of walking available in northern England.

Accommodation and transport

Accommodation is plentiful at the end of each of the 13-mile sections and some days have villages perfectly positioned for a pub lunch. The route could be wild-camped or you could make use of campsites along the way. Some sections are supported by local bus services but the nearest train station is about 15 miles from the route, so getting to the start requires planning.

Best day-walk

If you like to walk high, then park in Keld and catch the bus to Reeth, walking back to your car over

Melbecks Moor and down the wonderful Swinner Gill. If you prefer a low-level walk then use the bus between Hawes and Askrigg to walk beside the Ure.

Howgills and Limestone Trail

David and Heather Pitt, authors of *Howgills and Limestone Trail*

Kirkby Stephen to Settle: 76 miles/122 km
Difficulty rating: 4
Average days to complete: 7
Waymarking? No
Maps: OS OL19, OL2
Baggage courier? Yes
For more details: howgillsandlimestonetrail.org.uk

Describe the trail

A chance to see the splendour of the Howgill Fells and Limestone Country. The trail draws its inspiration from the two pictorial guides by Alfred Wainwright, *Walks on the Howgill Fells* and *Walks in Limestone Country* – recently revised. If it's combined with a return to Kirkby Stephen along the Pennine Journey route, making the expedition into a 134-mile walk, then the walker gains a real insight into this delightful area of North Yorkshire and Cumbria with a peep into Lancashire.

Highlights

Cautley Spout, Ingleton Falls, Ingleborough, Pen-y-ghent and Catrigg Force.

Lowlights

Those walkers who only find pleasure in hills may not appreciate the short pastoral stretch that links the end of the pothole area at Leck with Ingleton.

Why do you love it?

The two extraneous but linked themes that emerged during the preparatory work on the guidebook: the Quaker movement, which could be said to have started in the area, and the early railways.

History/background

It provided an opportunity to link two passions of Alfred Wainwright – his love of the area of the trail expressed in his two pictorial guides to the area and the medium of a long distance walk.

How challenging?

At 76 miles the trail is a relatively short one and could be described as a good beginners' long distance walk. However, by virtue of the fact that its route goes over two of the Three Peaks, with an option to take in the third, it is reasonably challenging. A good initial level of fitness and, above all, stamina will be required to complete the trail.

Accommodation and transport

The trail website has details of accommodation and local taxi firms, as public transport on most of the route is minimal. However some B&B providers pick up and drop off overnight guests, as a result extending stays to two nights. This is particularly useful in areas of scarce accommodation as well as in popular places with many visitors.

Best day-walk

The stage from Horton in Ribblesdale to Settle.

A waterfall on the Herriot Way. STUART W. GREIG

The Howell Fells, as seen on the Howgills and Limestone Trail. DAVID AND HEATHER PITT

Colin Bywater's re-interpretation of an Alfred Wainwright sketch of the Howell Fells.

Lady Anne's Way

Sheila Gordon (ladyannesway.co.uk), author of *Lady Anne's Way*

Skipton to Penrith: 100 miles/160 km

Difficulty rating: 3

Average days to complete: 6–9

Waymarking? Partly waymarked

Maps: The trail is not yet on maps, but the guidebook *Lady Anne's Way* by Sheila Gordon has large-scale strip maps

For more details: ladyannesway.co.uk

Describe the trail

A walk of great beauty, full of historical interest. The trail passes through the wonders of the Yorkshire Dales, through unspoilt villages and limestone pavements and progresses over the remote and rugged fellside of Mallerstang, to enter Cumbria and the hidden delights of the Eden Valley.

Highlights

The idyllic villages, Kettlewell and Askrigg. The traverse of Stake Moss and the views as you descend into Wensleydale with Addlebrough in the distance. Or my favourite, the climb out of Hawes up Cotter End followed by the walk along Lady Anne's Way all the way into Mallerstang, with Wild Boar Fell on your left and Mallerstang Edge to your right.

Lowlights

A couple of miles of road walking in the Eden Valley from Cliburn to Clifton Dykes, but at least there is plenty of grass verge to walk on and a cafe part way along.

Why do you love it?

The great variety of scenery, from the lush valley bottoms with their fascinating villages to the wild moorlands and dramatic limestone pavements. The fascinating ruined castles found along the route, devastated during the Civil Wars and subsequently restored during the seventeenth century by the indomitable Lady Anne Clifford, are also magnificent.

History/background

There is a great deal of historical interest along the route as you trace the story of the remarkable Lady Anne travelling through the landscape in her horse-litter accompanied by a host of retainers. The inspiration for the trail came from these incredible journeys that she undertook whilst supervising the work on her castles and other buildings.

How challenging?

This is a walk for anyone who is reasonably fit and will appeal both to the seasoned walkers and those seeking their first experience of a long distance path. Though originally conceived as a six-day walk, the way can be spread over nine days or more. The terrain is varied, encompassing a substantial amount of riverside walking and quiet pasture land. There are some modest fellside ascents and also two stretches of steeper terrain. Navigation shouldn't be a problem as there are no long stretches of remote moorland to negotiate. The signposting can be sporadic in the Eden Valley but the trail book is accompanied by large-scale strip maps, which show every wall. An application has also been made for official waymarking.

Accommodation and transport

Accommodation is usually plentiful in the Yorkshire Dales, but can be a problem in the Eden Valley. If doing the six-day walk, the only problem could be at Buckden where it's best to book ahead. If doing the nine-day alternative there are several places with limited accommodation and so it's advisable to check the trail website for details and book ahead. Youth hostels are situated at Hawes, Kirkby Stephen and Dufton just beyond Appleby. For backpackers there are campsites at Appletreewick, Kettlewell, Hawes, Kirkby Stephen, Appleby and Penrith. However, if you're not too fastidious about facilities, I have found that an enquiry at the local pub will often produce the name of a farmer willing to let you camp in a field or better still the pub garden. Transport can be limited but there are train stations at Skipton, Kirkby Stephen, Appleby and Penrith. Also once in the Eden Valley you are never too far away from the Settle–Carlisle railway line.

Best day-walk

It has to be the route out of Hawes over to Kirkby Stephen on Stage Four. Once up Cotter End the walking is delightful with stunning views all around. When you descend into Mallerstang you follow the River Eden past the romantic ruins of Pendragon Castle before finishing the day at the bustling town of Kirkby Stephen with its ancient church and market cross.

Limestone Way

Andrew Bowden, ramblingman.org.uk
Castleton to Rocester: 45 miles/72 km
Difficulty rating: 2
Average days to complete: 4
Waymarking? Partial
Maps: OS Explorer OL1, OL24, 259

Baggage courier? Yes

For more details: ramblingman.org.uk

Describe the trail

A walk through the south of the Peak District National Park. The Limestone Way is a tour of Derbyshire's limestone country, passing through farms and dales and attractive villages.

Highlights

Walking through several attractive dales, including the iconic Cave Dale near Castleton, with the ruined Peveril Castle looming overhead. Heading under the mighty remains of the former Miller's Dale railway viaduct. Fine views of the former spa town of Matlock.

Lowlights

Lots of road or track walking which can be hard on the feet. The section in Staffordshire is also a trifle dull, spending much of its time in farmed fields with few views. The northern section between Castleton and Matlock is far more impressive than the southern half.

Why do you love it?

The Limestone Way goes through some beautiful and rugged Peak District scenery. It takes you

TOP: River Eden at Thrang Bridge. BOTTOM: Brougham Castle. Both based on places sited on the Lady Anne's Way. FRANK GORDON

BELOW: Leaving Skipton, also on the Lady Anne's Way. TONY GROGAN/ SKYWARE

through quiet, almost hidden villages, and allows you to explore a lesser-known part of the National Park.

History/background

The trail originally ran from Castleton to Matlock, and was later extended to Rocester.

How challenging?

Good paths and tracks generally make this an easy walk to follow, with no long sections. There are hills to climb, but these are rarely taxing. It is well way-marked for most of the trail, however the section in Staffordshire has no specific Limestone waymarking and you will need to be confident using maps to find your way.

Accommodation and transport

Accommodation is plentiful in Castleton and Matlock, but can be much harder to find in other villages where there is limited accommodation on the route itself. There are railway stations at Matlock and Castleton, and buses at Rocester which will take you to stations at Derby or Uttoxeter. There are some local bus services near the route, although these are not always frequent.

Best day-walk

Moneyash to Castleton offers some of the trail's most stunning scenery, including the wonderful Cave Dale near Castleton. The section between Matlock and Moneyash is also recommended as it takes you through the scenic Cales Dale and the Robin Hood's Stride rock formation.

National Forest Way

Carol Rowntree Jones, the National Forest Company (nationalforestway.co.uk)

The National Memorial Arboretum, Alrewas, to Beacon Hill Country Park: 75 miles/120 km

Difficulty rating: 1–2

Average days to complete: 6

Waymarking? Yes

Maps: It will be marked on the next version of OS Explorer 245. Sections also use 233 and 246

Baggage courier? No

For more details: Leaflets with full descriptions and OS mapping can be downloaded from national-forestway.co.uk

Describe the trail

The route explores the varied and fascinating landscape of the National Forest, the boldest and biggest environmentally led regeneration project in the country, covering 200 square miles of the Midlands. The path leads through the Forest and through varying landscapes including industrial heritage areas, ancient deer parks, river valleys, granite outcrops, farmland, open space – all framed by woodland. Over 8 million trees have been planted in the National Forest since the early 1990s and in walking this trail you experience the story of this transformation.

Highlights

The start/finish at Beacon Hill Country Park. The magnificent stretch of varied-age woodlands between Rosliston and Moira. The wildlife haven across the river valley alongside the A38 and mainline railway line between Branston and Walton-on-Trent. The medieval spring at Blackfordby on a hot day. Carvers Rocks – a marooned outcrop of gritstone more usually found in the Peak District thrust up in south Derbyshire. Dimminsdale – a veritable 'Hobbitty' woodland, all dingley-dells, shady pools and a magical glade of snowdrops in February. Battlestead Hill and the panoramic views over the River Trent, the A38, the Trent and Mersey Canal, the Midland Railway – a history of transport – as well as wooded hills, farmland and the sheds and factories of Beer Town (Burton upon Trent).

Lowlights

The start/finish immediately from/to the National Memorial Arboretum has to use the A38 – not the most attractive stretch. Some of the farmland stretches – but hey, that's walking through farmland. What's great about the National Forest Way is that it changes so swiftly, so none of the less good stretches are *that* long – and the great stretches are like invigorating in-breaths of delight!

Why do you love it?

The variety. For instance, in one 4-mile stretch you begin in a tiny village in the ancient forest of Needwood, walk through a delightful new woodland, through a gorse-lined steep-sided little valley, then more new planting to open onto a vista of

wooded hills, over said hills past an ancient beech tree that is reminiscent of an Enid Blyton story, to open views over the river valley, then descent to walk alongside the sleepy Trent and Mersey Canal and end up at a nature reserve with wildfowl galore. All in the space of 4 miles.

History/background

The transformation of the landscape and the mining history. A recurring theme is the battleground between the Anglo-Saxon south and the Danelaw of northern Britain. You feel you're in ancient border country.

TOP: Bradgate Park. KEVIN TEBBUTT. CENTRE and BOTTOM: Beacon Hill Country Park. 2020vision/BEN HALL All on the National Forest Way.

Grangewood Estate in The National Forest. DIANA JARVIS

How challenging?

It's definitely beginner-friendly. It ties in perfectly with our aim to encourage all kinds of people to get out and enjoy the Forest and be out in the countryside. We like to think it is a definite introduction to long distance trail walking. It is waymarked: orange for walking west to east, purple for walking east to west. Some hills, but not a lot of ascent or descent. Much of it gentle walking.

Accommodation and transport

The route is divided into twelve stages, ranging from 4–7.5 miles in length. It can very easily be done as day walks, two stages a day is generally doable for a keen walker. All but one of the stages has *some* degree of public transport, though rarely frequent. Walkers should visit visitnationalforest. co.uk for information about accommodation on or near the route. There are a number of pubs and B&Bs, plus an eco-friendly youth hostel right in the middle of the route.

Best day-walk

Thornton Reservoir to Bradgate Park. The route takes you through beautiful Burroughs Wood, onto Martinshaw Wood across the M1, a breathtaking moment when you emerge from Lady Hay Wood, and a choice of tearooms at Newtown Linford. But a close second would be the aforementioned 4-mile walk, Rangemore to Branston, or the woodlands between Rosliston and Moira.

Pennine Bridleway (NT)

Julie Thompson, trail office

Middleton Top (near Middleton-by-Wirksworth) to south of Kirkby Stephen: 205 miles/330 km

Difficulty rating: 3

Average days to complete: 14

Waymarking? Yes

Maps: The northern section will not be present on older versions of OS maps. OS Explorer OL1, 2, 19, 21, 24 for the southern section; Pennine Bridleway South from Harvey Maps for the south-east

Baggage courier? Yes

For more details: nationaltrail.co.uk/pennine-bridleway

Describe the trail

An adventurous and entertaining journey made special by the views and the people you meet. On the Pennine Bridleway you can expect to meet cyclists and horse riders as well as other walkers. There are no stiles to tackle, just easy-to-open gates and no steps, just graded slopes. That said, it's a Pennine trail so it's still hilly and challenging, for example the steep-sided valleys which are characteristic of the South Pennine section. The trail passes through fantastic landscapes but also offers access to villages and pubs. A variety of tracks are followed from historic packhorse trails and drovers routes to old cobbled tracks and newly created grass gravel paths.

Highlights

There are many. User feedback suggests the experience in general with the fabulous views and the hidden gems that you didn't expect to find are what make it. More obvious is the section through the Dales with the glorious scenery and the variety of tracks used – enclosed grassy lanes near Austwick, new paths leading to an award-winning timber bridge near Selside. Living in Calderdale, I love the hilly sections in the South Pennines with the mills and chimneys and the old causey paths. A detour from the trail into Hebden Bridge for plentiful cafes and quirky shops is worthwhile.

Lowlights

To some the stretches along the dismantled railway lines at the southern end of the trail can be a bit samey, but on the other hand they can be an easy way to start and build your fitness. For others the final slog up the fell to High Dophinsty in Cumbria may not be much fun if the weather's bad. It's horses for courses really.

Why do you love it?

It takes you to places that you probably would never have known about or thought to visit otherwise. You may expect it to be good in the Dales, but you may not realize that there are some amazing views and lovely peaceful sections of route in the metropolitan boroughs surrounding Manchester!

History/background

The Pennine Bridleway was the brainchild of a rider, Mary Towneley, who wanted horse riders to have the same chance to experience the thrill of making a long distance journey as those on foot. Planning a trip from Northumberland to Derbyshire, she was struck by the fragmented nature of the bridleway network, which made it near impossible to safely plan a long distance ride. In 1986 Lady Towneley presented the then Countryside Commission with the challenge of creating a purpose-built National Trail for horse riders in the north of England. The Pennine Bridleway was finally opened in 2012 to be enjoyed by all – horse riders, walkers and mountain bikers.

How challenging?

The Pennine Bridleway is a flagship for the rights of way network, so the quality of the signing and waymarking is high and the gates and route in general are well maintained. It's been carefully aligned and built to avoid boggy terrain. This means a lot of the route is surfaced but with a variety of treatments, new and old, with grass sections reinforced with stone. Busy roads are avoided and any major-road crossings have a crossing control. Whilst you are never too far away from civilization on the southern section of the route, once you get into the Yorkshire Dales and the final push through Cumbria in particular, the route is more remote and services fewer.

Walker at Matley Moor Farm near Hayfield, Pennine Bridleway.
MIKE WILLIAMS

Accommodation and transport

There are plenty of accommodation options, ranging from campsites to hotels. The trail can be completed using public transport. In the Dales the picturesque Settle to Carlisle railway comes in very useful.

Best day-walk

Difficult one. Probably in the Yorkshire Dales.

Pennine Journey

David and Heather Pitt, authors of *A Pennine Journey*

A circular walk from Settle to Hadrian's Wall and back: 247 miles/396 km

Difficulty rating: 5

Average days to complete: 18

Waymarking? Yes

Maps: The route is included on OS's mapping database and in time will feature on all OS Landranger and Explorer maps – it's already on OL2 Yorkshire Dales (South and West). You will need: OS OL2, OL30, OL31, OL307, OL43, OL19, OL41

Baggage courier? Yes

For more details: penninejourney.org.uk

Describe the trail

A modern recreation of a walk done in 1938 by Alfred Wainwright. Arguably the most attractive long distance path in northern England, it traverses some of the delightful terrain the region has to offer. From limestone country, moorland, Hadrian's Wall, the Pennines and ending with more limestone country during which the Journey takes in two of the Yorkshire Three Peaks. The 'journeyer' enjoys walks along and in the valleys of most of the region's major rivers whilst passing through some delightful towns and villages.

Highlights

The walk along the River Tees, the 20-mile section of Hadrian's Wall and the Eden Valley attract the most favourable comments.

Lowlights

Without a doubt it is the lonely moorland sections where route-finding, especially in the mist, presents a challenge.

Why do you love it?

It is a showcase for the rich variety of terrain that northern England has to offer.

History/background

This was Alfred Wainwright's first long distance walk and his narrative description was written in 1939 but only published in 1986. In between those dates he compiled his incomparable pictorial guides to the Lake District Fells, after which he wrote, in his *Pennine Way Companion*, what many still consider the definitive guide to Britain's first long distance path. He followed that with his own coast-to-coast walk.

How challenging?

It is without doubt a challenging walk. A good level of fitness will be required to complete the journey in one go. It would also be sensible, for inexperienced long distance walkers, to take the first few days more easily. Half of the route's stages involve ascents of over 2,000 ft/600 m with the final two being over 3,000 ft/900 m and there are inevitably some boggy sections. The route is waymarked.

Accommodation and transport

The Pennine Journey website has information on accommodation and comprehensive details of local taxi firms as public transport on most of the route is minimal. However, there's a growing tendency for some B&B providers to pick up and drop off overnight guests and as a result extending stays to two nights. A baggage courier service is offered by Brigantes (brigantesenglishwalks.com).

Best day-walk

From the section along Hadrian's Wall, because it's here that history, scenery and the objective of Alfred Wainwright's Pennine Journey come together. Another alternative could be the opening stage, extended by the ascent of Pen-y-ghent and a look at Hull Pot before the return to Horton-in-Ribblesdale.

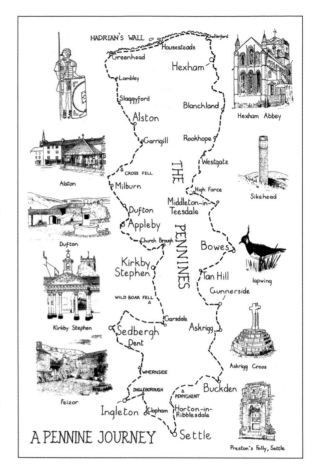

A Pennine Journey. DAVID AND HEATHER PITT

Is there a lonelier, more appealing view than the Tan Hill Inn in the middle of a windswept moor? DAMIAN HALL

Pennine Way (NT)

Damian Hall, author of *Pennine Way*

Edale to Kirk Yetholm: 268 miles/429 km

Difficulty rating: 5

Average days to complete: 16–18

Waymarking? Yes

Maps: The official guide, Aurum's *Pennine Way*, has full OS mapping. Alternatively you'll need nine OS maps (OL1, OL2, OL21, OL21, OL16, OL19, OL31, OL42, OL43), or three from Harvey Maps, or two from Footprint Maps

Baggage courier? Yes

For more details: nationaltrail.co.uk/pennine-way

Describe the trail

England's oldest and toughest National Trail and some of the wildest, remotest and best upland walking in the country. The Pennine Way travels

Descending into Teesdale on the Pennine Way. DAMIAN HALL

Autumn on the Pennine Way.
DAMIAN HALL

along the Pennines, the backbone of England, all the way from Edale in Derbyshire to little Kirk Yetholm just over the border in Scotland. Wayfarers tramp their muddy boots across the bleakly beautiful gritstone plateaus and melancholy moorlands, up and down secret wind-tickled dales, along rugged ridges with endless views and big, big skies, past limestone splendour, following singing rivers past crashing waterfalls, through wild-flower-strewn meadows, up stout mountains and many more lonely and dreamy wild places. It tiptoes through landscapes that inspired great writers. It's a history lesson on northern England. It's a fascinating geological field trip. It's a tour of cosy pubs, welcoming cafes and numerous charming villages

you've probably never heard of and may never want to leave. But most of all it's a walk through life-affirming natural beauty. I'm a bit biased, but it's pretty good.

Highlights

You get the rugged Peak District, the glorious Yorkshire Dales – especially the wonders around Malham – stirring Hadrian's Wall and the criminally underrated Cheviots. The Way includes England's highest waterfall above ground (Hardraw Force), the highest pub (Tan Hill Inn), the coldest place in the country (Cross Fell), one of the Yorkshire Three Peaks (Pen-y-ghent), totemic Kinder Scout and the compelling yet terrifying chasm of High Cup – the greatest view in England.

Low Force (in background) on the River Tees, Pennine Way.
DAMIAN HALL

Lowlights

It can get a bit boggy. The section between Alston and Greenhead is a bit fiddly. Not everyone loves Cross Fell.

Why do you love it?

Above all, the sense of remoteness and wildness right in the middle of an island we often think of as excessively busy and crowded. And the powerful sense of history the trail has.

History/background

The Pennine Way, which celebrate its fiftieth birthday – England's first National Trail to do so – in 2015, is strongly linked to the Mass Trespass on Kinder Scout in 1932. Those wonderful law-breakers greatly improved this country for us and we shouldn't forget that. Plus Alfred Wainwright wrote an amusingly grumpy guidebook, entitled *Pennine Way Companion*. Brian Clough walked some of it, too.

How challenging?

It can be tough, but not as tough as its reputation. It's long, plus the Pennines are often plateaus so if the weather turns unfriendly you're kind of stuck up there for a bit.

Accommodation and transport

Accommodation is good throughout, with some excellent B&Bs. Transport does get a bit trickier as you get further north.

High Force on the River Tees, Pennine Way. DAMIAN HALL

High Cup: the greatest moment on the Pennine Way. DAMIAN HALL

Classic Yorkshire Dales scenery near Thwaite. DAMIAN HALL

Best day-walk

Middleton in Teesdale to Dufton. Skipping through flowery meadows, following the playful Tees, Low Force tickles your fancy and High Force tickles you somewhere fancier, before Cauldron Snout snorts at you. That's a pretty good day by anyone's standards, but the best bit of the whole walk is still to come ... plus Dufton's a gem, too.

Raad Ny Foillan (Isle of Man Coastal Footpath)

Rachele Quayle, from visitisleofman.com/walking
Douglas and back again: 100 miles/160 km
Difficulty rating: 3
Average days to complete: 5

Waymarking? Yes
Maps: Isle of Man Outdoor Leisure Map, 1:25,000 recommended
Baggage courier? Yes
For more details: visitisleofman.com/walking; *Isle of Man Coastal Path* by Aileen Evans
Describe the trail

The only long distance walk in the British Isles which goes round an entire country. Raad Ny Foillan is 100 miles of terrain so varied every day is a completely different type of walking, ranging from stunning glens to remote moorland, dramatic coastal cliffs and isolated beaches.

The criminally under-rated Cheviots: the Pennine Way's grande finale.
DAMIAN HALL

TALKING WALKING – STEVE WESTWOOD

Steve has over twenty years' experience in developing and managing trails. Prior to his role as Pennine Way National Trail Officer he managed the seven-year upgrade of the West Highland Way and worked previously as a maintenance ranger for the Yorkshire Dales National Park. He has walked, cycled and paddled on trails around the world including the John Muir Trail, the GR20 and the Bowron Canoe circuit. He is the training officer and an active call-out member of his local Mountain Rescue team.

Steve Westwood.

What do you remember about your first multi-day walk?

It was the Pennine Way when I was sixteen years old. I set off with a couple of friends, who both dropped out at Dufton. I had no knowledge of suitable hill food. I recorded what I ate in my guidebook: 'Malham – two litres of cola and seven packets of cheese and onion crisps!'

What effect did your first long walk have on you?

At times I remember being scared and lonely after my friends had dropped out. To this day, every time I walk down the Corpse Road from Cross Fell, 'Echo Beach' from Martha and the Muffins comes into my head. I listened to it on a transistor radio whilst walking in the fading light.

Which is your all-time favourite trek and why?

All-time favourite has to be the John Muir Trail and of course the Pennine Way!

What is it about long distance walks that appeals to you?

I love the journeying, the time to think and the detail of things along the way.

How much do you obsess over equipment?

If I was really obsessed about carrying the weight it would be cheaper to go on a diet!

What advice do you have for fellow long distance walkers?

You can spend a lot of time planning multi-day trips, but to me much of the pleasure is just going with the flow and not planning it too much. As long as you have reasonably good-quality kit you can adapt to situations as they arise. One thing that really makes a difference to how enjoyable a long trip turns out for me is how well I sleep – you will never regret buying a good sleeping bag.

Highlights

Magnificent coastal and interior scenery and views, varied walking, a feeling of remoteness yet you're never far from a village or town, and wildlife and fauna abound.

Lowlights

A couple of sections are tide-dependent, but the alternative route is along very quiet country lanes. A little road walking in places, but no roads on the Isle of Man are especially busy. The beach walking section can be very tiring, hard on the ankles and desolate especially if the weather is poor.

Why do you love it?

Stunning countryside, quiet but not too isolated and superb views.

History/background

The walk can be completed during the Isle of Man Walking Festival as the Coastal Challenge. The walk is guided, all transport is provided. An ideal way to raise money for charity by sponsorship.

How challenging?

Enough of a challenge for experienced walkers to complete it in five days and feel they have achieved something. It's not beginner-friendly as some sections are very remote, but can be completed by an average walker in seven days. One section is particularly remote and a compass/GPS is recommended if the weather is poor. This section is also very hilly with three separate steep ascents. Signposting is very good, but sometimes the posts are blown over in the wind and/or pushed over by wild wallabies or sheep.

Accommodation and transport

From Peel on the west of the island to Ramsey on the east coast, accommodation is limited and it may be necessary to use accommodation off the coastal path. There are no problems between Douglas and Peel. Campsites are limited in the north of the island. All sections can be done as day walks, but public transport is limited in the north of the island, between Kirk Michael and Ramsey. Transport between Douglas and Port Erin is very good, with the opportunity to use Victorian steam trains during the summer – and between Ramsey and Douglas there's an opportunity to use a Victorian electric railway during the summer. It is not recommended to walk the Raad Ny Foillan during the Tourist Trophy Race (TT) and the Festival of Motorcycling. The island is extremely busy then with accommodation booking up at least a year in advance and, with road closures, several areas of the island cannot be accessed.

Best day-walk

First choice would be Port St Mary to Port Eri; second choice, Ramsey to Laxey; third choice, Port Erin to Peel.

Ribble Way

Dennis Kelsall, co-author (with Jan Kelsall) of *The Ribble Way*

Longton (near Preston) to the Ribble's source high on Cam Fell: 71 miles/114 km
Difficulty rating: 2.5
Average days to complete: 7
Waymarking? Yes

Maps: OS Explorers 286, 287, OL41, OL2
For more details: visitribblevalley.co.uk, yorkshiredales.org.uk

Describe the walk

A wander through the Ribble Valley from its estuary to the river's source on Cam Fell in the Yorkshire Dales. This is a walk of contrast that progresses through an increasingly spartan agricultural landscape. Preston is the only major conurbation passed, but the route through the city largely follows pleasant riverside parkland. Although rarely dramatic, the scenery is engaging, with long views up the valley to the hills of the Yorkshire Dales.

Highlights

The last section beyond Settle is the most scenically dramatic as the route passes through the Yorkshire Dales Three Peaks triangle, but there's plenty of other interest too. Ribchester was a Roman fort. Upstream, Hurst Green is home to the impressive Stonyhurst College (with connections to Sir Arthur Conan Doyle and J.R.R. Tolkien amongst others), Clitheroe has an impressive little castle, while nearby Sawley has the remains of a Cistercian abbey. Picturesque Settle is one end of the famous Settle–Carlisle Railway, the most impressive viaduct on the route being passed at Ribblehead.

Lowlights

With sections across stock farmland and moor, prolonged periods of rain can render the going tough and the river does occasionally flood, making short sections temporarily impassable.

Why do you love it?

It is a fine walk in itself but offers great scope for any number of day walks to explore the surrounding landscape. Many of those completing the trail add on a couple or more days to tackle Yorkshire's Three Peaks and Pendle Hill is readily accessible from Clitheroe.

History/background

The idea was conceived in the 1960s, but access difficulties meant the project did not get off the ground for some twenty years and the first leg was only opened in 1985 by Mike Harding, then President of the Ramblers Association.

Ribblehead Viaduct and Ingleborough, Six Peaks Trail. TONY GROGAN/
SKYWARE PRESS

How challenging?

Long enough to present a satisfying challenge but
without great technical or logistical difficulty, it
is an ideal introduction to long distance walking.
Though moorland ground can be heavy-going,
signage is generally good.

Accommodation and transport

Accommodation is not always plentiful, particularly in Lancashire, where the trail is largely
through farmland providing few options for wild
camping. As ever, the secret lies in advance planning. Alternatively the route can be completed
as seven or eight separate one-day walks, using a
combination of circular routes and public transport
options.

Best day-walk

It has to be from Settle to the source, but throw in an
extra day or so to incorporate the Three Peaks.

Settle to Carlisle Way

Jacquetta Megarry, author and publisher of *Settle to
Carlisle Way*

Settle to Carlisle: 97 miles/156 km
Difficulty rating: 4
Average days to complete: 7–8
Waymarking? No
Maps: Not marked on OS maps, but it is on Harvey's
waterproof *Settle to Carlisle Way*
Baggage courier? No
For more details: foscl.org.uk, rucsacs.com

Describe the trail

A route that runs from station to station within
sight of Britain's best-loved mainline railway.
The Settle to Carlisle Way goes for 97 miles (156
km) northward from Settle, passing great views of
the Three Peaks on its way through the Yorkshire
Dales National Park, past Ribblehead Viaduct and

Settle Walker's Group. rucsacs.com

Armathwaite, on the Settle to Carlisle Way. rucsacs.com

over Blea Moor tunnel. Entering Cumbria, the Way passes beneath Wild Boar Fell and descends gently through the delightful valley of the River Eden. Here it passes Long Meg and her Daughters (stone circle) and, after Armathwaite, it ends in the historic border city of Carlisle.

Highlights
Passing Ribblehead Viaduct and its memorial, hearing a train passing through Blea Moor

tunnel 500 ft/152 m beneath, enjoying views over the River Eden, visiting the Brief Encounter cafe (Langwathby Station), Long Meg and her Daughters, St Constantine's Cells (monks' cells), and the riverside approach to Carlisle.

Lowlights
During and after heavy rain much of the route is prone to bogginess. Also there is some roadside walking.

Why do you love it?
I'll never forget the thrill of seeing and hearing the *Fellsman* steam-hauling its train up the Long Drag between Settle and Aisgill. (Steam services run on Wednesdays throughout summer.) Using the railway makes the logistics much easier and you can walk the sections in any order.

History/background
The railway was an amazing feat of Victorian engineering, and the route passes many of its viaducts and uses its stations. When British Rail tried to close the line, the Friends of the Settle to Carlisle Line mounted a vigorous campaign whose success in 1989 resulted in the restoration of Ribblehead Viaduct.

How challenging?
It isn't waymarked, so you have to follow guidebook directions and/or your map carefully, so it isn't

Corby, Settle to Carlisle Way.
rucsacs.com

Pen-y-ghent rising behind Horton-in-Ribblesdale, Six Peaks Trail.
CHRIS GROGAN

ideal for a beginner. The terrain is not that difficult except after rain when it can be very boggy, but there are also quite a few stiles. None of the sections are particularly long and the ease of railway connections means you can walk them in any order.

Accommodation and transport

There's plenty of choice of accommodation in Settle, Kirkby Stephen, Appleby and Carlisle, but smaller villages have only a few B&Bs. Great access by mainline train means the route can easily be completed in sections/day walks.

Best day-walk

Ribblehead to Garsdale Station is a great 11-mile section: you begin at the magnificent twenty-four-arched viaduct, soaring over 98 ft/30 m above the ground, and follow moorland tracks over Blea Moor to a high point of 1,640 ft/500 m. From there you see Dent Head and Arten Gill Viaducts, and descend past rapids to Dent Head, later following the River Dee. After a stiff climb beside Arten Gill, you enjoy contouring the flanks of Great Knoutberry Hill with amazing views gradually unfolding.

Six Peaks Trail

Chris Grogan, co-author of *Dales Rail Trails*
Settle to Kirkby Stephen: 48 miles/78 km
Difficulty rating: 4

Average days to complete: 4
Waymarking? No
Maps: OS Explorer 2, 19, 41
Baggage courier? No
For more details: dalesrailtrails.co.uk

Describe the trail

A 48-mile walk follows the line of the Settle–Carlisle railway line, crossing six peaks on the route from Settle to Kirkby Stephen. It's a linear route over Pen-y-ghent, Ingleborough, Whernside, Great Knoutberry, Swarth Fell and Wild Boar Fell which takes the walker off the well-known challenge route but includes the Yorkshire Three Peaks followed by three less-well-known ones.

Highlights

Pen-y-ghent, Ingleborough and Whernside, plus three more Yorkshire peaks. Walking the Wild Boar Fell ridge. Following the spectacular Settle–Carlisle railway line.

Lowlights

The Yorkshire Three Peaks area can be very crowded. There's a stretch of road walking between Great Knoutberry and Garsdale. It's an exposed route with little shelter in bad weather.

Why do you love it?

The contrast between the popular peaks of Pen-y-ghent, Ingleborough and Whernside and the

The view from Knoutberry, Six Peaks Trail. CHRIS GROGAN

solitude of Great Knoutberry, Swarth Fell and Wild Boar Fell.

History/background

It was created as a way to take walkers into the landscapes of the Yorkshire Three Peaks area without joining the crowds on the challenge route.

How challenging?

It's very challenging. It is exposed with a mile/3 km of ascent in 48 miles/77 km. It is not waymarked, walkers need navigation skills. It's isolated and boggy in places.

Accommodation and transport

Good. Each of the four sections starts and finishes at a railway station. Accommodation can be found at the end of each section or the train can be used to walk from a single base. It can be walked as a continuous route or as four separate days.

Best day-walk

Day four from Garsdale to Kirkby Stephen over Wild Boar Fell.

Staffordshire Way

Sarah Matthews, leader of the Staffordshire National Women's Register Golden Challenge Walk

From Kinver to Mow Cop: 93 miles/150 km
Difficulty rating: 3
Average days to complete: 7
Waymarking? Yes
Maps: Working northwards, OS OL218, 242, 244, 259, 24, 268

The nab and summit of Wild Boar Fell, Six Peaks Trail.
CHRIS GROGAN

Baggage courier? No

For more details: staffordshire.gov.uk

Describe the trail

A walk up the middle of Staffordshire. Walking almost 100 miles within one county, you gain a good picture of its wide variety of scenery including heathland, rolling pastureland, sandstone ridges and water meadows, and learn something of its history from canals, lime kilns, stately homes and the Glacial Boulder.

Highlights

The highlights of the Way are the scenery and views on Kinver Edge, on Cannock Chase, in the Churnet Valley and on Boseley Cloud. The Caldon Canal towpath, near Cheadle, and the towpath along the Trent and Mersey near Shugborough are also very pleasant.

Lowlights

Parts of the Way, such as the dove meadows between Rocester and Uttoxeter and the country park area around Laddergate and Deep Hayes can become mudbaths in wet weather. Polytunnel land, south of Penkridge, can be unappealing, especially in poor weather. North of Abbots Bromley there are some vast prairies to cross. You may feel that your glimpse of Shugborough is not worth the trek along the A513 and the estate road.

Why do you love it?

The aforementioned scenic highlights are worth a visit at any time of the year, and the sheer variety is fascinating.

History/background

There is much geological interest, such as the sandstone ridges and the Bunter pebble beds. If you have time to spare, the Kinver Rock Houses at the southern end are worth a visit. You could stop for lunch in Codsall Station, a pub that is also a working station with a restored vintage waiting room and ticket office. There are many reminders of Staffordshire's industrial past, especially in the Churnet Valley. Penkridge, Colton and Abbot's Bromley are all villages full of interesting old buildings, and there are many others, such as the Gothic turrets of Alton Towers visible from the summit of

View from Kinver Edge on the Staffordshire Way. SARAH MATTHEWS

Walking into the Sherbrook Valley on the Staffordshire Way.
SARAH MATTHEWS

Toothill Wood and Arkwright's mill at Rocester, now the JCB Academy.

How challenging?

Most of the walkers on the Staffordshire National Women's Register Golden Challenge Walk had never walked a long distance trail before, but they managed to complete the Way over one week. The steepest ascents are up Bedall Bank onto Cannock Chase and up Boseley Cloud, but anyone reasonably fit will manage them. The signposting is generally good, but I would strongly advise the use of the appropriate OS maps.

Accommodation and transport

There are few campsites and only one self-catering youth hostel along or close to the Way. As long as you are prepared to walk 16 miles or so in a day, it should be perfectly possible to find overnight B&B or pub accommodation as the Way passes through or close to many towns and villages. However, if you want to return home after each day's walk, the lack of public transport can be a difficulty in the more rural areas, such as that between Kinver and Codsall, and you may need to ask for lifts or summon a taxi.

Best day-walk

Denstone to somewhere near Leek.

Tributaries Walk

Stuart W. Greig (lonewalker.net; @LoneWalkerUK), author of *The Tributaries Walk*

A circular walk starting in Ingleton, Yorkshire Dales: 96 miles/155 km

Difficulty rating: 3

Average days to complete: 7

Waymarking? No

Maps: OS Landranger 98, 92

Baggage courier? Yes

For more details: tributarieswalk.co.uk

Describe the trail

As its name suggests, the Tributaries Walk is focussed on the rivers, becks and gills that flow through the valleys of the Yorkshire Dales. Beginning in Ingleton, the trail explores beautiful valleys and the high heather-clad moors that separate them. Visiting as many dales as possible, the route meanders, picking out waterfalls, hidden caves, rocky escarpments and old packhorse bridges. The guidebook encourages interaction and includes a quiz to help walkers get the most out of their visit, with a final map challenge to test the grey matter.

Highlights

The walk has so many highlights, but the high path above the River Swale as you leave Muker and ascend up the wonderful Swinner Gill is

The Tributaries Walk focuses on the rivers, becks and gills that flow through the Yorkshire Dales. STUART W. GREIG

spectacular, as is the ascent of Satron Moor on the day into Askrigg, high above the diminutive Oxnop Gill. If limestone pavement is of interest, then there is none better than that above Malham Cove, a wonder in its own right and a sight that everyone should experience at some point.

Lowlights

There are none.

Why do you love it?

The route visits thirteen dales and each has one or more rivers, becks or streams running through it. Crossing between dales takes you over some wonderful high moorland and mountain terrain, past remote tarns, and the trail visits some of the most picturesque villages anywhere in the country. The diversity of scenery and terrain makes this path a firm favourite.

How challenging?

The walk builds up from the first day of 10 miles/17 km to the final day of 17 miles/27 km. No single day is particularly difficult, but the final two days cover 34 miles/55 km and over 5,000 ft/1,524 m of ascent. There are some exposed sections and good navigation skills are required if some of the high route options are taken.

Accommodation and transport

The Tributaries Walk is well served by Settle train station, as it sits right on the route. Accommodation is plentiful in most overnight stops except in Yockenthwaite; there is only one B&B, with only a couple of beds. As such, advance bookings should be made before departure. Campers may have to extend some days and divert uphill if wild camping is desirable, as this is primarily a low-level route. The baggage services provided by Brigantes Holidays (briganteseng-lishwalks.com) work in both a clockwise and anti-clockwise direction.

Best day-walk

The first day from Ingleton to Dent offers plenty of route options, including an ascent of Yorkshire's highest mountain, Whernside. The lower-level valley route through Kingsdale, on the other hand, allows for a visit to Yordas Cave, the ancient home of a baby-eating giant.

Sherbrook Valley on the Two Saints Way. CANNOCK CHASE AONB UNIT

Two Saints Way

David Pott, route creator and author of *The Two Saints Way* (twosaintsway.org.uk)

Chester Cathedral to St Chad's Lichfield: 92 miles/148 km

Difficulty rating: 3

Average days to complete: 7

Waymarking? It's 95 per cent waymarked

Maps: OS Explorer 266, 257, 258, 244

Baggage courier? No

For more details: *The Two Saints Way*: twosaintsway.org.uk

Describe the trail

A revived pilgrimage through the heart of middle England. A unique aspect of the trail is that it links with the revival of interest in Mercian England following the discovery of the Staffordshire Hoard. The trail provides an opportunity to walk through old Mercia, visiting key pilgrimage sites both well known in Chester and Lichfield and several lesser known places such as Barthomley, Trentham, Stone and Stafford. The trail passes by the Potteries Museum in Stoke where the Staffordshire Hoard can be viewed. It is not idealized England as in say the Cotswold Way, but 'a real slice of England' which includes urban stretches and ordinary farmland as well as beautiful villages like Bunbury, Burston and the Cannock Chase Area of Outstanding Natural Beauty.

Highlights

Chester Cathedral and city, Bunbury, Llangollen Canal, Nantwich, Wybunbury, Englesea Brook Chapel, Barthomley, Festival Park Stoke, Potteries

TALKING WALKING – CHRIS TOWNSEND

Chris is an outdoor writer and photographer who has written over twenty books, including the award-winning *The Backpacker's Handbook*. His latest book is *Rattlesnakes & Bald Eagles*, the story of his walk along the Pacific Crest Trail. He has a blog at christownsend.com and is on Twitter @townsendoutdoor.

What do you remember about your first multi-day walk?

My first was the Pennine Way in 1976, when I was twenty-five. It was April and I remember it snowed at Tan Hill. There was also a great deal of rain! But I enjoyed it.

What effect did your first long walk have on you?

I realized how much I loved backpacking and wild country and that I wanted to do much longer walks.

How many long distance trails have you done since?

Taking 500 miles as the minimum distance, I've done thirteen including the Pacific Crest Trail, Continental Divide Trail, Canadian Rockies End-to-End (a first), Yukon Territory End-to-End (probably a first), Norway and Sweden South to North, the Munros and Tops (a first), the Arizona Trail, the Pacific Northwest Trail and the Scottish Watershed.

What is it about long distance walks that appeals to you?

I love spending days and weeks in wild places. I love the freedom of the hills. I love nature. I love wild camping. In fact every possible aspect of long distance walks appeals to me!

How much do you obsess over equipment?

I review gear for *The Great Outdoors* so obsessing about it is work. However on a long walk I like to forget about it. If gear is doing its job properly it should be unnoticeable.

Chris Townsend on the TGO Challenge 2014.

What luxury item do you take on a trek, if any?

There are two others might consider luxuries. An e-reader for use in the tent in bad weather and on boring road walks (it used to be paperback books but I can carry a whole library on an e-reader) and a pair of mini-binoculars for wildlife watching.

Do you do any fitness preparation beforehand?

No. But that's because I'm out regularly anyway. In fact in the weeks leading up to a long walk I usually get less exercise than usual as there's so much else to do.

What advice do you have for fellow long distance walkers?

Enjoy it! And realize that there will be times when it won't seem enjoyable. Keep walking. It will get better.

Museum Stoke, Etruria Junction Stoke, Trentham Estate, Burston, Beacon Hill, St Mary's Stafford, all of Cannock Chase, Cross in Hand Lane, Lichfield Cathedral and St Chad's Well.

Lowlights

The hardest parts are along some of the canal towpaths especially during or after wet weather. The stretch between Calveley and Barbridge close to the A51 is one of these and another is between Burston and Salt. The Canal and River Trust hopes to improve this stretch soon. Parts of Stoke show urban deprivation with a grotty underpass and decaying buildings, but fascinating curiosities and surprises are never far away!

The last mile into the centre of Stafford is rather boring.

Why do you love it?

I love its great variety. There is such incredible beauty and it opens up unlikely places not on popular tourist routes. I like the fact it doesn't avoid urban stretches or the sewage works at Stafford! It's a genuine pilgrimage route with every opportunity to seek healing in body, mind and soul.

History/background

The idea for the Two Saints Way came to me soon after my wife Pam and I came to Stone in 2007. I quickly became intrigued by the foundational story of the town, the legend of the two princes St Wulfad and St Rufin. I noted that apart from various sites in Stone itself, there were other places in the Trent Valley between Trentham and Salt that had connections with the legend, such as the Saxon hill-fort at Bury Bank (formerly called Wulpherecestre) and St Rufin's Church in Burston. I conceived of the idea of linking these sites together in a story trail.

How challenging?

Relative to most routes, a 2–3 rating. As well as some bits of canal towpath there's an appropriately named Watery Lane just south of Cannock Chase that can be a bit tricky. The Staffordshire section is much hillier than in Cheshire.

Accommodation and transport

The route is conveniently divided into four sections, each of which have four stages 3–8 miles long. There are lots of accommodation and transport options. See *The Two Saints Way* for more, and check out: transportdirect.info, travelinemidlands. co.uk, traveline-northwest.co.uk.

Best day-walk

A very difficult question! I have a soft spot for Stoke-on-Trent and the route through that much maligned city has a great deal of interest with fascinating industrial heritage along the canal stretches, the quirky Festival Park with remnants of the exhibition such as statues and exotic plants around, the Potteries Museum and Saxon Cross at Stoke Minster. The Two Saints Way across Cannock Chase is fantastic and several walkers have said how much they like the stretch between Trentham and Stone.

North-East England

Cleveland Way (NT)

Jacquetta Megarry, co-author of *Cleveland Way*
Helmsley to Filey: 108 miles/174 km
Difficulty rating: 3
Average days to complete: 9
Waymarking? Yes
Maps: OS and Harvey Maps (which covers the whole route on one sheet and is waterproof)
Baggage courier? Yes
For more details: nationaltrail.co.uk/cleveland-way; rucsacs.com

Describe the trail

One of the oldest and most popular of England's National Trails, this one is strangely shaped like a lopsided horseshoe. It sets off westerly from Helmsley, swings north with wide views over heather moorland, through the Hambleton Hills and north-east through the Cleveland Hills, undulating to reach the coast at Saltburn. From there it heads decisively south-east and becomes a cliff-top trail along unspoiled coastline past fishing villages and smugglers' coves.

Highlights

Helmsley Castle, the White Horse of Kilburn, Mount Grace Priory, the summit of Cringle Moor, the ascent of Roseberry Topping, cliff lift at Saltburn-by-the-Sea, coastal villages such as Staithes and Runswick, Robin Hood's Bay and Scarborough.

Lowlights

There's a short stretch of beach at Runswick Bay which may be impassable in stormy weather or at extreme high tide. A few parts can be very boggy after heavy rain.

Why do you love it?

Superb wildlife in the North York Moors National Park and North Sea coast, and a great sense of satisfaction in completing what is, in effect, two National Trails in a single expedition.

History/background

Very early Christian heritage visible in moorland crosses and marker stones, also the wonderful ruins of buildings such as Rievaulx Abbey, Whitby Abbey and Mount Grace Priory. Maritime heritage

Robin Hood's Bay from Ravenscar, Cleveland Way. NORTH YORK MOORS NATIONAL PARK AUTHORITY AND MALCOLM HODGSON

As the Cleveland Way is a National Trail it's well waymarked.
rucsacs.com

includes Captain Cook's Memorial and shipbuilding in Whitby.

How challenging?

The inland section is more obviously hilly and undulating, with a high point of 1,490 ft/454 m on Round Hill. The coastal section is lower-lying and easy to underestimate, with frequent descents to sea level, followed by ascents, often on steps. However, the waymarking is excellent and the terrain generally sound. Beginners could readily manage this walk if they allow plenty of time; ideally a novice might divide it into two expeditions. On a nine-day itinerary there is a 17-mile day, but if spaced over ten days it is readily divided.

Accommodation and transport

Accommodation is plentiful along the coastal section but still needs to be booked. Inland the

The Cleveland Way includes plenty of coastal scenery. rucsacs.com

TALKING WALKING – JULIE WELCH

At *The Observer* Julie became the first woman to report on football for a national newspaper. Her books include *26.2: Running The London Marathon*, *The Ghost Of White Hart Lane* (with Rob White), and the hilarious *Out On Your Feet: The Hallucinatory World of Hundred-Mile Walking*. Julie edits the Long Distance Walkers Association's membership magazine, *Strider*.

What's your long distance walking background?

I was told about the Long Distance Walkers Association around eighteen years ago and the whole idea of challenge walks really intrigued me. It was such a quirky, magical world – seeing beautiful parts of the countryside, doing harm to no one, crashing around in wild places while the rest of humanity was getting on with humdrum existence.
The LDWA is a lovely organization, too, full of some of the nicest people you'll ever meet anywhere. Their events are very well organized and extremely good value for money. I've probably done more than a hundred.

How did your first challenge walk go?

It was 100 km, which was MUCH further than I'd ever walked before. I gave up, sodden, crippled and exhausted, after 43 miles. But like a lot of walkers, I was completely hooked.

Why do a challenge walk?

A question I frequently ask myself, particularly when standing in a sheep field in pouring rain at 2 a.m., trying to find the way out. Seriously? It's a great way of taking yourself a little bit (or a whole lot) out of your comfort zone. But you get this sort of self-affirmation. 'Yes, I can do it! I haven't been found wanting!' It's given me tremendous confidence – if I can do a 100 km, other things in life are possible too.

Was *Out On Your Feet* a fun book to write?

It's been the most fun of any book I've written. I LOVED it, absolutely loved it. People seem to have enjoyed it, apart from one indignant older lady who marched up and said, 'I was shocked, SHOCKED, by your language.'

How important is equipment?

Take a compass – learn how to use it. A survival bag for really long events – 99.9 per cent of the time you won't need it, but one day you might, and you'll be grateful you packed one. Choose your rucksack carefully. It needs to feel comfortable and not chafe. Germolene is useful for the inevitable scratches/nettle stings. And also because, um, when you've been striding along for hours your bum can get rather sore! Honestly, though, you don't have to spend a lot on the latest technical gear. I've got a top I was given as a freebie in 2001. It can get a bit whiffy but it does what it's meant to do. Basically, by the end of 100 km you're not going to look like a supermodel, whatever you wear.

route crosses sparsely populated moorland, with no B&Bs at Clay Bank and only one near the trail at Kildale. As of 2012 there were hostels at Helmsley, Osmotherley, Whitby, near Robin Hood's Bay and near Scarborough. Public transport is patchy, and it can be difficult to reach Helmsley and Sutton Bank. There are good rail services to Whitby and Scarborough/Filey, connecting to the East Coast mainline. Coastliner buses from Leeds connect to resorts on the east coast and there are buses along the coast through Whitby and Scarborough.

Best day-walk

From Saltburn-by-the-Sea to Runswick Bay is 12 miles of fine walking along the North Yorkshire and Cleveland Heritage Coast. Starting from the Victorian seaside resort of Saltburn, head south through Hunt Cliff Nature Reserve, past Guibal Fanhouse and through Skinningrove Bay along Rock Cliff – the highest cliff on England's North Yorkshire coast – to the fishing village of Staithes and then on to Runswick Bay.

Hadrian's Wall (NT)

Anthony Burton, author of *Hadrian's Wall Path* and National Trail Video Guides (tvwalks.com)
Wallsend to Bowness-on-Solway: 84 miles/135 km
Difficulty rating: 2
Average days to complete: 7 (there's a lot to stop and see)

Waymarking? Yes

Maps: OS (1:50,000) 85, 86, 87, 88; Harvey Maps; Footprint Maps

Baggage courier? Yes

For more details: hadrians-wall.org

Describe the trail

The walk follows the entire length of Hadrian's Wall. The obvious appeal is that you get to see virtually all the physical remains of the wall. The plus factor is that you also get a rich variety of scenery – one of Britain's best urban riverside walks is in Newcastle, the wild and hilly central section and the final walk beside the estuary.

Highlights

The highlights are undoubtedly the sections in the middle of the walk where the wall itself is best preserved. There are also some fascinating museums to visit and the well-preserved forts, particularly Housesteads, Corbridge and Birdoswald.

Lowlights

The lowlight for me is not, as some people think, the first part walking along the Tyne through Newcastle – that's fascinating. The dullest part comes in the section from Heddon-on-the-Wall to Chollerford, where remains of the wall are slight and the path runs alongside a road.

Why do you love it?

This really is a walk to appeal to those who, like me, have a love not just for landscape but also for the history of the land. It's unique.

History/background

History all the way!

How challenging?

In general the going is really quite easy, in a clement time of year. In winter the central section in particular is really bleak and inhospitable. Walkers should be aware that this is very open countryside for most of the way, so if you do get bad weather it really hits you – nowhere to shelter. It is, however, generally pretty easy to break it up into reasonable lengths.

Accommodation and transport

Transport is good in summer, when a special Hadrian's Wall bus service runs. Accommodation is limited – there are four YHAs – but B&Bs and hotels are few and far between. This is a very popular walk so anyone expecting to spend the night under a roof should think of booking well ahead.

Best day-walk

To see the wall at its most spectacular, start where the path finally veers away from the B-road and heads for Sewingshields Crags and stay on as far as Thirlwell. The central section near Steel Rigg is the most popular with tourists, but if you want to get away from the crowds and see one of the best sections of wall then the section a little further west at Walltown Crags is superb.

Hadrian's Wall National Trail offers plenty of history but dramatic scenery too. DAMIAN HALL

Ravenber Way

Ron Scholes (landscapeheritage.co.uk), author of *Coast to Coast on the Ravenber Way* and *Walking in Eden: Circular and Linear Routes in the Eden Valley*

Ravenglass to Berwick-upon-Tweed: 210 miles/336.8 km

Difficulty rating: 3–4

Average days to complete: 14

Waymarking? Yes (with normal footpath markers, but not with specific Ravenber Way ones).

Maps: It's not marked on OS maps, but author's route maps accompany text, hand-drawn at a scale of 2.25in to the mile; or OS 4, 5, 6, 7, 16, 19, 31, 42, 43, 307, 332, 339, 346

Baggage courier? Yes

For more details: landscapeheritage.co.uk

Describe the trail

Alfred Wainwright approved of the route and made suggestions to improve it. Sadly he died just after I had completed my long walk and didn't get to see the first edition of the Ravenber Way guidebook (though I was delighted Betty Wainwright agreed to write the foreword). The walk – whose title is derived from the words Ravenglass and Berwick – passes through two National Parks and other Areas of Outstanding Natural Beauty. There are mountains, high hills, rolling moorland, expansive forests and lush river valleys; charming villages and towns, and a wealth of fascinating history: prehistoric sites, ancient highways and settlements, medieval farming patterns, Roman remains, fortified peles and bastle houses, motte and bailey earthworks and castles. This coast walk passes Lakeland's high peaks, crosses the pastoral Eden Valley, climbs over the high Pennines, traverses the northern moors and heads on into the ancient kingdom of Northumbria. Beyond the Roman Wall lies the remote Cheviot Hills, where reivers and mosstroopers once roamed. The journey ends as it follows the leafy valley of the River Till and along the banks of the mighty River Tweed, to Berwick-upon-Tweed.

Highlights

Lakeland, Dufton to Garrigill, Simonside Hills, the Cheviot Hills, Till and Tweed Valleys, the historic town of Berwick-upon-Tweed.

Lowlights

The walk from Wark, through Birtley to Small Burn, is rather featureless.

Why do you love it?

The tremendous variety of landscape and the quality of the rights of way. There are so many views and viewpoints to enjoy. This walk excels in the solitude factor. Civilization and a bed for the night are also keenly anticipated.

History/background

The line of the Roman Road over High Street; a complex of stone circles on Moor Divock; the impressive ruins of Lowther Castle; the Tynehead area, where the Romans worked for lead ore; the fine estate village of Blanchland, with its warm-coloured stone cottages and abbey founded by

Alfred Wainwright helped design the Ravenber Way. RON SCHOLES

Premonstratensian monks in 1165; Hexham Abbey and its fine skyline of medieval buildings; the Roman fort of Brocolitia and the Temple of Mithras and many, many more examples like these.

How challenging?

A beginner may struggle on the Lakeland, Pennine and Cheviot sections with a full pack, but would easily cope with the early Eskdale, Eden Valley, and along the Till and Tweed. Even so, I recommend that for the Ravenber, even beginners should have had some experience in wild country walking. There are mountain and hill ascents and descents, high moorland terrain, and long sections are inevitable when the area is remote and sprawling, as in the Cheviot Hills.

Transport and accommodation

In one or two locations accommodation is thin on the ground and needs to be booked well in advance. You *may* see a local bus or minibus in deepest Lakeland. There's a railway station at Appleby, if anyone feels like giving up. Public transport is thin on the ground in the Eden Valley, Dufton, Garrigill and Nenthead. There is a link at Allenheads and Blanchland. Hexham has real buses and a railway station; the area between Wark and the Cheviots is a transport desert, so don't bother enquiring. During the planning of a long distance route I compile a list of local taxi operators. It's an important backup.

Best day-walk

Not in any particular order of preference: Ravenglass to Wasdale Head, Dufton to Garrigill and Alwinton to Westnewton Bridge.

Six Dales Trail

John Sparshatt, author of *Six Dales Trail: A 38 mile route from Otley to Middleham*

Otley to Middleham: 38 miles/61 km
Difficulty rating: 2
Average days to complete: 2–3
Waymarking? Yes
Maps: OS Landranger 99 and 104
Baggage courier? Yes
For more details: sixdalestrail.org.uk
Describe the trail

The Six Dales Trail takes its name from the six dales traversed as it makes its way northward from Otley, across the length of the Nidderdale Area of Outstanding Natural Beauty to Middleham. The trail was devised by a small team from the Otley Walkers are Welcome group keen to introduce walkers to little-known but superb Dales scenery. The trail passes through ancient dry-stone-walled sheep pastures, high heather moorland with gritstone outcrops, quiet riverbanks, and the landscaped parkland surrounding the ruins of Jervaulx Abbey, to finish at the magnificent ruins of Middleham Castle.

Highlights

The many wonderful views across the Dales; bluebell woods; the amazing variety of old stone stiles; the riverside paths; the ginnels and cobbled side-streets around Otley's Buttercross Market; the atmospheric ruin of Jervaulx Abbey, a Cistercian monastery founded in 1156; the imposing ruin of Middleham Castle, the childhood home of Richard III; Leeds Pals Memorial, a monument to the volunteers or 'Pals' from Leeds who went off to fight in the Great War; tranquil Guisecliff Tarn; the pretty village of Ramsgill with its spacious green surrounded by stone cottages with flower-filled gardens; the diverse birdlife; the extraordinary variety of wild-flowers within the walls of Jervaulx Abbey; and the bustling little town of Pateley Bridge.

Lowlights

One short section of road walking just before Jervaulx Abbey.

Why do you love it?

The variety of terrain and landscape views.

History/background

The Leeds Pals Memorial in Colsterdale.

How challenging?

It's a challenging route with 4,800 ft/1,463 m of ascent – a good one for a beginner to try a long distance walk over two to three days. There's varied terrain from field paths to good tracks at the side of reservoirs. There are two short sections over open moorland but in the main good underfoot conditions. It's well waymarked with easy-to-follow directions in the accompanying guidebook.

Accommodation and transport

Good public transport links at Otley (buses to Leeds/Bradford/Skipton and Harrogate). An hourly bus service from Pateley Bridge to Harrogate. A bus service to Leyburn and Ripon from Middleham. Various accommodation options with some places offering pickup and drop off services (see accommodation links on the trail website).

Best day-walk

Either Otley to Pateley Bridge (18 miles) or Pateley Bridge to Middleham (20 miles). Both are excellent day walks in their own right. Otley to Blubberhouses (some 10 miles) is a good walk.

St Oswald's Way

Adam Dawson, adamswalk.com
Heavenfield to Holy Island: 96 miles/154 km
Difficulty rating: 2
Average days to complete: 6
Waymarking? Yes
Maps: OS 42, 43, 316, 325, 332, 340; Harvey Maps
Baggage courier? Yes
For more details: stoswaldsway.com

Describe the trail

A walk from Hadrian's Wall to Holy Island, over wild Northumberland moors and along spectacular coastlines. An amazing contrast between wild moors and stunning coasts, with lots of historical interest along the way.

Highlights

The beach walk from Warkworth to Craster is amazing – views stretching to infinity, and Dunstanburgh Castle looming in the distance.

Lowlights

I didn't particularly enjoy the long stretch from Rothbury to Warkworth. Partly because it was pouring with rain, but mostly because it was along banks of the attractive but unremarkable River Coquet, through fields with innumerable stiles and slightly menacing herds of cows.

Why do you love this trail?

The long walks along the beaches were exhilarating and uplifting. With fantastic castles to visit along the way, it's hard to beat.

History/background

The castles at Dunstanburgh, Bamburgh and Lindisfarne are absolutely fascinating and it's worth allowing an extra hour or two to look round each one.

How challenging?

This is a pretty straightforward walk. It's mostly well waymarked, but you still need a map. There is plenty of accommodation, so short days of 12–15 miles are perfectly possible. There are a couple of boggy sections between Kirkwhelpington and Rothbury but mostly it's easy going. The sections along the beaches are good, though you need to keep an eye on the tides – at high tide you have to walk close to the shoreline, where the sand is very soft.

Accommodation and transport

We took taxis at a couple of points. There are plenty of B&B options but they tend to get full. I booked in July for the following October and many places already had no vacancies. I didn't notice a lot of campsites along the way. Many of the more attractive and frequently visited spots had conspicuous 'no camping' signs. It could be done in sections if preferred – the main transport route is the East Coast main railway line, with stops at Newcastle (branch line to Hexham), Alnmouth and Berwick.

Best day-walk

Probably the day from Craster to Bamburgh, which combines uplifting beach walking with historical interest at Dunstanburgh and Bamburgh castles. There are plenty of opportunities for refreshment along the way, at Low Newton-by-the-Sea, Beadnell and Seahouses.

Viking Way

Debby Braund, Rights of Way and Countryside Access, Lincolnshire County Council
Humber Bridge to Oakham: 147 miles/237 km
Difficulty rating: 2
Average days to complete: 10
Waymarking? Yes
Maps: OS Explorer 15, 247, 272, 273, 281, 282
Baggage courier? Yes
For more details: lincolnshire.gov.uk/countryside

Describe the trail

The Viking Way goes through the rural and unspoilt countryside of Lincolnshire and Rutland visiting pretty villages, bustling market towns, the historic city of Lincoln with its magnificent cathedral and the impressive Rutland Water. The walk crosses the Lincolnshire Wolds Area of Outstanding Natural Beauty as well as other typical Lincolnshire landscapes including the Lincolnshire Limewoods, heathland, fenland and escarpments.

Highlights

Lincoln, the Wolds AONB, Lincolnshire Limewoods and Rutland Water.

Lowlights

Lincolnshire is a rural farming county so some of the route crosses arable farmland.

Why do you love it?

The variety of landscapes and the pretty towns and villages.

History/background

The trail was opened in 1976 by a partnership between Lincolnshire, Leicestershire and Humberside Councils and the Ramblers. The name was suggested by the Ramblers Association to reflect the influence of Danelaw in the eastern counties of Britain.

How challenging?

There are few steep gradients. The route is well waymarked along its length with the Viking Way logo, a Viking helmet.

Accommodation and transport

The guidebook is divided into easy-to-walk sections linking towns and villages with facilities. For information on facilities and accommodation go to visitlincolnshire.com; for information on public transport go to lincsbus.info.

Best day-walk

Sections through the Wolds AONB, the Lincolnshire Limewoods, Lincoln Cliff villages, Rutland Water.

Yorkshire Wolds Way (NT)

Tony Gowers, author of *Yorkshire Wolds Way*
Hessle to Filey: 79 miles/127 km
Difficulty rating: 2
Average days to complete: 6

THE ENGLAND COAST PATH

In 2020, all coastal walks in England – and many more that haven't quite been ironed out yet – become part of the England Coast Path. The Marine and Coastal Access Act in 2009 provided both a right to walk along the full 2,700 miles/4,345 km of England's coastline and a permanent right of access to a coastal margin around the coast, including beaches and access to sea cliffs. Outdoor organizations including the BMC and the Ramblers have campaigned hard for improved coastal access and finally this ambitious and wondrous plan looks likely to come to fruition. It is massively exciting news and the ECP already has a website: nationaltrail.co.uk/england-coast-path.

Waymarking? Yes
Maps: OS Explorer 293, 294, 300, 301
Baggage courier? Yes
For more details: nationaltrail.co.uk/yorkshirewoldsway

Describe the trail

It's a wonderfully varied walk and an ideal introduction to long distance walking. Of all the National Trails, the YWW is the quietest and least walked. That makes it the perfect trail for peace and solitude in a fascinating and often overlooked part of the country.

Highlights

There are some wonderful dry valleys especially around Thixendale.

Lowlights

Not too many as it's a short trail with lots of variety – city, river, countryside, villages and coast. Accommodation can be hard to find in places and the weather can be awful in winter and when that easterly wind blows!

Why do you love it?

It takes walkers to a part of the country that is virtually unknown. However, it is the peace and quiet that make it so appealing.

History/background

David Hockney so loves the trees and this landscape that he has produced many of his most famous works of art here.

How challenging?

The trail is quite short and not too tough and makes an ideal introduction to long distance walking. Waymarking is generally good – up to the usual National Trail standards. The northern section is through sparsely populated countryside, making accommodation difficult to find and resulting in longer sections at times. There are a few short steep hills but overall it's not too challenging.

Accommodation and transport

Accommodation and public transport are very sparse along parts of the trail. Both ends however are served by public transport and it is generally recommended to leave the car at home. The route can be done in short sections though using car/taxis options.

Best day-walk

The 12 miles from Millington to Thixendale make a superb walk through the most magnificent dry valleys of the Yorkshire Wolds.

Wales

North Wales

Isle of Anglesey Coast Path

David Canning, LDWA member

Holyhead to Holyhead: 125 miles/200 km

Difficulty rating: Mostly 1–2, some sections 3

Average days to complete: 12 (but can easily be done in 8–10)

Waymarking? Yes

Maps: OS Explorer 262, 263; OS Landranger 114

Baggage courier? Yes

For more details: *Walking the Isle of Anglesey Coastal Path* by Carl Rogers

Describe the trail

A relatively easy and almost entirely coastal walk with some stunning scenery. This is a wonderful path around Anglesey and the Holy Island, which takes in fine beaches, some stunning cliff scenery, lovely historic towns and villages, and some very fine historical monuments. It's physically fairly undemanding compared to some other UK coastal paths, but because of its length and a couple of

Anglesey Coast Path. DAVID CANNING

tougher sections, you will still feel you've achieved something special. This would be a great long distance path for someone wishing to try one for the first time.

Highlights

Many great beaches, such as at Aberffraw, Church Bay and Porth Trecastell; the stunning cliffs at South Stack Lighthouse; beautiful coastal villages and ports such as Moelfre, Camaes and Amlwch Port.

Lowlights

The walk across the Stanley Embankment from Valley to Holyhead is a bit dull. The section between Menai Bridge and Beaumaris is virtually all on tarmac and has little of interest. However, both of these sections are fairly short and don't detract from the path as a whole.

TALKING WALKING – TRISTAN GOOLEY

Tristan is the author of award-winning and bestselling outdoor books, including *The Natural Navigator* and *The Walker's Guide to Outdoor Clues and Signs*. He set up a natural navigation school and edits the natural navigation website naturalnavigator.com. He is on Twitter @naturalnav.

Tristan Gooley.

What do you remember about your first multi-day walk?

When I was fourteen, I walked with three friends for five days on the Brecon Beacons.

Any rookie errors you'll admit to?

Our initial route plans were ludicrous! They ignored footpaths almost entirely and included one plan to walk straight up the near vertical south face of Pen–Y–Fan, the highest point in southern Britain. Fortunately, before we set off, these plans were gently laughed at and then 'amended' by my father who had got to know the Beacons very well as an SAS officer.

What effect did your first long walk have on you?

I fell in love with tea and OS maps.

How many long distance trails have you done since?

I enjoy picking my own routes, so not that many.

Which is your all-time favourite trek?

Cwm Idwal in North Wales and walking across the Libyan Sahara with Tuareg nomads.

What is it about long distance walks that appeals to you?

It is the best way I know of blending fresh air with the perfect levels of exercise for body and mind.

How much do you obsess over equipment?

Quite a bit in the early days, not so much these days.

What luxury item do you take on a trek, if any?

If remote, then an Emergency Position Indicating Radio Beacon (EPIRB). If UK, then silk thermals.

Do you do any fitness preparation beforehand?

I walk a bit most days for my work, but nothing extra.

What advice do you have for fellow long distance walkers?

Stop earlier than you think you should on day one, as day two is often the one to worry about.

Why do you love it?

The scenery and landscape are always changing with great views just about around every turn you take.

History/background

There are many fine historical sites directly on the path. These include Beaumaris Castle (one of the few in the UK with water in its moat), Penmon Priory, Amlwch Port, and Thomas Telford's famous suspension bridge.

How challenging?

This is generally an easy path with very gradual ascents and descents. However there are two more demanding sections. One is the 12-mile/20 km section from Holyhead to Trearddur where the total ascent is around 2,000 ft/600 m and the second, which would normally be walked over two days, is the 20 miles/32 km between Portreath and Amlwch Port with a total ascent of around 3600 ft/1,100 m. Signposting and the terrain underfoot are pretty good.

Accommodation and transport

There is abundant accommodation to suit all styles and budgets, and costs on the island are generally below the UK average. The island is also well served by a good bus network. If you plan carefully, you could arrange, for all sections of the walk, to catch a bus between your start and end points each day. As some are infrequent, it's probably wise to catch the bus first if possible from your end point to your start point. You will occasionally have to walk inland for a short distance to reach the bus route, but quite often the routes are virtually on the path itself. Full details of bus routes and timetables can be found at anglesey.gov.uk.

Best day-walk

The most strenuous is from Holyhead to Trearddur. This 12-mile/19-km walk takes in the northern section of Holy Island. There are increasingly great views along this most rugged coastline of the coast path. It's really worth making the time to climb down all of the steps (and later back up again!) and cross the bridge to visit the South Stack Lighthouse (check opening times if you wish to climb the tower). A short detour from the path up Holyhead Mountain will also award you with spectacular views.

A more gentle walk is the 11 miles/18 km from Cemaes to Church Bay. Early on you bypass the Wylfra Power Station and reach the unusual lagoon and nature reserve at Cemlyn Bay. From there, you follow the most remote part of the coast path to the fine beach at Church Bay.

Mid-Wales

Glyndŵr's Way (NT)

Andrew Bowden, ramblingman.org.uk
Knighton to Welshpool: 135 miles/217 km
Difficulty rating: 4
Average days to complete: 9
Waymarking? Yes
Maps: OS Landranger 124, 125, 126, 135, 136, 137, 147, 148; Explorer 201, 214, 215, 216, 239, OL23; Harvey Maps
Baggage courier? Yes

For more details: nationaltrail.co.uk/glyndwrs-way

Describe the trail

A tour of a quiet but beautiful part of Wales. A hugely varied route, it doesn't follow any particular geographic features or any historical trail. It simply connects together some of the finest tracks, lakes, hills and valleys in the area. With plenty of hills, it's a challenging walk with lots of ascents and descents; however, fine views more than make up for the hard work.

Highlights

Stunning panoramic views every day, and several beautiful lakes such as Lake Vynwy where you can sit in the hotel bar and watch the sun set.

Lowlights

There's a lot of hill climbing, with several ascents and descents every day, which many people will find tiring. There are also several stretches on (quiet) roads, and some landowners have even been known to padlock gates.

Why do you love it?

The views and the quietness of the walking.

History/background

The trail's named after Owain Glyndwr, the last Welshman to hold the title of Prince of Wales. Glyndwr attempted to overthrow English rule in the fifteenth century. Although the trail doesn't follow any particular route Glyndwr took, it does go through several places that have connections to him.

How challenging?

There is lots of ascent and descent, which can be tiring, and there are long distances between accommodation sources. Most days are 15 miles or more. Signposting is good, and generally easy to follow.

Accommodation and transport

B&B accommodation can be sparse, and difficult to find, especially when searching online. However, there is always at least one place to stay at the end of each day's walking. Public transport is mostly non-existent except at Knighton, Welshpool and Machynlleth. It's possible to split the route into two, by breaking at the mid-point at Machynlleth.

Best day-walk

Abbeycwmhir to Llanberis offers a perfect example of a typical day – great views and hilly walking.

Wye Valley Walk

Anthony Burton, author of *The Wye Valley Walk*

Plynlimon to Chepstow: 136 miles/219 km
Difficulty rating: 3
Average days to complete: 12
Waymarking? Yes
Maps: OS (1:50,000) 136, 147, 148, 149, 161, 162
Baggage courier? Yes
For more details: wyevalleywalk.org

Describe the trail

The walk follows the River Wye from its source to its confluence with the Severn. This is a walk of great contrasts, starting high in the hills, with tough walking in rugged surroundings, with a gentle middle section around Hereford and ending with spectacular gorges and high cliffs.

Highlights

The upper sections offer the wildest and most remote walking and the final section between Tintern and Chepstow offers a high-level route with splendid views.

Lowlights

There is a problem with the start, which is not easily accessed – most people find they have to walk up from Llangurig and then retrace their steps – or alternatively walk 8 miles along paths from Llanidloes – or arrange private transport of some sort.

Why do you love it?

I love the contrast – you see the river in all its different moods, dashing and placid – and there are plenty of sites of interest along the way.

History/background

Historically the Wye has been a frontier between England and Wales, so you find the great castles of Goodrich and Chepstow and the fortified bridge at Monmouth. There is also the great cathedral of Hereford and the beautiful if ruined Tintern Abbey.

How challenging?

Don't be misled by the fact this is a walk down a river – it's no gentle stroll along grassy banks. The upper sections are tough, and there are some steep sections at the end as well.

Accommodation and transport

Accommodation on the whole is good. Transport is excellent in the lower sections, but a good deal less so in the higher reaches – and as mentioned the start offers a problem.

Best day-walk

Monmouth to Chepstow – it offers wonderful scenery, passes Tintern Abbey and has good transport at both ends.

South-West Wales

Pembrokeshire Coast Path (NT)

Dave Maclachlan, Pembrokeshire Coast Path trail officer

Amroth to Poppit: 186 miles/300 km
Difficulty rating: Whole trail 5, but some sections are 1
Average days to complete: 11
Waymarking? Yes
Maps: Not needed – just follow the path and pay attention in towns; Harvey Maps
Baggage courier? Yes
For more details: nationaltrail.co.uk/pembroke-shire-coast-path, nt.pcnpa.org.uk

Describe the trail

Wow! The PCP is the way to see the amazing maritime landform that led to Pembrokeshire's coast being designated the UK's only coastal National Park.

Highlights

All of it except Stack Rocks to Freshwater West; Angle to Milford; Poppit to St Dogmaels.

Lowlights

Stack Rocks to Freshwater West includes an Army shooting range; Angle to Milford is trouble-free walking but lacks the outstanding coastal character; Poppit to St Dogmaels includes road walking (with no pavement).

Why do you love it?

Knocks me out every time I walk it.

History/background

Over fifty beaches; over fifty Iron Age forts; seven

The Pembrokeshire Coast Path includes over fifty beaches. PCNPA

medieval castles; over twenty World War II sites; Stonehenge and more.

How challenging?

There is a variety of conditions and topography offering something for everyone. St Dogmaels to Newport is 16 miles/25 km and 3,500 ft/1,066 m of ascent/descent; Stack Rocks to Stackpole Quay is 7 miles/11 km of pretty flat limestone cliff and beach-walking.

Accommodation and transport

An excellent range of accommodation covers this National Trail but book early. There's not much between St Dogmaels and Newport so if that's the first day consider getting the bus (in season) to Ceibwr and splitting it. Public transport coverage is comprehensive (if not cut) in season; it needs some

St Justinian: the old lifeboat station and a new one being built. PCNPA

focus to work out how to use it best. See pembroke-shiregreenways.co.uk for more details.

Best day-walk

Any of the walks involving some of the picturesque, charming towns and villages en route, such as Tenby, St Davids, Solva and Newport.

All Wales

Cambrian Way

George Tod, cambrianway.org.uk
Cardiff to Conwy: 288 miles/463 km
Difficulty rating: 5
Average days to complete: 2–4
Waymarking? No
Maps: The route is not marked on OS maps, but OS Explorer maps are recommended due to the difficulty of navigation: 151, 152, OL13, OL12, 187, 213, 214, 215, OL23, OL18 & OL17 (214 is only needed for a few kilometres)
Baggage courier? No
For more details: *Cambrian Way* by A.J. Drake
Describe the trail
A mountain connoisseur's walk. A high-level route traversing the highest and wildest parts of Wales, from Cardiff on the south coast to Conway on the north coast.

Highlights

Some of the finest mountain scenery of Wales – the Black Mountains, Brecon Beacons, Carmarthen Fans, Plynlimon, Cadair Idris, the Rhinogs, Snowdon, the Glyders and the Carneddau plus many more.

Lowlights

Being a high-level walk it can be subject to bad weather at times. Route-finding can be difficult, especially in bad weather over wild terrain. There is a total of about 67,000 ft/20,400 m of ascent, which requires a high level of fitness and stamina.

Why do you love it?

Providing the weather is fair, it has some of the most spectacular and varied scenery to be found in Britain.

History/background

The Cambrian Way is the brainchild of Tony Drake (1923–2012), who was awarded an MBE for Services to Public Rights of Way. The founding member of the Gloucestershire Mountaineering Club and Ramblers Footpath Secretary for much of his life, Tony hand-drew maps for the first guidebook and loved getting postcards from Cambrian Way finishers. He was also instrumental in the formation of the Cotswold Way.

How challenging?

This is a very challenging walk with difficult

TALKING WALKING – JENNY WALTERS

Jenny's walking career began with a climb up Twmbarlwm – aka the Pimple – in South Wales when she was five. She landed the job of her dreams on *Country Walking* magazine eight years ago and has been walking all over the place, and writing about it, ever since. Find the magazine at livefortheoutdoors.com and tweeting @countrywalking.

What do you remember about your first multi-day walk?

My first was the Thorsbome Trail, a four-day wilderness hike on the Australian island of Hinchinbrook. I was utterly unprepared for how hard and how wonderful it would be. But years later I can still remember the damp cool of walking through mangroves, watching turtles frolic in the turquoise sea, treading barefoot across sandy beaches so white it made my eyes hurt, and the panorama across rainforest and ocean from Nina Peak.

What effect did your first long walk have on you?

Despite the pain, I was totally hooked. I spent the next couple of months walking one trail after another in Australia and New Zealand. I'm a bit cautious by nature and it made me happy to feel like a proper adventurer – I'd walked into the wilderness (albeit often with comfy huts at day's end) and could think of myself as brave.

What is it about long distance walks that appeals to you?

Getting away from it all. I love day-walks too, but the return to the worries and deadlines of the working world can loom all too soon. On a multi-day trail, that all fades away and it becomes just about the walking, the elements, the challenge, and the landscape around you, for day after beautiful day. Oh, and you can eat cake at every opportunity and call it fuel.

What luxury item do you take on a trek, if any?

Jenny Walters.

I have a Winnie-the-Pooh bear that always travels in my rucksack.

Do you do any fitness preparation beforehand?

I walk. In fact, I use an upcoming trail as a great excuse to hike all weekend, every weekend, and call it training. I loathe the gym, so I tell myself the best preparation for walking is walking!

What advice do you have for fellow long distance walkers?

Just do it! Start with a two to three day walk – the Long Distance Walkers Association has a great database at ldwa.org.uk where you can choose the distance, region and scenery you like – and see how you like it. My guess is you'll love it …

navigation through many wild and remote areas with virtually no waymarking. The walk involves about 3,000 ft/9,000 m of ascent a day for a typical schedule. In parts, the route goes over rough open moorland, which is sometimes boggy and often difficult underfoot. It's not suitable for beginners and should only be undertaken by experienced walkers with a considerable level of fitness and stamina plus good orienteering skills.

Accommodation and transport

In some parts there is very limited accommodation in the form of B&Bs or hostels and this can involve some long sections, sometimes with lengthy diversions for accommodation. The use of a tent or bivvy bag may ease some of these problems, although the extra weight can be a burden with all the ascent. Public transport varies considerably along the route, being quite good in some places but with very

Garn Wen from ascent of Blorenge, Cambrian Way. GEORGE TOD

Looking back at Sugar Loaf from ascent of Garn Wen, Cambrian Way. GEORGE TOD

Fan y Big from Cribyn, Cambrian Way. GEORGE TOD

infrequent rural services in others. However, some people have managed to do the walk in sections using public transport.

Best day-walk

Some of the most spectacular scenery lies in the northern section through the Snowdonia National Park, so any section there is recommended. If you prefer peace and quiet in the mountains, avoid Snowdon, though the scenery is spectacular. There are other very worthy sections such as the Black Mountains, the Brecon Beacons and the Carmarthen Fans.

Offa's Dyke Path (NT)

Tony Gowers, author of *Offa's Dyke Path*
Sedbury Cliff to Prestatyn: 177 miles/285 km
Difficulty rating: 4
Average days to complete: 14
Waymarking? Yes
Maps: Explorer Outdoor Leisure 13, 14. Recommended: OS 201, 216, 240, 256, 265; Harvey Maps
Baggage courier? Yes
For more details: nationaltrail.co.uk/offasdyke
Describe the trail
A magnificent hike along the ancient earthwork that borders England and Wales. Like Hadrian's Wall, Offa's Dyke Path follows a distinct and historic feature over the undulating landscape of the borderlands of England and Wales.

Highlights

There are superb sections of the route over the Black Mountains, Hergest Ridge and the Clwydian Mountains but some of the best sections of the Dyke are found between Kington and Knighton.

Lowlights

Although the numbers have reduced there are still a huge number of stiles to negotiate. The central low-lying section near the Upper Severn can be very boggy in the wet. You don't get many views of the River Wye as you are mainly in woodland.

Into the Lugg Valley, Offa's Dyke Path. TONY GOWERS

The upland sections will be especially bleak in poor weather.

Why do you love it?

It's such a historic route as it follows the remains of the ancient earthwork straddling the high ground of the English/Welsh borderlands.

History/background

The trail is symbolized by the earthworks of King Offa who built the dyke in the eighth century to divide Wales from Mercia.

How challenging?

It's a tough route as it has lots of ascents and descents. The famous quote is that walking Offa's Dyke Path is almost the equivalent of climbing Mount Everest! There is a very long and demanding section over the Black Mountains. Waymarking is of the usual high National Trail standard, but navigation can be difficult especially if the mist descends in places like the Clwydian and Black Mountains.

Accommodation and transport

Public transport is poor in places but both ends and Knighton in the middle are served by rail. Accommodation is also scarce in places and may require a long diversion from the trail. Outside of towns, shops and services are very limited and many pubs are only open in the evenings.

Best day-walk

The long upland section between Pandy and Hay-on-Wye is spectacularly rewarding on a fine summer's day. The Kington to Knighton section has much variety and follows lots of fine parts of the dyke.

Wales Coast Path

Paddy Dillon (paddydillon.co.uk), author of *The Wales Coast Path*

Chester to Chepstow: 870 miles/1,400 km

Difficulty rating: 3 (some might say 5 owing to length)

Average days to complete: 60

Waymarking? Yes

Maps: Free, detailed 'Static Maps' available from the Wales Coast Path website (see below), which are OS Explorers overlaid with the route

Baggage courier? Yes

For more details: walescoastpath.gov.uk

Describe the trail

Follows the coast of Wales as closely as possible. Wales claims to be the only country in the world with a continuous coastal path. It's a remarkably

Wye Valley above Redbrook, Offa's Dyke Path. TONY GOWERS

varied trail, including beaches, salt marshes, promenades, rugged cliffs, along with villages, towns and cities. Mostly rural and scenic, but also urban and industrial in places.

Highlights

The cliff coasts of Anglesey, Llŷn, Ceredigion and Pembrokeshire. On the urban front, the chance to climb over the scary Newport Transporter Bridge!

Lowlights

The backstreets of Margam and the busy road leaving Cardiff.

Why do you love it?

It's very long, with sustained interest and amazing variety. Despite its length, several walkers have combined the Wales Coast Path with the Offa's Dyke Path to walk all the way round Wales. Clearly, it inspires walkers to walk ever onwards!

History/background

The geology of the entire coast. The 'Iron Ring' castles on the north coast; the ever-present reminders of the history of Wales, its language and culture. Some splendid urban renewal schemes.

How challenging?

No stretch of the coast is particularly difficult, but there are some remote and rugged paths, and some steep ascents and descents. However, this should be balanced against considerable stretches of easy walking through gentle terrain. The main difficulty is the sheer length, and therefore the need for sound planning if the whole trail is to be walked at once. Walking in summer is likely to be much easier than walking in winter. Surprisingly, the trail has been completed by people who have limited experience of long distance walking. The signposting is usually very good. While the coastal path is usually obvious, there are diversions inland from time to time where greater care with route-finding is needed.

Accommodation and transport

Most towns and villages offer plenty of lodgings, but places can fill up in summer, and may close for winter. Some stretches have little accommodation, and it is wise to know what is available. There are plenty of campsites. Public transport is available

Climbing up from Three Cliffs Bay, Gower Peninsula, Wales Coast Path. DAMIAN HALL

TALKING WALKING – PADDY DILLON

Paddy is a prolific outdoor writer and photographer. He is an author and illustrator of over sixty guidebooks, contributor to thirty more guidebooks, and regular contributor to outdoor magazines. Paddy enjoys anything from simple day-walks to challenging long distance walks, from coastal walks to high mountains. In short, plenty of variety! His website is paddydillon.co.uk.

What do you remember about your first multi-day walk?

At sixteen I decided to walk half of the Pennine Way, then continued to and through the Lake District, and headed back home via the Yorkshire Dales. I camped every night for four weeks and I spent £17.33 (that's £182.91 in today's money), which didn't leave much for food, drink and campsite fees. But I survived.

Were there any rookie errors you'll admit to?

I begged, stole and borrowed all the wrong kit, and when I couldn't lift my pack, I decided to leave out non-essential things such as pots, pans, stove, and a monstrous Big Ben alarm clock that my father seemed to think I needed. As I left the house, he said I'd be arrested for vagrancy. Two weeks later, the police were questioning me by the roadside, wondering if I was a vagrant.

What effect did your first long walk have on you?

Most of the time, I was exhausted, which wasn't helped by walking 30 miles on my first day, and 46 miles non-stop later in the trip. Due to limited funds I also got very hungry and thin towards the end. Most of my kit was useless. On the plus side, I gained a lot of experience in a short time.

Which is your all-time favourite UK trek?

The Pennine Way, as it was once the standard measure of whether you were a 'serious' walker.

Paddy Dillon.

What is it about long distance walks that appeals to you?

I've always wanted to see what was over the next hill, and always enjoyed the sense of continual change and variety while walking from one place to another over an extended period of time.

How much do you obsess over equipment?

I like to pack lightweight and low-bulk, so that I can enjoy walking without being overburdened. I'm prepared to pay whatever it costs to achieve that, but I don't obsess about it. I'll modify kit or even make it from scratch if I can't buy exactly what I need.

---

on a daily basis, but varies from regular to occasional, depending on the area. Sunday services are sometimes rare or absent. Walking daily stages that link with public transport works well along most parts of the coast. Pembrokeshire has a remarkable network of coastal bus services.

Best day-walk

The cliff coast of Llŷn, beyond Nefyn. The cliff coast near St Davids. The cliff coast of the Gower.

Scotland

Southern Scotland

Annandale Way (GT)

Ross Gemmell, countryside ranger, Dumfries and Galloway Council

The Devil's Beef Tub, near Moffat, to Newbie Barns, Annan: 53 miles/85 km

Difficulty rating: 2
Average days to complete: 4
Waymarking? Yes
Maps: OS Explorer 314, 322, 323, 330
Baggage courier? Yes (local taxi services)
For more details: annandaleway.org (includes a free guide to download or one to purchase)

Describe the trail

History and secrets of a tranquil part of Scotland. The walk starts high above the source of the River Annan, then drops down to trace the river along the valley bottom into pretty Moffat. Heading south out of Beattock it meets the Southern Upland Way and continues over the high ground of Cragielandshill and down onto the Lord of Annandale's Estate where the route zigzags through ancient oak forests and down the valley to Millhousebridge. Here, there's a choice between Lockerbie or Lochmaben. Lockerbie takes in the scenic Lockerbie Wildlife Trust's Eskrigg Nature Reserve, whilst the western Lochmaben route takes in Castle Loch with its ruined castle and sculpture trail and fantastic views from Joe Graham's monument. The two arms meet near Hoddam Bridge to follow the enchanting River Annan as it passes down through Annan and to its end at Newbie Barns on the coast.

Highlights

Getting a flavour of all the towns and villages along its route while having the continual theme of the River Annan and its tributaries. The feeling of remoteness while knowing that the next town is only a few miles away.

Lowlights

Cattle-poked fields in the winter – but on the plus side, these give the route character! The bog at the

Waypost near Corehead Farm, Moffat. SUSAN KEVAN

top of the Devils Beef Tub with the final cairn to the side – I truly hate this and always think it should have been built on a pallet so we could shift it somewhere else without having to rebuild it!

Why do you love it?

The views appearing from nowhere. There are eight viewpoint benches situated at some of the best views, which, when combined, give an overall flavour of Annandale life and the trail itself.

History/background

The route is fairly new, established in September 2009 by Sulwath Connections. There are several places with strong links to the Wars of Scottish Independence en route.

How challenging?

It's beginner-friendly. There's 4,577ft/1,395m of ascent and the Annandale Way has been designed to be achievable in 4–5 days.

Accommodation and transport

Accommodation is pretty good – the Way is created with overnight stops in small market towns and

The Annandale Way bequeaths the history and secrets of a tranquil part of Scotland. BECKY DUNCAN

Views appear from nowhere on the Annandale Way.
BECKY DUNCAN

villages: Moffat, Johnstonebridge/Annandale Estate, Lochmaben or Lockerbie, Brydekirk and Annan. As always with transport, plan ahead, but most places are reachable with public transport. There's more info at annandaleway.org.

Best day-walk

I really enjoy the section from Moffat, where the path heads south following the Crooked Road up out of Beattock and meets the Southern Upland Way.

Arran Coastal Way

Jacquetta Megarry, author of *The Arran Coastal Way*

A circular walk from Brodick: 65 miles/104 km
Difficulty rating: 3
Average days to complete: 6–7
Waymarking? Yes
Maps: Harvey Maps
Baggage courier? Yes
For more details: coastalway.co.uk

Describe the trail

Scotland's finest circular walk on an enchanting island. Accessible from Glasgow, Arran is often described as 'Scotland in miniature'. This coastal walk features varied scenery from mountain paths to deserted beaches, and widely varying terrain, from road walking to boulder hopping and Arran's wildlife is unusually approachable.

Highlights

Brodick Castle, Goat Fell (detour to the summit), Lochranza Castle, Isle of Arran Distillery, boulder hopping on the south coast, Glenashdale Falls and the Giants' Graves.

Lowlights

Of the 18 miles (29 km) from Lochranza to Blackwaterfoot, about 11 miles (18 km) consists of road walking.

The Arran Coastal Way is said to be Scotland's finest circular walk.
rucsacs.com

Arran also has plenty of geological intrigue. rucsacs.com

Why do you love it?

The coastal views, the approachable wildlife and the friendly Arranachs (locals).

History/background

Arran is so famous for its visible geology that it's considered a mecca for geology field trips. Its features include raised beaches, cliffs and sea caves and, above all, Hutton's Unconformity near Lochranza. There are also various castles, graveyards and other sites of historic interest, including the King's Cave (Robert the Bruce). The Machrie Moor Stone Circles detour takes you to Bronze Age stone circles.

How challenging?

The most challenging terrain is the boulder fields, but the difficulties can be avoided by using the road. The distances look deceptively modest but challenging terrain and the need to be aware of tidal windows make it sensible to take your time. Waymarking is in place throughout, but is not always easily spotted.

Accommodation and transport

There is plenty of choice of accommodation in Brodick and Whiting Bay, with restricted choice elsewhere. However, nowhere in Arran is much more than 30–40 minutes away by road and the excellent bus services mean that even as an unsupported walker you can stay several nights in one place; use the bus to reach the start and to return from the end of each section.

Best day-walk

I most enjoyed the section from Brodick to Sannox including the option to summit Goat Fell, which has a spectacular panorama with distant mountain views. It's also well worth making the excursion by ferry to the Holy Isle which has fascinating history and wildlife all of its own and an entertaining walk clockwise around the island.

Arran is often described as 'Scotland in miniature'. rucsacs.com

TALKING WALKING – JACQUETTA MEGARRY

Jacquetta hikes, writes and publishes guidebooks for long walks in weatherproof format. She is an active member of the Outdoor Writers and Photographers Guild. Her company's website is rucsacs.com and can also be found at facebook.com/rucsacs.

What do you remember about your first multi-day walk?

I had just turned fifty and together with three friends we walked the West Highland Way. We had a wonderful time, though I thought the official guidebook was hopeless in rain and wind. One thing led to another, and I stumbled into publishing guidebooks.

Which is your favourite UK trek?

The Arran Coastal Way, because of its scenic variety, its castles, standing stones and distillery, its very approachable wildlife, the untamed nature of the walking (in places including boulder-hopping), the panorama from Goat Fell and above all the warm welcome from Arranachs.

What is it about long distance walks that appeals to you?

The world becomes a simpler place when you carry your possessions on your back and propel yourself from A to B without relying on anybody else for transport. Walking alone, you see a lot of wildlife and scenery, and there's nothing to disturb your tranquillity or interrupt your thoughts. Each step away from the noise of 'civilization' is a step towards inner peace. John Muir expressed it better: 'Nature's peace will flow into you as sunshine flows into trees … cares will drop off like autumn leaves.' He later said, 'Only by going alone in silence, without baggage, can one truly get to the heart of the wilderness.'

Jacquetta Megarry.

What advice do you have for fellow long distance walkers?

Don't spoil the experience by committing yourself to overlong daily distances. For sustained multi-day walking, including stops for meals, rests, wildlife and photographs, don't expect much more than about 2 mph (3.2 kph) overall for each day. That way, you will finish early, and enjoy yourself more the next day. After all, if you were really in a hurry you wouldn't be walking! Also, travel light: apart from plenty of socks, leave the rest behind.

Ayrshire Coastal Path (GT)

James Begg, route manager and author of *Ayrshire Coastal Path: The Official Guide Book*

Glenapp Kirk to Skelmorlie: 100 miles/161 km

Difficulty rating: 2

Average days to complete: 5–10 days

Waymarking? Yes

Maps: It's due to be included in the next revision of OS Explorer Maps; OS Landranger 1:50,000 sheets 76, 70, 63; OS Explorer 1:25,000 sheets 317, 326, (333), 341

Baggage courier? Yes

For more details: ayrshirecoastalpath.org; focrt.org

Describe the trail

Panoramic beauty, wildlife in abundance, challenging, yet gentle. Dominated by the silhouettes of Ailsa Craig and Arran, the trail runs for 100 miles along one of the finest panoramic coastlines in the British Isles, from Glenapp Kirk to Skelmorlie. From the wild cliffs of Glenapp to the sands of Ayr and Ardrossan, the ever-changing perspectives of 'the Craig' and 'the Sleeping Warrior' provide a feast for both eye and camera as walkers are drawn

The Ayrshire Coastal Path boasts panoramic beauty and wildlife in abundance. JAMES BEGG

slowly northwards towards the sheltered waters of Largs and Skelmorlie and the upper Firth of Clyde.

Highlights

The ever-changing sea panorama and perspective of Ailsa Craig and Arran when walking from south to north along the wild coastline from Glenapp to Heads of Ayr; and the wonderful views of where you have just been, and the road ahead, from the Iron Age fort on Knock Hill above Largs.

Lowlights

The Ayrshire Coastal Path isn't a constant paved path, so in some places walkers may encounter muddy, cattle-trodden field-edge paths in winter. Or in a wet summer, perhaps paths overgrown with bracken and long grass – till our 'Pathminder' squad of between fifteen and twenty retired Rotarians and other volunteers manage to strim and mow

their way along miles of cliff-tops and foreshore. Unlike some of the long distance Big Boys, we have no Scottish or local government maintenance funding. So please be understanding – and any wee (or big) donations towards upkeep would be much appreciated.

Why do you love it?

Apart from the wonderful, ever-changing scenery, in spring, summer, autumn or winter, there is always something special to see – from seals to basking sharks, foxes, otters, deer, wild goats, 135 recorded species of bird, a great variety of wild-flowers, and interesting geology.

History/background

Ayrshire is a land with a long and turbulent history – it has seen the Bronze Age, Iron Age, Romans, Vikings, Scottish Wars of Wallace and Bruce, Cromwell, warring Lowland clans, and two World Wars. The evidence is strewn along the coast in ruined headland forts and castles. And Ayrshire is also the land of Robert Burns, with a visit to his Birthplace Museum in Alloway marked by a short

The Ayrshire Coastal Path runs for 100 miles along one of the finest coastlines in the British Isles. JAMES BEGG

You might see seals, basking sharks, foxes or otters on the Ayrshire Coastal Path. BECKY DUNCAN

Path detour. *The Official Guide Book* is full of information on the area's social and natural history.

How challenging?

The short sections of 6–9 miles (10–14 km) are designed for middle-aged walkers, while young fit things can aim for two or three sections per day. There are only three sections of 9–11 miles. The South section (from Glenapp to Ayr) involves undulating wild cliff-top paths and rocky shores, and is more challenging than the North (from Ayr to Skelmorlie), where most walking is at beach level, on sandy beaches, promenades, and cycle tracks. Total height gain over the 100 miles (161 km) is about 2,625 ft/800 m and the route is well waymarked. Several short 492 ft/150 m sections are affected by high tide levels, which might cause delays of a few hours on a few days each month. Consult the *Official Guide Book* for advice.

Accommodation and transport

It has good regular trains and buses running alongside for most of the way. The Trail website provides up-to-date links to bus, train, and tide timetables. It's easy for walkers to leave their cars; take a bus down to the starting point and walk back to your vehicle. Or use public transport both ways. The route's website also contains an excellent accommodation section, to suit all tastes, most of which can also arrange baggage transfers on request. The short sections make it ideal for day-walkers.

Best day-walk

The short but classic walk from Turnberry (or Maidens) to Dunure encompasses Turnberry Castle, Lighthouse, and Golf Course, Maidens old fishing harbour, NTS Culzean Castle and Country Park with a choice of cliff-top, woodland and formal garden through-walks, followed by a long sandy beach, and then a spectacular cliff-top walk and descent to the medieval Dunure Castle, a pretty old fishing harbour – and a welcome pint.

The first section – of wild moorland and cliff-top scenery from Glenapp to Ballantrae – is a firm favourite with the more energetic walkers.

Berwickshire Coastal Path (GT)

Euan Calvert, Scottish Borders Council

Berwick-upon-Tweed to Cockburnspath: 30 miles/45 km

Difficulty rating: 2

Average days to complete: 2

Waymarking? Yes

Maps: Harvey Maps

Baggage courier? Yes

For more details: Download a free brochure from scotborders.gov.uk

Describe the trail

The Berwickshire Coastal Path follows a rugged coastline that's arguably the most spectacular in Britain. The Path passes through Burnmouth, Eyemouth and St Abbs, crossing farmland and traversing the second-highest cliffs on the east coast of Britain. A short extension to the route takes advantage of the paths of the National Nature Reserve of St Abbs Head.

Highlights

Coldingham for its sandy bay and St Abbs Head for its impressive cliffs and birdlife.

Lowlights

Siccar Point to Dowlaw has vast views of East Lothian countryside and Bass Rock from rotational grazing. However there's some uninspiring walking on farmland and road.

The Berwickshire Coastal Path follows a rugged and spectacular coastline. BECKY DUNCAN

The trail includes characterful fishing villages tucked away in concealed coves. BECKY DUNCAN

The path has impressive geology on show too. BECKY DUNCAN

Why do you love it?

The impressive geology on show and the lovely little characterful fishing villages tucked away in concealed coves.

History/background

The northern end of the Berwickshire Coastal Path links with the Southern Upland Way, whilst the John Muir Way (which continues round the coast of East Lothian) can be accessed via the John Muir link.

How challenging?

There's a decent amount of elevation (5,630 ft/1,716 m ascent) for a comparatively short long distance path. But it's well waymarked. Strong walkers might manage the route in two days, but there is so much to see I recommend three relaxing days.

Accommodation and transport

Transport is excellent: take a bus locally or a train nationally from Berwick. Accommodation availability is good in the Coldingham/Eyemouth area and Berwick, but there's not so much in the Scottish Borders.

Best day-walk

Berwick to St Abbs, or a circular route in the 'Paths Around Eyemouth' brochure: Coldingham, Linkim Shore, St Abbs and back.

Borders Abbeys Way (GT)

Susan Kevan, Scottish Borders Council

Circular walking route including Hawick, Melrose and Kelso: 68 miles/109 km

Difficulty rating: 2–3

Average days to complete: 5–6

Waymarking? Yes

Maps: OS Landranger 73, 74, 79, 80; Explorer 331, 338, 339, OL16; the route guide (download from scotborders.gov.uk/bordersabbeysway)

Baggage courier? Yes

For more details: scotborders.gov.uk/borders-abbeysway; rangers@scotborders.gov.uk; (for accommodation) jedburgh@visitscotland.com

Describe the trail

A circular route linking the historic border towns and villages of Jedburgh, Denholm, Hawick, Selkirk, Melrose, St Boswells, Kelso and Jedburgh.

Combining the walk with visits to the four Borders Abbeys offers history and scenery.

Highlights

The Borders scenery at Roxburgh Viaduct, Selkirk Hill, Hartwoodmyres Forest, Dryburgh Bridge, Abbotsford House and the Tweed riverside. The friendly pubs and cafes in Denholm. Dryburgh Abbey and the nearby riverside.

Lowlights

Some sections are on quiet tarmac roads and farm tracks. Although it's very well waymarked, the route is designed to be walked in conjunction with a map or guide. The section on Black Hill near Jedburgh needs to be walked with a trail guide or map and compass as visibility can be low. Adequate time needs to be allowed if visiting the abbeys.

Why do you love it?

It's a great way to explore the countryside of the central Scottish Borders with a variety of scenery and habitats: woodland, forest, upland farmland, hill ground, riverside paths and lowland farmland and meadows.

History/background

The route links the historic ruined abbeys of Melrose, Dryburgh, Kelso and Jedburgh. King David I developed Scotland's trading economy, including the extension of trading privileges at the Royal Burghs of Berwick, Roxburgh, Jedburgh, Selkirk and Peebles. He's credited with establishing Scotland's first coinage and a royal mint was located at the now ruined Roxburgh Castle by the River Teviot on the route. David also established monasteries in the region.

How challenging?

The Borders Abbeys Way is a well-waymarked route suitable for an introduction to long distance walking. The route splits easily into 5–6 days of around 12 miles, or sections of differing lengths, still linked by public transport. It's possible to walk the route staying in one local location. Many people take a car to the end of their day's walking and take a bus to the start of that day's walk, and walk back to their car. Terrain is mainly paths and tracks.

Accommodation and transport

There's a range of accommodation options at the

Borders Abbeys Way is a circular route linking historic border towns. BECKY DUNCAN

The route links the historic ruined abbeys of Melrose, Dryburgh, Kelso and Jedburgh. BECKY DUNCAN

five to six most common stops. Using public transport opens up a wide range of other accommodation within the Scottish Borders, including Galashiels.

Best day-walk

Kelso to Jedburgh (13.5 miles/22 km) includes two abbeys, riverside, old railway lines and farmland. Also, Selkirk to Hawick (12 miles/19 km) includes the historic Haining Estate, and Hartwoodmyres Forest with views to Bowhill House. Also upland farmland with views to the Liddesdale hills and Hawick.

Centenary Way

John Sparshatt, author of *The Centenary Way*

York to Filey Brigg: 83 miles/134 km

Difficulty rating: 2

Average days to complete: 5–6 days

Waymarking? Yes

Maps: OS Landranger 100, 101, 105; OS Explorer 290, 300, 301

Baggage courier? No

For more details: ldwa.org.uk (includes free, downloadable eguide)

Describe the trail

A meandering route from York to Filey across the Howardian Hills and Yorkshire Wolds via Castle Howard and Wharram Percy, linking York and the Foss Walk with the Yorkshire Wolds Way and Cleveland Way National Trails. Meeting the Derwent and Foss, it combines riverside walks in deep valleys with forest tracks.

Highlights

York Minster, the ancient village of Wharram Percy, Castle Howard, Sherrif Hutton Castle, Kirkham Abbey and the finish at Filey Brigg.

Lowlights

Only one short steep climb through the wood at Deep Dale Plantation, near Wintringham.

Why do you love it?

The incredible variety of terrain and spectacular landscape views. There are rivers, forests, moorland, reservoirs, farmland, historic villages and monuments, a stunning abbey and castle along the trail.

History/background

A route devised to celebrate the hundredth anniversary of Yorkshire County Council.

How challenging?

Easy walking apart from one short steep climb. It's suitable for a beginner to tackle in easy stages. There's 6,000 ft/1,829 m of ascent and varied terrain from easy riverside paths, woodland tracks and fieldside paths.

Accommodation and transport

B&B accommodation is good between York and Malton and there are some B&B options along the A64 between Malton and Filey. Good options in York, Malton and Filey. A bus service runs between Filey, Malton and York.

Best day-walk

Malton to Wharram le Street (16 miles), visiting the Yorkshire Wolds and Wharren Percy. Bus back to Malton from Wharram le Street.

Clyde Walkway (GT)

Simon Pilpel, landscape and access development manager, South Lanarkshire Council

Glasgow city centre to Falls of Clyde at New Lanark: 40 miles/60 km

Difficulty rating: 2

Average days to complete: 2

Waymarking? Yes

Maps: OS Explorer 335, 342, 343

Baggage courier? No

For more details: southlanarkshire.gov.uk, scot-landsgreattrails.org.uk

Describe the trail

A riverside route along one of Scotland's iconic rivers from the centre of Glasgow to the World Heritage Site of New Lanark and the spectacular Falls of Clyde.

Highlights

Clyde Valley Orchards and Falls of Clyde/New Lanark.

Lowlights

Some sections of the route pass through urban and industrial areas in the Glasgow conurbation.

Why do you love it?

Because it takes you on a journey from the centre of Glasgow, the city of culture which drove Scotland's industrial and economic development, to Robert Owen's New Lanark, birthplace of the Industrial Revolution in Scotland, passing through the Garden Valley of the River Clyde. From vibrant urban culture to bucolic rural idyll.

History/background

The Clyde Walkway was created as a joint enterprise by the Glasgow City, South Lanarkshire, and North Lanarkshire Councils and completed in 2005.

How challenging?

The route is suitable for novice walkers and whilst there are some short sections of ascent and descent they should not pose any problems to the reasonably able walker.

Accommodation and transport
Public transport is good to all sections of the route. The route can easily be done in sections as day walks.

Best day-walk
From Strathclyde County Park to Falls of Clyde or vice versa.

Cowal Way
Jacquetta Megarry, editor and publisher of Rucksack Readers guidebooks (rucsacs.com)
Portavadie to Inveruglas: 57 miles/92 km
Difficulty rating: 3
Average days to complete: 5
Waymarking? Yes
Maps: OS 362, 363, 364
Baggage courier? Yes
For more details: *The Cowal Way* by Michael Kaufmann and James McLuckie; cowalway.co.uk

Describe the trail
A traverse of the peaceful Cowal Peninsula. Easily accessible from Glasgow, this trail combines the wildness of its Highland scenery with glorious views over several sea lochs and the Firth of Clyde and its islands, with great opportunities to spot wildlife.

Highlights
Former fishing villages such as Tighnabruaich, Caladh Harbour, Kilmodan Church and Carved Stones, the Allt Robuic Falls, Curra Lochain, views over the Clyde and the rugged mountains.

Lowlights
The section between Tighnabruaich and Glendaruel contains a rocky, steep, overgrown path, which after heavy rain can become very muddy and slippery. This is too difficult for some walkers, especially around high tide when the sea-water dictates the passable route. However, plans to upgrade this section are under way.

Why do you love it?
The scenery is rugged and varied and the wildlife very approachable.

History/background
Several historic castles, many fine Victorian mansions (some ruined), Millhouse Powder Mill (gunpowder) and Strachur Smiddy Museum (blacksmith heritage).

How challenging?
Cowal is prone to heavy rainfall and, during or after rain, conditions can become very muddy or boggy in places. The first two sections are low-lying, whilst the next three rise successively to 1,180 ft/360 m, 1,150 ft/350 m and 1,640 ft/500 m. The longest section is Glendaruel to Strachur (16 miles/25 km). The most hilly section (Lochgoilhead to Inveruglas) is 15 miles (24 km) but can readily be split. The trail is not ideal for beginners: north of Strachur, if mist or cloud descends, walkers may

Cowal Way is a traverse of the peaceful Cowal Peninsula.
rucsacs.com

TALKING WALKING – ALASTAIR HUMPHREYS

Alastair is an adventurer, author and blogger. He's cycled round the world, walked across southern India, rowed across the Atlantic Ocean, completed a crossing of Iceland, trekked 1,000 miles across the Empty Quarter desert and 120 miles round the M25 – one of his pioneering micro-adventures. Alastair has written six books and was named as one of *National Geographic*'s Adventurers of the year for 2012. His website is alastairhumphreys.com and he tweets at @al_humphreys.

What do you remember about your first multi-day walk?

I walked Hadrian's Wall on a school trip aged about ten. I remember mostly that we were sleeping in a barn – lots of straw and it smelled of poo. I was ill and very unhappy. Mum had to come and pick me up!

What effect did your first long walk have on you?

To be honest I was more influenced by bike travel – I found walking too slow. It was only after cycling round the world that I started to yearn for the simplicity, slowness and good-old-fashioned misery of trying to walk a long way!

How many long distance trails have you done since?

I walked the length of the Kaveri river in India and across the Empty Quarter desert in Arabia.

What is it about long distance walks that appeals to you?

The feeling of reaching the top of a big hill, looking back and knowing that – all the way to the Earth's horizon – you have covered every inch of that on foot. And the excitement and challenge of looking forward at all that still lies in wait.

Alastair Humphreys.

How much do you obsess over equipment?

Not at all. I think people who obsess over shaving 500g of their pack weight by spending £50 on a lighter spoon would be better off doing fifty press-ups every morning and losing a bit of weight!

Do you do any fitness preparation beforehand?

I try to be always fit, so I don't. However I would always advise a beginner to train in advance, building up their distances gradually to avoid injury.

---

need map and compass skills. Waymarkers exist, but are not always very visible.

Accommodation and transport

Cowal is mainly reached as if an island: most people arrive on one of four ferries, some by bus or car from Glasgow. There is little public transport within Cowal, with only an infrequent bus service (West Coast Motors) and no railways. The route has been designed to make its section breaks at villages that offer accommodation and shops, but these are small places with limited choice so it's essential to book ahead. The marina at Portavadie now offers B&B accommodation, but there's no accommodation at Inveruglas (though plenty at Arrochar, only 5.5 miles before the end).

Best day-walk

I found the final section the most varied and rewarding: starting from Lochgoilhead, the trail climbs to a pass in the range of mountains dividing two sea lochs, Lochs Goil and Long. The views from the pass are superb, then there's a fine descent to Loch Long, and the option of a side-trip to climb the iconic Cobbler (2,890 ft/881 m). From Arrochar, the trail heads north through secluded Glen Loin to reach the banks of Loch Lomond at Inveruglas.

Cross Borders Drove Road (GT)

Vyv Wood-Gee, the countryside management consultant who set up the route

Little Vantage (A70 south-west of Edinburgh) to Hawick: 52 miles/83 km

Difficulty rating: 2

Average days to complete: 4–5

Waymarking? Yes

Maps: OS Explorer 344, 336, 337, 338, 331

Baggage courier? Yes

For more details: southofscotlandcountryside-trails.co.uk

Describe the trail

Steeped in history, this spectacular trail follows the route along which thousands of cattle and sheep were herded for hundreds of years through the Scottish Borders. From the historic pass over the Pentland Hills, over rolling hills and through sheltered glens, the Cross Borders Drove Road combines great walking through stunning and varied scenery with a wealth of cultural interest. The character of the trail varies as much as the scenery, from narrow moorland paths and grassy loans to farm and forest tracks.

Highlights

Perhaps the best bits of this route are where it runs between the original twin dykes (walls) built to help the drovers stop their cattle from straying.

Lowlights

You won't find any refreshments or shops other than in West Linton, Peebles and Hawick.

Why do you love it?

Few, if any, other trails offer the chance to step back in history as this route does, and allow you to follow in the footsteps of the drovers. It showcases some of the best and most diverse walking the Borders has to offer. You will meet very few people and have only cows, sheep and wildlife for company. It's often hard to believe you can have such a fantastic sense of being away from it all, yet never that far from civilization, and within relatively easy reach of Edinburgh.

History/background

The Cross Borders Drove Road is part of the 155-mile (250 km) South of Scotland Countryside Trails network, a spiderweb of linking routes offering fantastic walking, mountain biking and horse riding in Southern Scotland.

How challenging?

The whole route is clearly signed and waymarked throughout, and easy to follow with a map. The steepest hill is the climb up from Gypsy Glen, south of Peebles, which is more than justified by the 360-degree views from the top of Yellowmire Hill with the Tweed Valley stretching out below you.

Cleghorn Glen on the Cross Borders Drove Road. VYV WOOD-GEE

Cross Borders Drove Road follows a route used for centuries to herd cattle and sheep. YVV WOOD-GEE

Accommodation and transport

There are plenty of accommodation options in and around Peebles and Hawick, but choices are more limited in West Linton and Traquair. Accommodation is hard to find at other points along the route without a short deviation. There's a bothy on the Minch Moor above Traquair for the self-sufficient. A public bus service goes between Peebles and West Linton, and from Peebles to Traquair, but there's no direct link between the start and finish of the route.

Best day-walk

A toss-up between West Linton (or Halmyre) to Peebles because of the variety from fertile farmland and forestry to hidden glens and open hills, including sections of original drove road; and Peebles to Traquair, which is more hilly and remote, best on a clear day when you can fully appreciate the views. Both are equally as good on a crisp winter's day as at any other time of year.

Fife Coastal Path (GT)

John Henderson, Walking Support (walkingsupport.co.uk)
Kincardine to Newburgh: 116.5 miles/186 km
Difficulty rating: 3
Average days to complete: 7
Waymarking? Yes
Maps: OS 65, 66, 59; Footprint Maps

Baggage courier? Yes (walkingsupport.co.uk)
For more details: fifecoastalpath.net

Describe the trail

A mainly coastal walk offering commanding views across the Firth of Forth to the City of Edinburgh, over to the Isle of May, then north to the Angus coast and the Firth of Tay. Starting from the south-west border of Fife the Way heads east, then north before turning west along the Tay estuary, concluding at the county boundary with Perth and Kinross.

Highlights

Sections of the walk in the East Neuk of Fife and St Andrews.

An ancient settlement with links to royalty, Kinghorn has a small harbour and two sandy beaches that offer spectacular views across the Firth of Forth. JOHN HENDERSON

View over Newport on Tay on the new section from Newport on Tay/ Tay Road Bridge to Newburgh, Fife Coastal Path. JOHN HENDERSON

Lowlights

The way from Kincardine through to Leven has several sections that are industrial, although this can also be broken up with some historic and attractive communities. Although industrial they do tell a story of the heritage of this part of Fife.

Why do you love it?

With the exception of Newport on Tay to Newburgh, the route is generally level and easy walking. The route passes through some quant fishing communities.

History/background

St Andrews is steeped in history as well as having the pride of being the home of golf. Pettycur and Newport on Tay are the south and north points of the main eighteenth-century links to the north of Scotland. North Queensferry has links to Margaret, a Saxon princess who fled the Norman Conquest of England and married Malcolm III of Scotland, becoming queen and, in time, a saint.

How challenging?

The greatest challenge is the length of the whole way, but many will walk only the original route from North Queensferry to Newport on Tay, which is 85 miles.

Accommodation and transport

Accommodation in all stopping points is adequate or good and linking buses are frequent. Some sections also have good links to the rail system.

Best day-walk

Any of the sections from Lower Largo to St Andrews, this being the East Neuk area.

Forth and Clyde Canal and Union Canal Paths (GT)

Brian Cowan, long distance walker

Bowling to Fountainbridge, Edinburgh: 66 miles/106 km

Difficulty rating: 4–6

Average days to complete: 3

Waymarking? Yes

Linlithgow Basin, at the end of the first day's walk from Falkirk, Forth and Clyde Canal and Union Canal Paths. BRIAN COWAN

The Kelpies at Carronshore, by sculptor Andy Scott, FCCUCP.
BRIAN COWAN

Maps: Free map available from walkhighlands.co.uk

Baggage courier? No

For more details: walkhighlands.co.uk

Describe the trail

An easy and very pleasant walk. As the name (FCCUCP) hints, the route is a tale of two canals, the Forth and Clyde and the Union, which meet, at the Falkirk Wheel boatlift, to form a footpath route from the mouth of the River Clyde on the west coast of Scotland to Edinburgh on the east.

Highlights

For those of a mechanical bent, the Forth and Clyde has some unique features: the drop lock at Dalmuir, the rotary boatlift near Camelon, and the Kelpies, standing 30 m high beside the canal at Carronshore. The Union Canal passes through the former shale mining area of Scotland, which in the early 1900s was producing about 2 per cent of the world's supply of mineral oil. The canal is one of the few linear canals following the same contour its entire length, so there are no locks. The very best bit? For me, the stretch between Clydebank and Port Dundas close to Glasgow city centre.

Lowlights

I really can't think of any. There's not really much variation in the altitude, so there are no sweeping panoramas to see, and much of it passes through urban areas, all of which many walkers may find too boring.

Why do you love it?

The surrounding landscape, and the industrial history of the towns it passes through.

History/background

Opened in 1790, the Forth and Clyde is the oldest of Scotland's four remaining canals. Much of the canal follows the line of the Antonine Wall, parts of it being uncovered during the canal's construction.

How challenging?

This is as easy an introduction to long distance walking as anyone could wish for, and, since it's all done on a towpath, it's impossible to go astray.

Accommodation and transport

Since the walk passes through several fair-sized towns, accommodation shouldn't be a problem. There are good public transport options should anyone decide to break it down into day walks, using the excellent Traveline Scotland website (travelinescotland.com). But there are no camping facilities along the walk.

Best day-walk

A difficult choice between the Bowling–Port Dundas stretch offering special views of Glasgow and its

Near Philipston, on the second day of the walk between Linlithgow and Broxburn, FCCUCP. BRIAN COWAN

environs, and the final stretch from Auchenstarry basin to Carronshore, which takes in the Falkirk Wheel and the Kelpies.

John Muir Way (GT)

Jacquetta Megarry, co-author (with Sandra Bardwell) and publisher of *John Muir Way*

Helensburgh to Dunbar: 134 miles/215 km
Difficulty rating: 4–5
Average days to complete: 10
Waymarking? Yes
Maps: It's not on OS (as of 2014), but the route is covered by 347, 348, 349, 350, 351
Baggage courier? Yes
For more details: johnmuirway.org; rucsacs.com

Describe the trail

A low-level route that runs across central Scotland to Dunbar, the birthplace of John Muir. Apart from its western section, the route runs close to many centres of population so you are never far from facilities and good public transport. Unusually, it's equally suitable for both walkers and cyclists with many route alternatives to suit both. This coast-to-coast route has immense variety and includes some surprisingly remote sections.

Highlights

The Hill House at Helensburgh is Charles Rennie Mackintosh's masterpiece of domestic architecture. The Forth and Clyde and Union Canals have great heritage and wildlife. They are linked by the Falkirk Wheel, a masterpiece of engineering and the world's only rotating boatlift. Other points of interest include Callendar Park and House, Avon Aqueduct, Linlithgow Loch and Palace, Blackness Castle, Hopetoun House, the Forth Bridge, Arthur's Seat (823 ft/251 m), Dirleton Castle and Preston Mill. The ascent of North Berwick Law (613 ft/187 m) is rewarded by a superb summit panorama. The route culminates at the John Muir Birthplace and museum.

Lowlights

The route officially bypasses the best of Linlithgow (easily overcome by a small detour); the route through Edinburgh avoids the World Heritage Site of Edinburgh's Old and New Towns, instead

The John Muir Way finishes in Dunbar, the birthplace of its namesake. rucsacs.com

making a long, strange diversion to the south-west. (You can download a much better, shorter city-centre route from rucsacs.com/books/jm).

Why do you love it?

It's very easy to tackle in sections and offers huge variety.

History/background

John Muir, world-famous as the father of National Parks, grew up in Dunbar and completing this route is a good way to celebrate his contribution. The route is steeped in canal heritage and there are many castles and Roman remains (e.g. Antonine Wall and its forts) en route.

How challenging?

The trail is mainly beginner-friendly with the exception of the 18-mile Balloch–Strathblane section. The difficulty rating of 4–5 mainly reflects its overall length if tackled as a coast-to-coast; tackled in sections it's generally easy, with moderate gradients and never going above 885 ft/270 m. The waymarking is consistent, although the frequent options for cyclists to diverge from walkers means you have to be vigilant, and spotting waymarkers at some street junctions in Edinburgh can be tricky.

Accommodation and transport

There is a wide choice of B&B-style accommodation almost throughout, but you are very restricted in smaller places such as Strathblane where booking is essential. There are no hostels or bunk-houses other than in Edinburgh. (Although wild camping is allowed in Scotland, much of the route passes through farmland and urban areas where it is unlikely to be an option.) Public transport is good, other than in the western section where it is much sparser.

Best day-walk

The final section from North Berwick to Dunbar offers the option of a trip up North Berwick Law with its fine summit panorama, with glorious coastal walking through the John Muir Country Park across the sands of Belhaven Bay to end in Dunbar at the John Muir Birthplace museum.

Kintyre Way (GT)

Sandra Bardwell, co-author of *The Kintyre Way*
Tarbert to Southend: 87 miles/140 km
Difficulty rating: 3
Average days to complete: 7
Waymarking? Yes
Maps: OS (1:25,000) 357, 356
Baggage courier? Yes
For more details: kintyreway.com
Describe the trail

A remote route criss-crossing the Kintyre Peninsula. The Way explores Scotland's only 'main-land island'. It's a very varied route, looking both outward to the Atlantic Ocean and inward to the Firth of Clyde. Its terrain includes coastal walking, moorland, and forest paths and tracks.

A Scottish stronghold, Kintyre Way. SANDRA BARDWELL

Highlights

Wild and remote coast and moorland between Machrihanish and Southend, views from high points between Tarbert and Claonaig.

A boat returning to harbour, Kintyre Way. SANDRA BARDWELL

Lowlights

Wind turbines and conifer plantations between Tayinloan and Carradale.

Why do you love it?

The sense of remoteness from the rest of Scotland, fine coastal scenery and wide views.

History/background

Whisky-making (near Campbeltown), medieval gravestones and several imposing castles.

How challenging?

It's not beginner-friendly. There are some steep ups and downs, and boggy terrain in several places. The southern part has three long days (16, 20 and 21 miles). It's well waymarked, though careful navigation is needed in poor weather.

Accommodation and transport

Accommodation, apart from hotels, is not plentiful, but a tent is far from essential as long as you book well in advance. It would be difficult to do the whole route as day walks because of infrequent or non-existent bus services in some places. Though there are adequate services to Tarbert (the start) and to Campbeltown, they are infrequent from the finish (Southend).

Best day-walk

The final section to Southend, officially from Campbeltown. Preferably take the bus to Machrihanish to reduce the route's length to 15.5 miles and avoid road walking.

The Mary Queen of Scots Way is a coast-to-coast walk across central Scotland. PAUL PRESCOTT

Mary Queen of Scots Way

Paul Prescott, route creator and author of *Mary Queen of Scots Way*

Arrochar to St Andrews: 107 miles/172 km

Difficulty rating: 4

Average days to complete: 6–10

Waymarking? No

Maps: The route isn't marked on maps. OS Explorer 364, 365, 366, 369, 370, 371

Baggage courier? No

For more details: maryqueenofscotsway.com; rucsacs.com

Describe the trail

A coast-to-coast walk across central Scotland. The scenery is very varied: the Way starts at a rugged sea loch and ends on a sandy beach, going through hills, forest and moorland and passing castles, forts, towns and villages on the way. Although it runs close to the densely populated central belt, many parts of the Way are surprisingly remote.

Highlights

Every stage is different, so the best bits are a very personal choice. Mine are the Loch Katrine aqueducts, the panorama from Dumyat, Dollar Glen and Castle Campbell, the ascent into the Lomond Hills, the descent of Maspie Den and the conservation village of Falkland with its palace.

Lowlights

Because the route is unofficial it can be affected

The Mary Queen of Scots Way goes through hills, forest and moorland, and passes forts, villages and castles such as Doune Castle (left). rucsacs. com

without notice by landowner actions, particularly forestry operations and ploughing.

Why do you love it?

Its great variety of scenery.

History/background

The route passes through and overlooks many places that were important in the life of Mary Queen of Scots.

How challenging?

The going underfoot is good, on footpaths, forest tracks, cycle routes or country lanes almost throughout. The terrain is undulating and in places (such as the ascent of Dumyat) there are steep sections. The route is not recommended as a beginner's first long distance path because of its unofficial status and the need for navigation.

Accommodation and transport

Because of its easy accessibility to the population centres of the Scottish central belt, this route lends itself to day walks and shorter sections. Public transport is not plentiful, but car access is good with buses sparse. For through walkers there is adequate accommodation everywhere along the route. Camping is not advised.

Best day-walk

First choice: Glenfarg to Falkland (10 miles/16 km).

Second choice: Loch Lomond to Aberfoyle (16 miles/26 km).

Mull of Galloway Trail (GT)

Tom Stevenson, mullofgallowaytrail.co.uk

Mull of Galloway to Stranraer: 26 miles/42 km

Difficulty rating: 3

Average days to complete: 1–3

Waymarking? Yes

Maps: OS Explorer 309

Baggage courier? No

For more details: *27 Circular Walks Based on the Mull of Galloway Trail* by Robert Clark (available from mullofgallowaytrail.co.uk); an illustrated leaflet that includes a full route description is available in tourist information offices and other local outlets.

Describe the trail

A varied walk with some beautiful coastal scenery. The trail runs from the Mull of Galloway, the most southerly point in Scotland from which it's possible to see Northern Ireland, the Isle of Man, Cumbria and the Machars. The terrain is very varied, starting along cliff-tops and following the coast of Luce Bay to Clayshant where it diverts inland along minor roads and across farmland and woods before

Looking south to the Mull. The lighthouse is just visible on the promontory. TOM STEVENSON

arriving at Stranraer. The trail connects with the Loch Ryan Coastal Path at Stranraer which keeps to the shores of Loch Ryan and then climbs north of Cairnryan to give views of the North Rhins, Northern Ireland and the Isle of Man.

Highlights

The most scenic part is along the coast from the Mull to Maryport with rugged cliffs and beautiful views. The trail incorporates woodland walks and a huge variety of wild flowers, especially in spring and summer, can be seen along the trail, as well as seals, roe deer and red squirrels. With a very mild climate in south-west Scotland with little snow and frost the trail is used throughout the year.

Lowlights

The road walking from Clayshant to High Barnultoch isn't the most exciting part of the trail, although the surrounding countryside is pleasant. There's some stony foreshore walking, but these sections are short and parts of the trail were recently rerouted to cut down on these.

Why do you love it?

The scenery, the variety of the terrain, the wildflowers and the opportunity to see wildlife.

History/background

The Rotary Club of Ayr completed the Ayrshire Coastal Path from Glenapp to Skelmorlie and thereafter the Rotary Club of Stranraer created firstly the Loch Ryan Coastal Path and then the Mull of Galloway Trail. Other Rotary clubs later became involved, linking the Ayrshire Coastal Path at Skelmorlie to the newly formed Clyde Coastal Path, which crosses the Erskine Bridge and ends at Milngavie.

How challenging?

The most difficult part is from the Mull to Maryport where care is required along the cliffs. This section also involves some ups and downs while other parts are fairly level. Sandhead to Stranraer is the easiest section with no climbing and partly on minor roads. The trail is well waymarked.

Accommodation and transport

The Mull to Stranraer can be completed in a day, but it can be easily broken down into two or three sections for day walks. Numbered waymarkers along the route break the trail into ten sections which are shown in the aforementioned leaflet. The *27*

Looking north on the Mull of Galloway Trail. TOM STEVENSON

Circular Walks Based on the Mull of Galloway Trail provides options for shorter walks using parts of the trail. There is a bus service from Drummore to Stranraer (except on a Sunday), but unfortunately no public transport from the Mull to Drummore. There are hotels and guesthouses in Drummore, Sandhead and Stranraer and good cafes/restaurants at the Mull, Drummore, Sandhead and Stranraer. There are also several caravan parks en route.

Best day-walk

The most spectacular part is from the Mull to Drummore where perhaps the best views can be appreciated. New England Bay to Ardwell gives a variety of terrain, including a wooded section, with masses of wild-flowers in spring and summer. Often seals are seen along this section of coastline.

Rob Roy Way (GT)

John Henderson, Walking Support (walkingsupport.co.uk)

Drymen to Pitlochry: 77 miles/124 km or 94 miles/151 km

Difficulty rating: 3

Average days to complete: 7

Waymarking? Yes

Maps: OS Landranger 57, 51, 52; Harvey Maps; Footprint Maps

Baggage courier? Yes

For more details: robroyway.com; *The Rob Roy Way* by Jacquetta Megarry

Describe the trail

A walk across the Southern Highlands of Scotland taking in some of Scotland's finest lochs and glens. Linking Drymen with the Perthshire tourist hub of Pitlochry, this walk follows the tracks and paths used by Rob Roy MacGregor in the seventeenth and eighteenth centuries. Sense the history of Scotland as you travel through glens, along rivers and burns and past mountains and lochs, soaking up some of Scotland's greatest scenery.

Highlights

Walking on the banks of Loch Lubnaig, ascending Glen Ogle via the old railway and viaduct, the descent onto Loch Tay with views across to Ben Lawers and Schiehallion, the Falls of Acharn, Birks of Aberfeldy and the descent from the Stone Circle at Carra Beag into Pitlochry.

Lowlights

Walking between Ardeonaig and Ardtalnaig then Ardtalnaig to Acharn on the south Loch Tay road, even although the views are wonderful.

Why do you love it?

Variety of scenery and the communities that are along the Way.

History/background

Rob Roy and the Jacobite period.

How challenging?

The route is well waymarked but walkers should also have supporting maps, especially on the extended loop going from Ardtalnaig to Amulree and then on to Aberfeldy. There are several ascents and descents but none of extreme gradient.

Accommodation and transport

The Way passes through interesting communities

where accommodation is plentiful with the one exception being Ardtalnaig (at the time of writing only one B&B) and on the extended loop at Amulree (none at the time of writing). Camping opportunities also exist at all points with the exception of Ardtalnaig and Amulree. Day sections are possible; however, bus links between Drymen, Aberfoyle and Callander, then between Killin, Ardtalnaig and Aberfeldy are limited to a Post Bus.

Best day-walk

Lochearnhead to Killin, Killin to Ardeonaig or Acharn to Aberfeldy.

River Ayr Way (GT)

Louise Kyle, from East Ayrshire Leisure (eastayrshireleisure.com)

Glenbuck Lock to Ayr (source to sea): 44 miles/66 km

Difficulty rating: 2

Average days to complete: 2–7

Waymarking? Yes

Maps: OS Explorer 326, 327, 328, 335

Baggage courier? No

For more details: eastayrshireleisure.com; *The River Ayr Way* by Dale Love

Describe the trail

The River Ayr Way is Scotland's first source-to-sea path, now used by around 150,000 people each year. Experience Ayrshire's most varied and beautiful countryside, enjoy relaxing accommodation, welcoming pubs and award-winning restaurants. The route passes through one of the most interesting river valleys in southern Scotland and, unlike many other long distance routes, can be walked over a weekend. The River Ayr inspired Robert Burns, helped hide William Wallace from English troops and powered the Industrial Revolution. Find out more about some of Ayrshire's most famous worthies on this walk – Wallace, Burns, John Loudoun Macadam and Tibbie Pagan are just a few. Discover more of the rich industrial past of the area and the bloody Covenanting times which led to almost fifty years of strife in the area. The route also has diverse wildlife including otters, badgers, herons, hen harriers and much more.

Autumn on the River Ayr Way. EAST AYRSHIRE LEISURE

The River Ayr Way is Scotland's first source-to-sea path.
EAST AYRSHIRE LEISURE

The trail could be walked over a weekend. EAST AYRSHIRE LEISURE

Highlights

The range of scenery and landscapes, from open moorland to shaded woodland areas, plus the wildlife and history.

Lowlights

Some areas can be quite wet or boggy in the winter due to weather and the rise of the river in wetter months.

Why do you love it?

The range of scenery, wildlife and history is fantastic.

History/background

The River Ayr Way opened in 2006 and is Scotland's first source-to-sea path network. It passes through areas steeped in history with links to many famous Scottish figures including Robert Burns, William Wallace, John Loudoun Macadam and many Covenanters. The route also has a wide range of habitats and diversity of wildlife including otters, badgers, herons, hen harriers and much more.

How challenging?

Some sections are easier than others. The terrain is mostly built path and there are some inclines but nothing too challenging. Signposting is sufficient.

Accommodation and transport

Public transport to Glenbuck can be difficult. The bus route ends at Muirkirk which is about 2 miles from the start of the walk. A local taxi company in Muirkirk can be used and if you are staying along the route, some accommodation providers will arrange a drop off/collection service. There is a range of accommodation – from camping and caravanning to B&Bs and hotels. Car parking is available at Glenbuck. The River Ayr Way can easily be walked in sections.

Best day-walk

Ayr Gorge, a Scottish Wildlife Trust reserve at Failford, is a popular circular walk. The areas around Muirkirk have a rich history and Muirkirk also has a village audio tour. Catrine Voes is East Ayrshire's first nature reserve, and Neolithic cup and ring markings are at nearby Ballochmyle Viaduct. Catrine Ice Cream Parlour is also on this section and is a lovely place for lunch, coffees and suchlike.

Romans and Reivers Route (GT)

Vyv Wood-Gee, the countryside management consultant who helped set up the route

Ae to Hawick: 52 miles/83 km
Difficulty rating: 2
Average days to complete: 3–4
Waymarking? Yes
Maps: OS Landranger 89, 79
Baggage courier? No
For more details: southofscotlandcountrysidetrails.co.uk

Describe the trail

This linear route through the 'debatable lands' just north of the Scottish border follows old Roman roads and some of the trails once used by the notorious thieving Border Reivers. Much of the western half of this route follows forest tracks, or winding quiet lanes. Emerging from the forest at Craik, the character of the trail changes, following grassy former drove roads and farm tracks across rolling hills, with spectacular views across the Borders.

Highlights

Marching in the footsteps of the Romans and standing at the Roman signal station where Dumfries and Galloway meets the Scottish Borders, looking across to the hills on which other beacons were lit in Roman times.

Lowlights

Quite a few stretches of the route are on forest tracks and forest roads, which are easy to follow but hard underfoot. Shops, refreshments and accommodation en route are relatively few and far between.

Why do you love it?

I love exploring how our ancestors traversed the troubled lands, where the Reivers hid their cattle after their midnight raids on unsuspecting farmsteads, having only birds for company, and opportunity to appreciate the diversity of southern Scotland.

History/background

The Romans and Reivers route is part of the 150-mile/250 km South of Scotland Countryside Trails network, a spiderweb of linking routes offering fantastic walking, mountain biking and horse riding in Southern Scotland.

Romans and Reivers is a historic route. VYV WOOD-GEE

The trail follows old Roman roads through the 'debatable lands'.
VYV WOOD-GEE

Walkers enjoy spectacular views across the Borders. VYV WOOD-GEE

How challenging?

The whole route is clearly waymarked throughout, and easy to follow with a map. There is one relatively steep section at Garrowgill, between Moffat and Eskdalemuir, but even that is still on a well-made path. The biggest challenge for walkers is the distance between services, and shortage of cake shops or cafes!

Accommodation and transport

There's plentiful accommodation in Moffat and Hawick, a farmhouse B&B at Craik, Wiltonburn and Eskdalemuir – or Samye Ling Buddhist monastery offers B&B, plus an evening meal if required, at Eskdalemuir. There are regular bus services to Moffat and Eskdalemuir but no public transport linking start/finish, or settlements on the route.

Best day-walk

Craik to Hawick, which offers great variation in character from forest rides and good tracks through enclosed farmland to the little-used hill path above Roberton where you'll have only sheep, cattle and curlews for company. The fantastic stretch at the head of the Dryfe Valley is also good on the section from Moffat to Eskdalemuir, although there's a fair bit on forest road either end.

St Cuthbert's Way (GT)

John Henderson, Walking Support (walkingsupport.co.uk)

Melrose to Lindisfarne (Holy Island): 62.5 miles/100 km

Difficulty rating: 3

Average days to complete: 4–5

Waymarking? Yes

Maps: OS Explorer 338, 339, 340, OL16; Harvey Maps

Baggage courier? Yes

For more details: stcuthbertsway.net

Describe the trail

It runs across the Scottish Borders to the Northumberland coast following in the footsteps of St Cuthbert. Starting from the historic border town of Melrose which lies on the bank of the River Tweed and below the iconic Eildon Hill, this route traverses the Scottish Border countryside before crossing into England and onto the Cheviot Hills. Following a stop in the market town of Wooler the walk soon reaches the Shiellow Hills and the first views of the Northumberland coast and the Holy Island. When the tide permits the walker can enter onto this unique island where early seventh-century saints brought Christianity to northern England.

Highlights

Views from the Eildon Hills, crossing Wideopen Hill, the peace and openness of the walk on the Cheviots, views from Shiellow Hill and the crossing onto the island especially by the Pilgrim's Way (across the sands).

Lowlights

The lack of accommodation directly on the Way in the Harestanes area. This requires an extra 3 miles' walk into Jedburgh or the use of support transport. The tidal times need to be consulted and plans made to get in and out of the Holy Island.

Why do you love it?

The variety of scenery, and the story behind the trail.

History/background

The history relates to St Cuthbert of the seventh century who started his monastic life in Old Melrose (2 miles from Melrose) and ended his life on the Holy Island where he was Bishop of Lindisfarne.

TALKING WALKING – CAMERON MCNEISH

Cameron has been climbing mountains and walking trails for over forty years. He was editor of *The Great Outdoors* magazine for twenty years and now writes, blogs and makes television programmes about Scotland's wild places. He lives with his wife in the Scottish Highlands.

What do you remember about your first multi-day walk?

It was a revelation. I camped high on a beach below Cairn Toul and woke to see reindeer grazing nearby. I then realized that to know a mountain fully, to really connect with the landscape, you have to sleep out on it.

What effect did your first long walk have on you?

It made me want to do more, and meet people who were more experienced in multi-day walking than I was. I joined the Backpackers Club (of which I'm now president) and met some wonderful individuals who greatly influenced me.

How many long distance trails have you done since?

I've honestly lost count. But few of them have been 'official' recognized trails. I tend to make up my own routes and in the past seven years or so I've been creating long distance routes, and walking them, for BBC Scotland television programmes. These include the Sutherland Trail, the Sky Trail, the Hebrides End to End, Scottish Coast to Coast, the Scottish National Trail, the Pilgrims' Trail (from Iona to Portmahomack in Easter Ross) and the Western Way, between the Mull of Galloway and Oban. We have produced books for some of these routes and DVDs for all of them (available from Amazon).

Cameron McNeish.

How much do you obsess over equipment?

I don't. Much of my gear is old, well loved and well used. I think most outdoor gear is over-hyped and over-expensive. I would much rather support small companies run by enthusiasts who make good, specialist lightweight equipment.

What luxury item do you take on a trek, if any?

A dram or two of whisky.

St Cuthbert's Way. BECKY DUNCAN

There are also strong Roman connections with Melrose and the Eildon Hills.

How challenging?

There are some ascents in terms of the Eildon Hills, Wideopen Hill (1,207 ft/368 m) and on the Cheviots around Green Humbleton and Yeavering Bell. The day from Melrose to Harestanes and Wooler onto Lindisfarne can be long for the less experienced walker but equally the sections can be split to remove this challenge.

Accommodation and transport

Accommodation is generally good and plentiful although the cost on the Holy Island is markedly higher. Hostel accommodation is limited to Kirk Yetholm and Wooler and no tents are permitted on the Holy Island. Transport into Melrose is good, but getting away from the Holy Island is very restricted and tide-dependent. Intermediate points have very restricted public transport with the exception of Wooler

Best day-walk

Melrose to Harestanes, or break off at points such as south of St Boswells on the A68. This is a varied section with Eildon Hills and River Tweed walks (and frequent buses on the A68 for connections back to Melrose).

Scottish National Trail

Cameron McNeish (cameronmcneish.wordpress.com), route creator, writer and TV presenter
Kirk Yetholm to Cape Wrath: 470 miles/756 km
Difficulty rating: 5
Average days to complete: 35–40

Waymarking? Three signposts: one at the beginning, one in the middle and one at the end!
Maps: See scottishnationaltrail.org.uk
Baggage courier? No
For more details: walkhighlands.co.uk/scottish-national-trail.shtml

Describe the trail

An end-to-end walk through Scotland. The Scottish National Trail links together a number of long distance routes in Scotland, i.e. St Cuthbert's Way, the Southern Uplands Way, the West Highland Way, the Rob Roy Way and many others to create a long and challenging route through Scotland. The northern sections of the route are particularly demanding.

Highlights

The section between Kintail and Cape Wrath.

Lowlights

Inevitably, on a long walk like this there will be several sections where the walker will be on tarmac but I have tried very hard to keep this to a minimum. A couple of days follow canal towpaths between Edinburgh and Glasgow and while some will find that comparatively boring others will be inspired by the relaxed walking it offers.

Why do you love it?

It traverses the entire country of Scotland offering an incomparable diversity of landscape.

History/background

There is history around every corner, from the tales of reiving (13th–17th century raiders along the Anglo-Scottish border) in the Border's debatable lands to the highland clearances in the north to

the immense feat of engineering that is the Falkirk Wheel.

How challenging?

It is extremely challenging. Most people tackle it in sections, although a team of fell runners in a relay has run it over a few days.

Accommodation and transport

There's plenty of accommodation in the southern sections but once past the Great Glen accommodation and transport are scarce.

Best day-walk

Probably the section into Sandwood Bay in Sutherland.

Southern Upland Way (GT)

Alan Castle, author of *The Southern Upland Way*

Portpatrick to Cockburnspath: 212 miles/341 km

Difficulty rating: 4

Average days to complete: 13–15

Waymarking? Yes

Maps: OS Landranger 82, 76, 77, 71, 78, 79, 73, 74, 67

Baggage courier? Yes

For more details: southernuplandway.gov.uk; southernuplandwayholidays.com

Describe the trail

Scotland's Coast to Coast, providing a succession of dramatic landscapes coupled with a wide selection of interesting places to visit. As the Way cuts across the grain of southern Scotland many different landscapes are unveiled: coastal cliffs, high moorland, rolling hills, remote mountains, forests, lochs, majestic rivers and sylvan valleys abounding in wildlife. The Way passes through regions that are exceedingly rich in archaeological and historical associations, from prehistoric standing stones to monuments commemorating the Killing Times of the seventeenth-century Covenanters.

Highlights

Too many to list. Scenically, the remote and beautiful Galloway Hills, the dramatic Loch Trool, the Annandale Valley, the shores of St Mary's Loch, the tranquil River Tweed, the triplet of the Eildon Hills and the wild and lonely Lammermuir Hills. Amongst the tourist attractions of particular interest are Castle Kennedy Gardens, the Lead Mining Museum at Warnlochhead, Traquair House, Melrose Abbey and Thirlestane Castle and Gardens.

Lowlights

A false impression of the route is that there are huge tracts of trail through plantations of sitka spruce. Although the trail does pass through several plantations, the majority of the route is on open hillside or pleasant rural valleys.

Why do you love it?

The satisfaction that comes from walking from coast to coast. The sheer variety and grandeur of the scenery and the amazing history of the Border region that unfolds across the route.

History/background

This trail is steeped in history. New Luce, encountered on the second day, is where the story of the Covenanters and the Killing Times starts to unfold. Loch Trool is the site of one of Robert the Bruce's victories over the English in 1307. At Sanquar it's possible to post a letter from Britain's oldest Post Office, dating from 1763. Warnlochhead is Britain's highest village and home to the Museum of Scottish Lead Mining. Tibbie Shiels Inn on the shores of St Mary's Loch is one of the most famous old hostelries in Scotland and was the haunt of James Hogg, the Ettrick Shepherd Poet. Melrose has its ancient Abbey ruins, formal gardens and links to Sir Walter Scott.

How challenging?

At 212 miles this is not the most beginner-friendly National Trail in Scotland. The waymarking is good but the ability to use a map and compass or GPS is required if cloud blows in on some of the upland sections. Some B&Bs provide pickup facilities to shorten the distance that has to be walked in a day.

Accommodation and transport

Accommodation is available throughout, but in some sections it's limited. There are two consecutive long sections but B&Bs provide pickup facilities so these sections can be spread over three days. Carrying a tent or bivvy bag will allow greater freedom and there are six bothies on or very close to the route. Like most rural areas public transport is not readily available and therefore day walks would usually need to be circular routes from a parked car.

Best day-walk

The 21-mile section from Beattock (Moffat) to Tibbie Shiels Inn (St Mary's Loch). The route skirts the south of Moffat over three major rivers, Evan Water, River Annan and Moffat Water. Good views of Moffat and the Annanwater Valley are followed by a delightful deciduous wood. A high-level ridge route provides excellent views to Hart Fell and the route then crosses Ettrick Head and finally descends to St Mary's Loch and Tibbie Shiels Inn.

Three Lochs Way (GT)

John and Anne Urquhart, authors of *The Three Lochs Way* (threelochsway.co.uk)
Balloch to Inveruglas: 34 miles/55 km
Difficulty rating: 2

Arrochar Alps, Three Lochs Way.
JOHN AND ANNE URQUHART

Walkers above Arrochar on the Three Lochs Way. JOHN AND ANNE URQUHART

Average days to complete: 3

Waymarking? Yes

Maps: It will be on OS maps soon. OS Explorer 347 and 364; Landranger 56

Baggage courier? No

For more details: threelochsway.co.uk

Describe the trail

The Walking Gateway is to Argyll and Bute, and a Great Trail links Loch Lomond, the Gareloch and Loch Long. Gentle landscapes are gradually replaced by the scenic drama of mountain, crag and loch as the Three Lochs Way crosses the Highland Boundary Fault and heads towards the mountains of the Southern Highlands. With Loch Lomond, the Gareloch and Loch Long as scenic backdrops, the Three Lochs Way takes you on a fascinating journey through place and time, linking a necklace of communities along the Clyde Sea Lochs fringe of Scotland's first National Park. With the West Highland railway never far away, it offers plenty of options for shorter day walks.

Highlights

Stoneymolan Road, a delightful ancient route linking Balloch and Cardross. The stunning view over Loch Lomond when you cross the Highland Boundary Fault at Goukhill Muir. Great views north of Garelochhead over Loch Long to the knobbly skyline of 'Argyll's Bowling Green' and the 'Arrochar Alps'. The craggy Cobbler, the area's finest mountain and a must-climb Corbett.

Delightful Glen Loin Woodlands, a Site of Special Scientific Interest and home to red squirrels.

Lowlights

Some might consider the Loch Lomond Shores commercial development to be unattractive and parts of the armed forces training area section north of Garelochhead can be a bit boring. Pylons and power lines can detract from views in some places.

Why do you love it?

Its variety and interest – it has something for everybody.

History/background

Interesting Highland boundary geology, clan battles, a World War 1 spy story, the Hill House … too much to describe here. See the route's guide-book and website.

How challenging?

It's beginner-friendly and doesn't have a lot of serious ascent or descent. No boggy terrain, although the section just south of Arrochar can be wet underfoot. Garelochhead to Arrochar is a longer section without B&B accommodation. Excellent signposting and a free route app make navigation easy.

Accommodation and transport

Satisfactory wild camping sites are rare and walkers are recommended to stay at B&Bs. Options for B&B accommodation are plentiful in the south – not so much further north, although Arrochar and Tarbet have plenty. There's no accommodation at Inveruglas. The route parallels West Highland Railway so transport options are plentiful. It can be completed without a tent/bivvy bag and it's a walk that can easily be done in sections/day walks.

Best day-walk

The most spectacular is from Glen Douglas to Arrochar, although Glen Loin is very scenic too as is Balloch to Helensburgh.

West Highland Way (GT)

Anthony Burton, author of *West Highland Way*

Milngavie to Fort William: 94.5 miles/152 km

Difficulty rating: 4

Average days to complete: 7

Waymarking? Yes

Maps: OS (1:50,000) 41, 50, 56, 57, 64; Harvey Maps; Footprint Maps

Baggage courier? Yes

For more details: west-highland-way.co.uk

Describe the trail

A walk that takes in some of the most dramatic scenery of the Western Highlands. The trail begins comparatively gently with a walk up the eastern side of Loch Lomond, and then heads up Glen Falloch, over the fringes of Rannoch Moor to the mountains surrounding Glencoe. The final section consists of two climbs over mountain ridges before heading down Glen Nevis.

Highlights

There are two spectacular climbs, one out of Glencoe up the Devil's Staircase, the other from Kinlochleven down to Glen Nevis.

Lowlights

It is a little disappointing to find the end of the walk is a trudge down a dull road into Fort William – but it's only short.

Why do you love it?

Simple – if you love mountain scenery then you'll love this walk.

History/background

In part the way follows the line of General Wade's military road of the eighteenth century and Glencoe is famous for the massacre.

How challenging?

The challenging sections are the two climbs of nearly 2,000 ft/609 m each.

Accommodation and transport

Transport to either end is excellent – both are served by train and road – in between the situation is more variable. Accommodation generally isn't a problem.

Best day-walk

The walk from Glencoe to Kinlochleven – you can get a bus back to the start.

West Island Way (GT)

Keith Sharp, long distance walker

Kilchattan Bay to Port Bannatyne, Isle of Bute: 30 miles/48 km

Difficulty rating: 2

Average days to complete: 2

Waymarking? Yes

Maps: OS Landranger 63 or OS Explorer 362

Baggage courier? Not necessary

For more details: visitbute.com

Describe the trail

An excellent way to see the varied landscapes of the beautiful island of Bute. The trail offers a pleasant way of exploring the isle in two days and shows the contrasting landscapes. The southern half of the island has a lowland feel with most of the land being used for arable farming and cattle grazing. The northern half has a more rugged and remote feel with less farming and development. At numerous points along the trail there are great views of the surrounding Clyde coastline and islands such as Arran and Cumbrae.

Highlights

The highlight of the southern half of the trail is returning to Kilchattan Bay and diverting to the summit of Suidhe Chatain, which gives great views on a clear day. Similarly in the northern half of the trail diverting to the summit of Windy Hill also gives great views. The beach walk along Stravannan Bay at Bute Golf Club is also very pleasant.

Lowlights

There are a couple of sections of path in the southern half of the trail that are damaged and can be difficult to cross. Just after the start of the trail,

The West Island Way shows off the varied landscapes of the island of Bute. BECKY DUNCAN

south of Kilchattan Bay, the path has been damaged by coastal erosion and has some mild scrambles. The section from the B881 to Loch Fad can be very muddy and boggy due to extensive cattle grazing. The trail has been redirected across the hillside to Kames Hill and Edinbeg Hill before descending to Port Bannatyne and depending on the vintage of your OS maps this change may not be shown. The waymarking on the hillside is not the best, with the gaps between markers being slightly too long. However the route change does allow for a diversion to the summit of Windy Hill, the highest point on the island, which has great views to Arran.

Why do you love it?
I love that the trail captures the diverse nature of Bute, from the urban small town of Rothesay, to the lowland agriculture of the southern half of the trail, to the more remote forestry and hillsides of the northern half of the trail. Given that Bute is such a small island, you're never far from the sea, so the trail gives many opportunities for views across the Clyde to the mainland and to the other islands.

History/background
The ruins of St Blane's Church and Monastery near the southernmost point of the trail are worth a visit if you are interested in early Christianity in Scotland: historic-scotland.gov.uk.

How challenging?
The trail is not very difficult as long as you are comfortable with day walks of 12–15 miles (20–25 km). You could spread the trail over more days, but transport arrangements would be more complex. If you book accommodation in Rothesay the trail can easily be completed over two days carrying only day packs.

Accommodation and transport
If you are comfortable walking 12–15 miles (20–25 km) in a day the trail can be broken into two days with day one finishing in Rothesay, which has a variety of accommodation. It's not the sort of trail for wild camping – there is a campsite in Rothesay. An advantage of the West Island Way is that it's accessible without a car from across the UK. Regular trains run from Glasgow Central Station to Weymss Bay where they connect with the ferry to Rothesay.

There is a bus service from Rothesay to the start of the trail at Kilchattan Bay and from the end of the trail in Port Bannatyne back to Rothesay. Taxis are also available on the island.

Best day-walk
The northern half of the trail, starting in Rothesay and continuing down the B875 to Ettrick Bay, a beautiful location that has a small cafe with great views where you can stop for morning coffee or lunch before retracing your steps to where the trail turns north towards Glenmore.

Northern Scotland

Cape Wrath Trail
Iain Harper, author of *The Cape Wrath Trail*
Fort William to Cape Wrath: 230 miles/370 km
Difficulty rating: 5
Average days to complete: 17–21
Waymarking? No
Maps: Harvey Cape Wrath Trail North and South Maps are highly recommended
Baggage courier? Yes
For more details: capewrathtrailguide.org; capewrathtrail.co.uk

Describe the trail
A tough trail across some of the wildest mountain country the UK has to offer. The Cape Wrath Trail is not an officially recognized UK National Trail. In truth, it is not really a trail at all, more a jigsaw of routes between Fort William and the most north-westerly point of the UK, to be assembled according to your preferences. Perhaps because of this unique flexibility and lack of formal status, it has become highly regarded by many backpackers. Cameron McNeish neatly summarizes the trail: 'It's the sort of long distance route that most keen walkers dream of. A long tough trek through some of the most majestic, remote and stunningly beautiful landscape you could dare imagine. The Cape Wrath Trail is a challenging and often remote route which could be described as the hardest long distance backpacking route in the UK.'

Highlights
The trail takes you to some of Scotland's finest

The Cape Wrath Trail is generally considered to be Britain's remotest trek. IAIN HARPER

'It's the sort of long distance route that most keen walkers dream of,' says Cameron McNeish. IAIN HARPER

country via Morar, Knoydart, Torridon and Assynt, winding through beautiful glens, lochs and mountains. It traditionally begins in Fort William and winds across Argdour towards Glenfinnan taking in the gloriously remote rough bounds of Knoydart, before striking north to Shiel Bridge, Strathcarron, Kinlochewe and Inverlael, near Ullapool. A popular alternative leaves Fort William via the Great Glen Way, turning north to cut across Glen Garry and Glen Shiel, rejoining the main route at Morvich. North of the Ullapool road, the route turns inland to Oykel Bridge before heading towards Glencoul via Inchnadamph and the majestic Ben More. Then, below the shadows of Arkle and Foinaven, the final stretch passes Rhiconich and on to the farthest west coast and over the moors to Sandwood Bay and the Cape Wrath lighthouse.

Lowlights

It's a tough test for anyone and you'll brave remote country, rugged terrain, rain, wind, midges, bog and tricky river crossings. Whatever the time of year, it will test the limits of your physical and mental endurance. But dark, boggy moments are quickly forgotten amidst a solitude and beauty rarely found in modern life.

Why do you love it?

Because of its difficulty and the lack of amenities, the Cape Wrath Trail has resolutely defied the commercialization that has come to other trails in the Highlands, such as the West Highland Way. This footpath has an intriguing capacity to draw people into some of the most wild and remote places Scotland has to offer. There can be few other long distance paths with such an inspiring finale as the Cape itself – and so aptly named. There is also something in the challenge of traversing such a vast, primal and largely unspoilt tract of land. Its beauty lies in its freedom. You'll find few signposts

TALKING WALKING – RONALD TURNBULL

To avoid having to get a proper job, Ronald has funded his idle lifestyle by writing the award-winning *Granite & Grit*, a walker's guide to the UK's mountain rocks, and twenty-nine other books. He enjoys multi-day treks through the Highlands and along UK coastlines, and has made twenty-one different coast-to-coast crossings of the UK. His website ronaldturnbull.co.uk includes accounts of the John Muir Trail, a hike in the Appalachians, and the Spanish 3000s.

What do you remember about your first multi-day walk?

Oh my word. It was a two-day Sea Cadet Force exercise (aged fourteen) in the Black Mountains. I remember the dreadful 'pup tent' with wooden poles and canvas sides, very heavy, very small, rather damp, very uncomfortable. We got a half-ration of rum at the end and learnt some interesting songs.

What effect did your first long walk have on you?

What effect? I got wet, tired, and blistered. What effect?! A mix of pride and misery.

Which is your all-time favourite trek?

Fort William to Cape Wrath – big beautiful mountains all the way. John Muir Trail – outstanding wilderness and scenery, easy path, very pleasant Americans (we didn't meet any bears). Least favourite: Southern Upland Way. Too many forest roads.

What is it about long distance walks that appeals to you?

I guess it must be the tiredness, the wetness and the misery.

Ronald Turnbull.

How much do you obsess over equipment?

Not until it breaks. Then a bit of string will fix it.

What luxury item do you take on a trek, if any?

Is a spoon a luxury? I carry a spoon, even though the corner of the compass works almost as well.

What advice do you have for fellow long distance walkers?

Start early. Walk slowly. Stop fairly early. And read *The Book of the Bivvy* (Cicerone, 2007).

---

around here. This one's for true connoisseurs of the wild lands, and it's down to you.

History/background

The trail has become part of the International Appalachian Trail (IAT), a backpacking trail running from the northern end of the Appalachian Trail in Maine, USA, through New Brunswick, to the Gaspé Peninsula of Quebec, Canada, after which it extends to Nova Scotia, Prince Edward Island, Newfoundland and Labrador. Geological evidence shows that the Appalachian Mountains and the mountains of Western Europe and North Africa are parts of the former Central Pangean Mountains, made when minor supercontinents collided to form the supercontinent Pangaea more than 250 million years ago. With the break-up of Pangaea, sections of the former range remained with the continents as they drifted to their present locations.

How challenging?

The Cape Wrath Trail is regarded as the toughest long distance backpacking trail in Britain. It crosses remote, sparsely populated, potentially dangerous mountain country. There is no waymarking and often not even any clear paths, only bogs and leg-sapping terrain. Limited resupply points require self-sufficiency for much of the journey and there will be stretches during which you'll need to carry many days' supplies. This is absolutely not a route for beginners or those unfamiliar with remote, rugged mountain areas.

Accommodation and transport

The remoteness means there are a limited number of points at which you can join or escape. Strathcarron is on the Inverness to Kyle of Loch Ailsh (Skye) train line. For information about train travel in Scotland see: scotrail.co.uk. Shiel Bridge, Kinlochewe, Dundonnell, Ullapool, Inchnadamph, Rhiconich, Kinlochbervie and Durness all have bus services. There is generally not a great deal of accommodation and availability is much dependent on the time of year. It's a good idea to book in advance, and some of the more remote accommodation closes outside peak season. Whilst it's technically possible to walk the route without carrying a tent, using a combination of bothies and other accommodation, it's not prudent to do so.

Best day-walk

If you want a real taste of the Cape Wrath Trail, it's hard to beat striking out from Glenfinnan (a short train ride from Fort William) towards the rough bounds of Knoydart. An overnight stop can be taken at A'Chuil or Barisdale bothies before continuing onwards to Inverie and a well-deserved pint at The Old Forge, Britain's remotest pub. A ferry will then take you to Mallaig, where a train will return you to Fort William.

Cateran Trail (GT)

John Henderson, Walking Support (walkingsupport.co.uk)

Circular route from Blairgowrie: 64 miles/103 km

Difficulty rating: 3

Average days to complete: 5

Waymarking? Yes

Maps: OS Landranger 43, 44, 53; Explorer 381, 387, 388; Footprint Maps

Baggage courier? Yes (walkingsupport.co.uk)

For more details: walkthecaterantrail.com

'This one's for true connoisseurs of the wild lands.' IAIN HARPER

Describe the trail

Scenic circular footpath in the heart of Scotland. This is a walking route full of breathtaking landscapes with a wide range of changing terrain. Situated on the southern end of the Highlands in the heart of Perthshire and the Angus Glens, it provides the walker with a true feel of Scottish landscape and offers a glimpse of the lifestyle of the Caterans in the fifteenth to seventeenth centuries.

Highlights

Enochdhu to the Spittal of Glenshee passing by the Upper Lunch Hut; Little Forter to Kirkton of Glenisla; Glenshee to Little Forter via Loch Beanie, if this route option is chosen.

The ascent to the Upper Lunch Hut, Cateran Trail. JOHN HENDERSON

The Cateran Trail is a scenic circular footpath in the heart of Scotland. BECKY DUNCAN

Lowlights

The road sections between Cray and Forter or Cray and Brewlands Bridge (if either of these options are taken on the section between Spittal of Glenshee and Kirkton of Glenisla). The reverse leg of the walk on the Blairgowrie to Bridge of Cally section (if using the longer route section between Alyth and Blairgowrie).

The route evokes the history of the Caterans and the Jacobite uprising. BECKY DUNCAN

Why do you love it?

For the fact it's a circular walk and the start and end points are the same. The variation in the scenery, with some great Highland landscapes, is wonderful too.

History/background

The route evokes the history of the Caterans and the association with the many cattle drove roads of the fifteenth to seventeenth century. There are also links with the Jacobite uprising.

How challenging?

This is a straightforward, waymarked route. If the Loch Beanie option is taken, this is in part over rougher ground and is only recommended for those who are prepared to walk over open hillside terrain.

Accommodation and transport

Accommodation is plentiful at Blairgowrie and Alyth but is more restricted at points, such as Kirkmichael, Spittal of Glenshee and Kirkton of Glenisla. Some accommodation providers will offer a four- to five-night stay with transport to and from each section. Transport runs regularly between Blairgowrie and Alyth and to the main cities of Dundee and Perth, but transport on all other sections is extremely limited.

Best day-walk

Kirkmichael to Spittal of Glenshee or Spittal of Glenshee to Kirkton of Glenisla.

Dava Way (GT)

David Binney, davaway.org.uk
Grantown to Forres: 24 miles/38 km
Difficulty rating: 2
Average days to complete: 1
Waymarking? Yes
Maps: See davaway.org.uk for map downloads
Baggage courier? Yes
For more details: davaway.org.uk

Describe the trail

The Dava Way is a varied route, mostly following an old railway line, from the Cairngorm National Park to the Moray Firth coast crossing Dava Moor. This is the only off-road route linking Speyside and the Moray coast. In only 24 miles the route traverses very varied habitats, from high moorland through forest glades, and crossing farmland, with views from the high points across much of Scotland north of the Moray Firth.

Highlights

Apart from the views and nature, there are eye-catching carvings. The Halfway Hut provides shelter from the elements. These and many more features are explained on the numerous discrete waypoint boards along the route.

Lowlights

Railway walks follow gentle gradients and curves. There are few unexpected, round the corner moments, where new landscapes suddenly appear.

Why do you love it?

Radio Scotland's outdoors programme described it as, 'the best long distance walk for families in Scotland'. We think it is also a great off-road cycle route for trail bikes (it's too rough for road bikes).

History/background

The route follows the line of the original Highland Railway link to Inverness. Railway stories and others are retold in the *Dava Way Companion*.

How challenging?

Except for a short stretch through woodland at the northern end, there is nothing seriously steep. The path is dry shod in normal conditions. Signposting is considered good but it's always wise to watch out for the signs when chatting!

Accommodation and transport

There's varied accommodation at the start/finish in Grantown and Forres but almost nothing along the route. Wild camping is possible mid-way. The walk breaks easily into three sections, but there is no public transport so cars/taxis would be needed.

Best day-walk

For most, it is a one-day walk!

Great Glen Way (GT)

Sandra Bardwell, Great Glen resident and co-author of *Great Glen Way*

Fort William to Inverness: 77.5 miles/125 km
Difficulty rating: 3 (Main Route) 4 (High Route)
Average days to complete: 6
Waymarking? Yes
Maps: OS (1:50,000) 41, 34, 26, but both Footprint

The Great Glen Way: 'A magnificent scenic traverse of Scotland's Great Glen.' rucsacs.com

Maps (1:45,000), and Harvey Maps (1:40,000) are waterproof and cheaper. At time of publication, the newer High Route was not yet marked on maps, but route info can be found at outdoorhighlands.co.uk
Baggage courier? Yes
For more details: greatglenway.com; rucsacs.com

Describe the trail

A magnificent scenic traverse of Scotland's Great Glen. The Way follows the Caledonian Canal and traverses slopes above Loch Oich and the famous Loch Ness. It also passes Ben Nevis, Britain's highest mountain and includes sections along a historic railway line, forest tracks and paths and minor roads. Between Fort Augustus and Drumnadrochit there's a choice between Low and High Routes, the latter being more strenuous and more scenic.

Highlights

The High Route between Invermoriston and Drumnadrochit with spectacular views over Loch Ness, and distant lochs and mountains. Reaching the end at Inverness Castle with a view far down the Great Glen.

Lowlights

The roadside pavement path through Drumnadrochit.

Why do you love it?

The views, the real sense of achievement from walking through the Great Glen, and the great variety of historical features.

History/background

The Caledonian Canal and its boat traffic working the locks is a constant source of interest; Cromwell's Fort (Fort William) at the beginning and Inverness Castle at the end; between the two are other castles, some disused railway and prehistoric forts.

How challenging?

Its terrain is mostly sound underfoot, even in the wet, on towpaths, forest tracks, moorland paths and minor roads. Its difficulty is mainly moderate, apart from the challenge of the 20-mile (32 km) section (read on for more on this). It is beginner-friendly by the Low Route, again only if you split the last section. Altitude gain by the Low Route is about 4,560 ft/1,400 m, and by the High Route approximately 6,560 ft/2,000 m. The Drumnadrochit–Inverness section is 20 miles (32 km), but can be split at Blackfold using a private transfer or by camping at Abriachan. Some B&B hosts in Drumnadrochit offer a two-night package including Blackfold pickup and drop off.

Accommodation and transport

There are plenty of options in most towns and villages en route, and camping is not necessary except if relying on Abriachan. The route can readily be completed in sections using the good bus service through Great Glen from Fort William to Inverness. Both ends of the route are served by mainline rail.

Best day-walk

Invermoriston to Drumnadrochit by the High Route for the most spectacular and varied views, including distant mountains on a clear day.

Formartine and Buchan Way (GT)

Andrew Lafferty, long distance walker

Aberdeen to Peterhead/Fraserburgh: 56 miles/87 km

Difficulty rating: 1

Average days to complete: 4

Waymarking? Yes

Maps: There is one supplied by Walk Highlands (see below)

Baggage courier? No

For more details: walkhighlands.co.uk

Describe the trail

Easygoing walk along a cycle route that used to be a railway line. A stroll into the Aberdeenshire countryside, following the old Formartine and Buchan line. Plenty of old railway features still exist, such as old stations, mileage signs, overhead stone bridges and railway worker huts providing shelter en route.

Highlights

Villages to visit between stages providing public transport (the route never strays too far), shelter huts, country views, abandoned houses, ruins.

Lowlights

It can be a little boring in places, where there are no views or features. Also you have to get out of the way for bikes that pass every so often.

Why do you love it?

It's certainly worth a walk once.

History/background

There's the history of the railway line of course.

How challenging?

It's beginner-friendly, very flat, with not many ascents or descents. There are occasional boggy areas after rain but I have heard parts of the route have been upgraded since I walked it. There's plenty of signposting at the beginning and end of each stage (between villages), but not many signposts on the actual route as it's not required. It's just a case of following the cycle path, pretty much in a straight line.

The Moray Coast Trail has some wonderfully varied coastal walking.
SANDRA BARDWELL

The Moray Coast Trail is great for spotting seabirds and bottlenose dolphins. SANDRA BARDWELL

Accommodation and transport

I'm not sure about accommodation as I didn't use any, I simply travelled back to Aberdeen by bus at the end of each day's walk. I know there are B&Bs/hotels in Peterhead, Fraserburgh, Ellon and Strichen. It's not great for wild camping (although it could be done) as it's mostly farmland and there are not many campsites en route either. It's definitely a walk that can easily be done in sections/day walks. Public transport links are good everywhere except for Maud.

Best day-walk

Maud to Fraserburgh: start at the old Maud Station, which is still intact including its splitting platform, pass through the old village of Strichen to arrive at the coast to see Fraserburgh Beach in all its glory, taking in the great views over Fraserburgh and the surrounding countryside from the top of the sand dunes (this involves a climb). You could even chill out on the beach for the rest of the day (weather permitting!).

Moray Coast Trail (GT)

Sandra Bardwell, author of *The Moray Coast Trail*
Forres to Cullen: 44 miles/70 km
Difficulty rating: 2
Average days to complete: 3–4
Waymarking? Yes
Maps: OS (1:50,000) 27, 28, 29
Baggage courier? No
For more details: morayways.org.uk

Describe the trail

Wonderfully varied coastal walking. The route opens up a little-known part of Scotland's north-east coast. It offers wide sea views, and passes many historical features. It's a great walk for spotting sea-birds and bottlenose dolphins.

Highlights

Wide expanses of Lossiemouth Beach; fascinating wildlife at Spey Bay, especially bottlenose dolphins; the cliffs between Findochty and Cullen, including the famous Bow Fiddle Rock.

Lowlights

Aircraft noise at Lossiemouth; the MOD firing range (intermittently); roads through Buckie.

Why do you love it?

Almost continuous wide sea views, with a largely unspoiled coastline.

History/background

Fishing heritage (from the seventeenth century); old railways (Great North of Scotland, Highland).

How challenging?

Beginner-friendly, assuming reasonable stamina, mainly on level or gently undulating terrain; some boggy bits possible through forests; one section of the four-day itinerary is 16 miles (26 km) from Lossiemouth to Buckie but this could be split further. The terrain is a mixture of paths, minor roads, forest tracks and sandy beaches; the way-marking is good.

Accommodation and transport

Accommodation is adequate at each end and also

The Skye Trail traverses the full length of the Isle, 'taking in some of the most breathtaking scenery anywhere in the world'.
STUART W. GREIG

at Buckie, with less choice elsewhere. Bunkhouses are very rare, but there are some campsites. Good public transport serves the start and finish and local buses serve most places in between, so day walks are possible.

Best day-walk

Either Buckie to Cullen with all the best features of the trail within 7 miles, or Lossiemouth to Buckie – a long beach, wildlife and historic interest spread over 16 miles.

Skye Trail

Stuart W. Greig (@LoneWalkerUK, lonewalker.net)
Duntulm to Armadale: 107 miles/171 km
Difficulty rating: 3
Average days to complete: 8
Waymarking? No
Maps: OS Landranger 23, 32, 33; Harvey Maps
Baggage courier? No
For more details: skyetrail.org.uk; *A Long Walk on the Isle of Skye* by David Paterson

Describe the trail

An exploration of the stunning landscape of Skye, without the need for ropes and pitons. The Skye Trail traverses the full length of Scotland's mystical isle, taking in some of the most breathtaking scenery anywhere in the world, from the iconic pinnacle of the Old Man of Storr to the rugged mountain range

of the Black Cuillins. Walk beside beautiful coral beaches and explore long abandoned settlements. Often using rarely walked paths, the trail takes a mostly low-level route through valleys and over-passes, running beside the coast to give the walker a taste of almost every terrain on the island.

Highlights

There are so many. At the southern end there is Camsunary Bay, a remote pebble beach with a wide green pasture behind. The views from here will live with you for a long time, almost completely sur-rounded by high mountains with the azure sea at your feet – you will want to stay. The nearby bothy makes this a possibility too. In the north, the Old Man of Storr is one of the highlights of Skye and the trail walks beneath it and then up and around it, giving you wonderful views of this iconic rock needle from all angles.

Lowlights

If you love meeting fellow walkers on a trail then this is not the walk for you. There will be the occa-sional encounter with day-walkers on the same path, but many days are wild and remote, using little-walked paths; self-reliance and good naviga-tion skills are essential. Not being able to walk into a pub/B&B/hotel at the end of the day may be a logistical headache for anyone not prepared to wild camp.

Why do you love it?

As a long distance walker, the trail's main appeal lies in its scenery and environment, which is truly special. In good weather there is nowhere in the world that can compare to Skye. The trail is still relatively unknown and therefore quiet, outside the usual tourist hotspots. The remote sections are unlike anything you will have encountered on a National Trail and will appeal to those who enjoy rough walking across testing terrain with no marked path.

History/background

The Scottish clearances are one of the most shameful periods of our nation's history; thousands of families, forcibly evicted from their homes and shipped off to the New World, so the land they occupied could be more profitably grazed by sheep. The Skye Trail passes through some of these old settlements, giving a tiny glimpse into the tough life they must have led in the midst of this glorious landscape.

How challenging?

The trail, despite its location, is mostly low level, walking between the high hills rather than over them. There are options on most days to go high should you wish and the Trotternish Ridge is a 16-mile day with no facilities, including a calf–busting 5,000 ft/1,524 m of ascent. Overall, this walk is not particularly physically challenging, but many sections include no paths and no way-markers, so the ability to navigate independently and make sensible decisions about terrain selection are vital.

Accommodation and transport

Most days will end in a village or settlement that offers accommodation, but there are a couple that don't and walkers will need to go off-route to a bus stop to reach a town. Hitchhiking is a possibility on Skye as locals are very friendly and will often stop to offer a walker a lift. It's that sort of place. Public transport is surprisingly good in that it reaches remote parts of the island, but it's not always very frequent, so planning is needed.

Best day-walk

If high-level ridge walks are your favoured exercise then the day between the Storr and the Quiraing will be heaven on earth. Climbing up to meet the Old Man of Storr, a gigantic rock pinnacle soaring over the path, is incredible. There follows a long, open ridge with incredible views, culminating in your arrival at the Quiraing, another splendid formation of rock pinnacles and broken hills.

Speyside Way (GT)

Alan Castle, author of *The Speyside Way*
Aviemore to Buckie: 66 miles/106 km
Difficulty rating: 2
Average days to complete: 4–5
Waymarking? Yes
Maps: OS Explorer 403, 418, 419, 424; Harvey Maps; Footprint Maps
Baggage courier? Yes
For more details: speysideway.org

Describe the trail

The beautiful Spey Valley, wildlife and whisky. Speyside is undoubtedly one of the most beautiful areas of Scotland, a diverse landscape of mountain heath and moorland, mixed deciduous woodland, conifer plantations, wide river valleys and rich alluvial farmland. Varied wildlife, a heritage railway and whisky distilleries add interesting diversions along the trail.

Highlights

Naturalists will no doubt enjoy the Abernethy Forest and take the half-mile detour to the RSPB Osprey Centre at Loch Garten. Whisky connoisseurs will want to visit one or more of the distilleries that are on or close to the route, whilst steam train enthusiasts will want to join a train at either Aviemore or Boat of Garten. All will enjoy the scenery of the Spey Valley and Moray coast.

Lowlights

Between Cromdale and Ballindalloch Station there is a fair amount of ascent and descent, the trail constantly changes direction and there are many squeeze stiles to negotiate. However, the scenery as you climb above the Spey Valley is ample recompense.

Why do you love it?

The sheer diversity of landscape and wildlife. The availability of other routes that link with the Speyside Way including the Badenoch Way, Dava Way and Moray Coast Path (all described in the book), allowing the walker to tailor a trip to suit both their experience and time available.

History/background

The Spey Valley witnessed the birth of legal whisky distilling and several famous distilleries that are open to the public are on, or close to, the Speyside Way.

How challenging?

The main route is ideal for less experienced trail walkers. It's very well waymarked and there are plenty of places providing food and accommodation. Ascent is a modest 2,600 ft/792 m on the entire route. The 15-mile/19-km Tomintoul Spur from Tomintoul which joins the main route of the Speyside Way at Ballindalloch Station has more ascent and descent and is over impressive but wilder terrain.

Accommodation and transport

Accommodation along the Speyside Way is plentiful. Backpackers are provided with a number of simple, basic but free sites along the trail. Public transport is available along the Spey Valley so day walks are possible.

Best day-walk

Difficult to choose. The 10-mile (16-km) section from Boat of Garten to Grantown-on-Spey provides gentle walking through the Abernethy Forest National Nature Reserve and the Anagach Woods, affording the chance to observe osprey, capercaillie and goldeneye. The Srathspey Steam Railway is encountered at Boat of Garten. The small, tranquil village of Nethy Bridge is passed on the route to the major settlement of Grantown-on-Spey. Very different scenery is encountered on the 10-mile (16 km) section from Fochabers to Buckie, which follows the Spey for its last 5 miles through woodland and yellow broom until it emerges at Spey Bay, passing the small harbour of Portgordon to the terminus of the Way at Buckpool Harbour in Buckie.

John O'Groats to Land's End

Brian Smailes, author of *John O'Groats to Land's End*

John O'Groats to Land's End/Land's End to John O'Groats: 910 miles/1,465 km (by road)

Difficulty rating: 5, it's very tough

Average days to complete: 37

Waymarking? No

Maps: The route isn't marked on maps because it isn't a set route. Part of the fun of the challenge is devising your own route. Many people link National Trails, such as South West Coast Path, Cotswold Way, Severn Way, Limestone Way, Pennine Way, West Highland Way, Great Glen Way, or similar

Baggage courier? Outdoorchallengeevents.co.uk run the only guided and supported walk including a vehicle carrying your bags, all food and accommodation.

For more details: landsend-johnogroats-assoc. com; landsendjohnogroats.info

Describe the trail

A fantastic, never to be forgotten, ultimate challenge. Some 910 miles on road but also over grass/paths. A chance to see the country from top to bottom. Magnificent scenery and a chance to meet many remarkable people en route.

Highlights

Walking through Scotland, Devon and Cornwall and over the Severn Bridge. A chance to walk through the three counties from top to bottom!

Lowlights

Blisters on the feet but it is a challenge to try to prevent them. Walking the section through the Midlands between Hereford and Preston.

Why do you love it?

Once you have done it you are a changed person. A short walk is 200 miles after this! It takes a long time to sink in that you have done it. I also love the quietness and gradual progression of getting nearer to your goal and finishing the walk.

History/background

Some famous people have walked this including Dr Barbara Moor and Ian Botham.

How challenging?

Signposting is good. It's hilly in Scotland in parts and in Devon and Cornwall but not too bad elsewhere. Not boggy anywhere.

Accommodation and transport

You need accommodation, which can be expensive for B&Bs, but camping is a cheap alternative with a lightweight tent.

Best day-walk

Walking over the Black Isle bridges and down towards Inverness is good, as is the scenery through Hereford and the Severn Bridge. The best days are through central Scotland but there aren't many amenities there. Going through Devon and Cornwall is also good.

It should be noted that though Brian's guide details walking John O'Groats to Land's End by road, many people follow established footpaths, including National Trails (see example above).

Further Information

Blogs and Walking Websites

alansloman.blogspot.co.uk
alastairhumphreys.com
backpackingbongos.wordpress.com
christownsendoutdoors.com
deanread.net/blog
keithfoskett.com
livefortheoutdoors.co.uk
phreerunner.blogspot.co.uk
terrybnd.blogspot.co.uk
thegirloutdoors.co.uk
flyingdogphotography.blogspot.co.uk
ramblingman.org.uk
rucksackrose.com
twoblondeswalking.com
walksaroundbritain.co.uk
walkingenglishman.com

Books (some recommended reading)

A Walk in the Woods, Bill Bryson
A Passion for Nature: The Life of John Muir, Donald Worster
As I Walked Out One Midsummer's Morning, Laurie Lee
Between a Rock and a Hard Place, Aron Ralston
Crow Country, Mark Cocker
Into the Wild, Jon Krakauer

Mountains of the Mind, Robert Macfarlane
Nature Cure, Richard Mabey
One Man and His Bog, Barry Pilton
Out On Your Feet, Julie Welch
Pennine Walkies, Mark Wallington
Rattlesnakes and Bald Eagles: Hiking the Pacific Crest Trail, Chris Townsend
The Book of the Bivvy, Roland Turnbull
The Last Englishman, Keith Foskett
The Old Ways, Robert Macfarlane
The Wild Places, Robert Macfarlane
The Wild Rover, Mike Parker
Wainwright: The Biography, Hunter Davies
Walden; or, Life in the Woods, Henry David Thoreau
Walking, Henry David Thoreau
Walking Home, Simon Armitage
Wild, Cheryl Strayed

Guidebooks

Most of the trails in this book have a guidebook; the popular ones (namely National Trails) have at least three each. To find guidebooks, as well as the obvious web search, the LDWA website database is a great place to start your research.

The three main publishers of long-distance trails guides are Aurum, Cicerone and Trailblazer. Each offers route descriptions, mapping of sorts, points of interest you'll see en route, general advice and such like. Each company has their loyalists and each offers something different.

Aurum concentrate mostly on the National Trails – they're the official guides for the walks. Their guides include full-page OS mapping, enough to get you along the trail without buying additional full maps (unless, of course, you stray too far from the path). Cicerone guides are a more pocket-friendly size and offer a waterproof cover on some, but their OS maps cover smaller areas. Trailblazers draw their own maps (though they're better than that sounds), but make up for that with more logistical information, such as accommodation. However, that can quickly go out of date of course; don't depend on it.

As well as that trio, there are some smaller, specialist publishers, such as Rucksack Readers (rucsacs.com). Their guidebooks for long-distance trails and treks at altitude are printed on rainproof paper, in a 'rucksack-friendly format', with open-flat binding and a dropdown route map, working well in all weather. They cover 20 titles in Britain, three in Ireland and selected routes worldwide. (Each page has links to galleries, free downloads and really detailed Google map overlaps that you can zoom in on.)

Footpaths that don't have a printed guidebook often have a downloadable guide on the local council website or sometimes a hobbyist website with good information.

Antill, Trevor, *Monarch's Way Book 1: Worcester to Stratford-upon-Avon* (Monarch's Way Association, 1995/2005)

Antill, Trevor, *Monarch's Way Book 2: Stratford-upon-Avon to Charmouth* (Monarch's Way Association, 1995/2016)

Antill, Trevor, *Monarch's Way Book 3: Charmouth to Shoreham* (Monarch's Way Association, YEAR)

Sharp, David and Colin Saunders, *The London Loop* (Recreational Path Guides, 1995)

Equipment

Facebook has an Outdoor Gear Exchange UK page that might be worth a peak for nearly new and often new equipment. Also try:

alpkit.com
backpackinglight.co.uk
blacks.co.uk
cotswoldoutdoor.com
gooutdoors.co.uk
mountain-lite.co.uk
outdoorkit.co.uk
snowandrock.com
sportpursuit.com
ultralightoutdoorgear.co.uk

Knowledge and skills

Collins Complete Guide to British Wildlife
Hill Walking: The Official Handbook of the Mountain Leader and Walking Group Leader
Food For Free, Richard Mabey
Nordic Walking for Total Fitness, Suzanne Nottingham and Alexandra Jurasin
The Backpacker's Handbook, Chris Townsend
The Natural Explorer, Tristan Gooley
The Natural Navigator, Tristan Gooley
The Walker's Guide to Outdoor Clues and Signs, Tristan Gooley
The UK Trailwalker's Handbook, The Long Distance Walkers' Association
Three Peaks, Ten Tors: And Other Challenging Walks in the UK, Roland Turnbull

Schemes

Schemes, Mountain Leader Training

Magazines

Country Walking
Outdoor Fitness
The Great Outdoors
Trail
Walk

Maps

Ordnance Survey: ordnancesurvey.co.uk
Harvey Maps: harveymaps.co.uk
Footprint Maps: stirlingsurveys.co.uk

Organizations

Backpacker's Club: backpackersclub.co.uk
British Mountaineering Council: thebmc.co.uk
Ramblers: ramblers.org.uk
The RSPB: rspb.org.uk

Transport

Plan your journey on public transport: traveline.info

Plan your journey by car: theaa.com/route–planner

Ultramarathon events

ultramarathonrunning.com/races/uk.html
100marathonclub.org.uk/new/events/uk_ultra_list.shtml

Youth Hostels

Youth Hostels Association: yha.org.uk
Scottish Youth Hostels Association: syha.org.uk

Other useful websites

National Trails: nationaltrail.co.uk
National Parks: nationalparks.gov.uk
Scotland's Great Trails: scotlandsgreattrails.org.uk
Wildlife Trusts: wildlifetrusts.org
Technique coaching: runningreborn.co.uk
Nutrition: eatwellfeelfab.co.uk
reneemcgregor.com

Index

Annandale Way   129
Arran Coastal Path   131
Ayrshire Coastal Path   133

Berwickshire Coastal Path   135
Borders Abbeys Way   136
Bournemouth Coast Path   52

Cambrian Way   124
Cape Wrath Trail   160
Capital Ring   64
Cateran Trail   163
Centenary Way   138
Chiltern Way   65
Choosing a trail 36
Clarendon Way   52
Cleveland Way   111
Clyde Walkway   138
Coast to Coast   78
Coleridge Way   53
Cotswold Way   53
Cowal Way   139
Cross Borders Drove Road   141
Cumbria Coastal Way   80
Cumbria Way   79

Dales Celebration Way   83
Dales High Way   81
Dales Way   82
Dava Way   164

Derwent Valley Heritage Way   84
Dillon, Paddy   129
Downs Link   65

Emergencies   47
Equipment   26
Equipment check list   28

Fife Coastal Path   142
Food and drink/nutrition   40
Formartine and Buchan Way   166
Forth and Clyde and Union Canal Paths   143
Foskett, Keith   74
Further information   171

Glyndŵr's Way   121
Gooley, Tristan   120
Great Glen Way   165
Great Stones Way   55
Greensand Way   66
Gritstone Trail   85

Hadrian's Wall   113
Heart of England Way   56
Herriot Way   86
Hiking downhill   21
Hiking uphill   20
How to pack your pack   35
How to wear your pack   22
Howgills and Limestone Trail   88

Humphreys, Alastair   140
Hypothermia   43, 47

Icknield Way Path   57
Isle of Anglesey Coast Path   119

John Muir Way   145
John O'Groats to Land's End   170

Kintyre Way   144

Lady Anne's Way   89
Limestone Way   90
London Loop   67

Mary Queen of Scots   147
Mcneis, Cameron   154
Megarry, Jacquetta   133
Mid Wilts Way   57
Monarch's Way   58
Moray Coast Trail   167
Mull of Galloway   148

National Forest Way   92
Navigation   39
New Lipchis Way   68
North Downs Way   69

Offa's Dyke Path   126

Peddars Way and Norfolk Coastal Path   70
Pembrokeshire Coast Path   122
Pennine Bridleway   01
Pennine Journey   95
Pennine Way   97

Raad Ny Foillan (Isle of Man Coastal
   Footpath)   100
Ravenber Way   115
Ribble Way   102
Ridgeway (The)   59
River Ayr Way   151
Rob Roy Way 150
Romans and Reivers Route   152

Sandlings Walk   72

Saxon Shore Way   71
Scottish National Trail   155
Settle to Carlisle Way   103
Six Peaks Trail   105
Somerset Coast Path   60
South Downs Way   73
Shakespeare's Way   61
Six Dales Trail   116
Skye Trail   168
Smith, Phoebe   71
South West Coast Path   62
Southern Upland Way   156
Speyside Way   169
Staffordshire Way   106
St Cuthbert's Way   153
St Oswald's Way   117
Stretches   23
Suffolk Coast Path   75

Thames Path   76
Three Lochs Way   157
Townsend, Chris   110
Training plan   24
Tributaries Walk   108
Turnbull, Ronald   162
Two Saints Way   109

Vanguard Way   77
Viking Way   117

Wales Coast Path   127
Walking form and fitness   17
Walking shoes/boots   27
Walters, Jenny   120
Waterproofs   31
Wealdway   77
Welch, Julie   113
Wessex Ridgeway   63
West Highland Way   158
West Island Way   159
Westwood, Steve   101
White Horse Trail   63
Wild camping   38
Wye Valley Walk   122

Yorkshire Wolds Way   118